Edition Derivatives
European Institute of
Financial Engineering and Derivatives

Derivatives

An authoritative guide to derivatives for
financial intermediaries and investors

by
Michael Bloss,
Prof. Dr. Dr. Dietmar Ernst
and
Prof. Dr. Dr. Joachim Häcker

Oldenbourg Verlag München

Bibliografische Information der Deutschen Nationalbibliothek

Die Deutsche Nationalbibliothek verzeichnet diese Publikation in der Deutschen
Nationalbibliografie; detaillierte bibliografische Daten sind im Internet über
<http://dnb.d-nb.de> abrufbar.

© 2008 Oldenbourg Wissenschaftsverlag GmbH
Rosenheimer Straße 145, D-81671 München
Telefon: (089) 4 50 51-0
oldenbourg.de

Lektorat: Wirtschafts- und Sozialwissenschaften, wiso@oldenbourg.de
Herstellung: Anna Grosser
Coverentwurf: Kochan & Partner, München
Gedruckt auf säure- und chlorfreiem Papier
Druck: Grafik + Druck, München
Bindung: Thomas Buchbinderei GmbH, Augsburg

ISBN 978-3-486-58632-9

Preface

Futures and options are among the most interesting tools in today's financial world. Years ago, when the DTB (one of Eurex's predecessor organizations) was founded, no one could have foreseen the triumphant success derivatives would have in Europe and worldwide. At Eurex alone, around seven million contracts are traded everyday.

Michael Bloss, Dietmar Ernst and Joachim Häcker have managed to create a textbook that incorporates this complex subject matter into a well-structured form that combines theory with practice, all under the assumption that readers have plenty of interest but limited time.

Due to its comprehensive set-up, this book serves as both a manual for practitioners and a classic textbook for students. It was written for academic newcomers and seasoned, professional investors alike. If after reading this book your understanding of derivatives trading has improved, and you have taken an interest in deepening your knowledge, we will have accomplished our goal.
We wish you enjoyable reading.

Dr. Axel Vischer
Eurex Market Development

Authors

Michael Bloss is Investment Advisor and Assistant Vice President at Commerzbank AG. Furthermore, he is Assistant Professor at the Master Programme International Finance at Nürtingen University (Germany) and Director of the European Institute of Financial Engineering and Derivatives (EIFD). His areas of expertise include equity sales and derivatives. Mr. Bloss is author of several publications focusing on derivatives and financial engineering.

Dietmar Ernst is Professor for International Finance at Nürtingen University (Germany) and Dean of the Master Programme in International Finance. Furthermore, he is Director of the European Institute of Financial Engineering and Derivatives (EIFD). His areas of expertise include Investment Banking and Derivatives. He is author of several books and numerous publications.

Joachim Häcker is Professor for Corporate Finance at Heilbronn University (Germany) and at the University of Louisville (USA). Furthermore, he is Director of the European Institute of Financial Engineering and Derivatives (EIFD). As Vice President at Rothschild in London and Frankfurt he carried out numerous transactions. His areas of expertise include all major fields of investment banking.

Introductory Note

Investments in derivative financial instruments have grown rapidly in recent years. Looking back at the past two decades, there has been triumphant success. Derivatives have become an integral part of the financial world. Along with traditional financial instruments, they now represent a separate category of tradable instruments which meet with quite a substantial market. Institutional investors use derivatives to safeguard against risks and speculate on possible stock-price movements.

With this book we want to shed some light on the complex matter of derivatives and outline possible investment strategies. Special emphasis is placed on the correct application of derivative instruments, as well as their opportunity-and-risk profiles.

Contents of this book

While the book pertains to contracts traded on derivatives exchanges – options and futures – we will also address off-market and exotic deals.

After providing some basic information in the first chapter, we will describe investment strategies and their implementation. We have included an additional questions and answers section in the end of the book. This section can aid in preparations for exams, or simply to conduct private studies on the subject.

Our intention in writing this book is to offer an easy-to-understand. Since many of our intention in writing this book is to offer an easy-to-understand comprehensive account of investments in derivative financial instruments. Since many of the strategies described are relatively complex, we have included examples and illustrations. Additionally, we have made a point of clarifying the differences between private (retail) and institutional investors.

The book is meant for both practitioners and students that have basic knowledge of the topic. Thus, it is useful for derivatives experts in their daily work, and also can serve as an academic lecture on derivatives. In short, this book can be both a self-study workbook and a textbook to accompany an academic course. It is also suitable for use in vocational training and advanced education.

The authors would like to thank the Eurex, which has generously sponsored our work and made available the necessary materials. In particular we have to thank Ms. Christina Bodler of Eurex for her energetic support and for paving the way towards an English version. Dr. Axel Vischer and Mr. Stefan Misterek have been kind enough to support us with their expertise and provide technical editing. We also thank Joem Joselal Kurumthottathil for his untiring cooperation and precise input, as well as the constructive dialogue during the final phase. Further thanks go to Marc Bachhuber, Wolfgang Pflug, Helga Gallina-Pflug and Ralf Burkhardt for their support in producing this book. Finally, we thank Jutta Scherer for providing the translation of our book into English, Stuart McCall, Kristin Rediker and Alexandra Reuber for final editing.

It is our sincere wish to meet our readers' needs. So, if you have any comments, suggestions or helpful ideas, please do not hesitate to contact us. We look forward to your email under the following address:

derivate@oldenbourg.de

Nürtingen and Frankfurt/Main, January 2008

Michael Bloss
Dietmar Ernst
Joachim Häcker

List of Abbreviations

CBOE	Chicago Board Option Exchange
CBoT	Chicago Board of Trade
CHF	Swiss Frank
CME	Chicago Mercantile Exchange
CoC	Cost of Carry
DAX®	Deutscher Aktien-Index
EUR	Euro Currency
FDAX	DAX Future
FGBL	Euro Bund Future
FESX	Dow Jones Euro STOXX 50 Future
OGBL	Options on the Euro Bund Future
OTC	Over the Counter
T-Bond	Treasury Bond Future, USA
JPY	Japanese Yen
USD	U.S. Dollar
X/Y-Index	Exemplary Index (not real)
X/L/V/C-equity	Exemplary Stocks (not real)

Contents

1 How derivative exchanges and markets are structured 1

2 Set-up and structure of derivatives exchanges – the Eurex case study 15

14 Over the counter derivatives 143

15 Credit derivatives 155

16 Structuring complex portfolios with derivatives 161

1 How derivative exchanges and markets are structured

This chapter deals with the following questions:

1. How have derivatives exchanges developed historically?
2. What are derivatives?
3. Why are most derivatives contracts currently traded standardized?
4. What functions do derivative exchanges fulfill?
5. Who are the market participants at derivative exchanges?
6. How are derivative exchanges organized?
7. What other basic definitions are needed to understand derivative exchanges and markets?
8. "Bursa Mater et Magistra" – or: What is a sensible trading approach at the derivatives exchange?

1.1 A history of derivative exchanges

The financial derivative transactions we know today originated in commodity futures trading at derivative exchanges. These instruments were created as a safeguard against price risks.

As early as two-thousand years B.C., the first forms of derivatives markets emerged in India. Faced with unertainty in regards to situations in different world regions and economic change, people transacted rudimentary futures contracts to lock in the prices of goods delivered by sea. From the Middle Ages we know of futures contracts in England and France. These were mainly commodity futures on goods to be delivered from Asia several months later. Again, the motive for these transactions was to lock in prices. Around 1630, the Netherlands experienced intense trading of options on tulip bulbs (later known as the Tulip Mania). Similar to the New Economy we faced at the turn of the century, it led to the forming of bubbles: due to excessive demand, tulip bulbs became increasingly expensive, resulting in an upward price spiral. When investors began to reap their profits and get rid of their investments, it instigated a selling surge causing the price of tulip bulbs to collapse. Most investors suffered losses of more than 90 percent. In Asia, a brisk trade in rice and silk was going on at the same time. The futures exchange there was called **"Dojima Rice Market"**. Today, it is considered the very first futures market worldwide, located in Osaka, Japan.

The triumphant rise of the Chicago Board of Trade as the "mother of all futures exchanges" set in after 1848 (it was founded on April 3 of that year). This was the first time in history that standardized futures contracts were listed and traded. In 1989, the Chicago Butter and Egg Board was established. Originally, only butter and eggs could be traded at this exchange. As the range of products widened over the years, the board was renamed Chicago Mercantile Exchange (CME) in 1919. In 2007, CME announced its intention to acquire the Chicago Board of Trade (CBoT).

The question that remains now concerns the causes in the rising popularity of futures contracts. The rapid increase of US-American public debt, along with the abolishment of fixed exchange rates (with contracts introduced on May 16, 1972 on the International Monetary Market IMM), resulted in a new economic environment accompanied by greater volatility. In response to the volatility concern, the first financial futures contract – an interest future – was introduced in Chicago in the 1970s. This marked the birth of financial futures trading. In 1972, the first foreign-currency futures on the seven major global currencies were traded. The first contracts on the S&P 500 were introduced on the CME in 1982. In 1988, the German Futures Exchange DTB ("Deutsche Terminbörse") was founded, merging in 1998 with the Swiss SOFFEX, to consolidate into what today is known as Eurex. In 1992, the CME's GLOBEX Trading System (a computer-based trading platform) was put into service.

1.2 What are derivatives?

Derivatives are financial instruments where the initiation (T_0) and fulfillment ($T_0 + X$) of transactions take place at different points in time, as opposed to spot transactions where fulfillment takes place "on the spot" (i.e., upon contract conclusion). A derivative is a mutually binding obligation to deliver and accept a certain good of a certain quality, in a certain quantity, for a previously agreed price, and at an agreed point in time.

This classic form of derivatives is called a **forward** or **future. A forward** is an individually crafted bilateral contract between two contracting parties. All of its components are adapted individually to match the respective transaction. By contrast, a **future** is standardized and therefore tradable on the (derivatives) exchange. Its components cannot be determined individually. As such, a future can

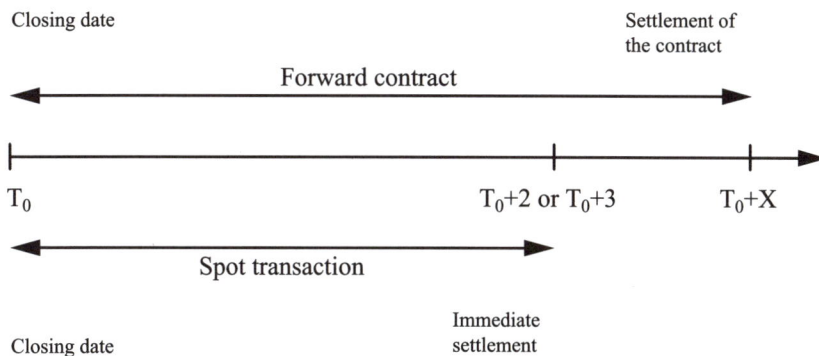

Figure 1.1: Point of fulfillment – derivative and cash transaction

always be transferred to another investor while a forward, due to its individual nature, cannot be transferred. Futures and forwards are also know as unconditional derivatives, as they must be fulfilled and executed under all circumstances. Their fulfillment does not require any further declaration of intent, and there is no right of choice.

A **future** is a derivative contract which must be fulfilled unconditionally. The buyer of the future assumes an increase, the seller a decrease of the underlying asset.

This is in sharp contrast to options, which also represent a class of derivatives. Contrary to a future or forward, an option does include a right of choice for the buyer. He can choose whether to exercise or abandon (not exercise) the option.

An **option** entails the right to buy or sell a certain quantity of an underlying within a given period of time, or at a certain point in time, and at a previously set price.

The option buyer decides whether the option will be exercised or not. After an option has been exercised, the seller (also referred to as "option writer") is required to assign (i.e., to cede) the underlying asset. As the silent partner in the transac-

```
                    ┌──────────────────────────────────┐
                    │     Unconditional derivatives     │
                    └──────────────────────────────────┘
        ┌───────────────────────┐        ┌───────────────────────┐
        │        Future         │        │        Forward        │
        └───────────────────────┘        └───────────────────────┘


                    ┌──────────────────────────────────┐
                    │      Conditional derivatives      │
                    └──────────────────────────────────┘
        ┌───────────────────────┐        ┌───────────────────────┐
        │        Option         │        │      OTC-Option       │
        └───────────────────────┘        └───────────────────────┘
```

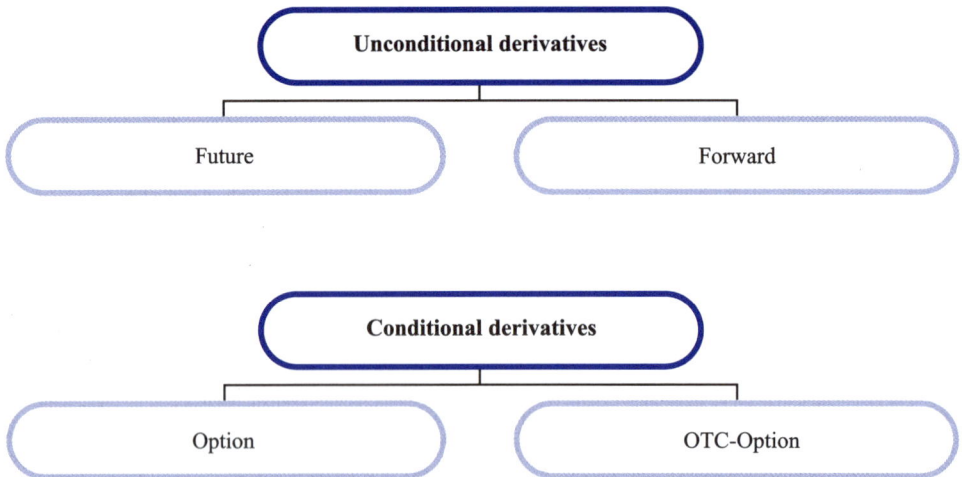

Figure 1.2: Conditional and Unconditional Derivatives

tion, the option writer has no right of choice. To compensate him for that he receives an option premium from the buyer.

As the buyer is not obliged to exercise his right but can alternatively choose to abandon it, options are also referred to as "conditional" derivative transactions. Contrary to futures, exercising options is not subject to any further declaration of intent on the buyer's part.

Options that are not standardized and traded on derivative exchanges, but agreed individually between the contracting parties are referred to as OTC options and they are traded "over the counter".

1.3 Standardized derivatives trading – Why is it common?

Most of the derivatives traded today are standardized. There are several reasons behind this standardization. For one thing, potential contract partners for a (non-standardized) forward can be difficult to locate. Also, with a forward it is almost impossible to close a position – i.e., contract out of the agreement by means of an offsetting deal. Standardized contracts, by contrast, allow the exiting party to be replaced by another. As contract details have been predefined, rather than individually agreed on between the contracting parties, a third party can take the place of the exiting party. Another important factor is that standardization facilitates swift and continuous trading. Derivatives positions can be opened and closed out (via a so-called offsetting order) at any time.

Table 1-1: Opening and closing

Opening (Initial order)	Closing (counter-order)
Long	Short
Short	Long

Contracts are standardized with regards to the following details:
- Underlying
- Contract size (quantity)
- Strike price
- Contract period
- Place & time of transaction
- Quality of the underlying

Underlying
The underlying is the object of the derivative transaction. It can be a Company share, an index, a commodity, or other financial good. The derivative transaction is based on this asset, or, in other words, it is the merchandise "underlying" the derivative transaction.

Contract size (quantity)
The contract size defines how many units of an underlying will have to be delivered or accepted under the derivative transaction in question. Thus, it specifies the quantity of a derivatives transaction.

Strike price
The strike price (or exercise price) is the price at which the underlying asset must be purchased or sold when an option is exercised. It can be considered the basic price of a derivative transaction. Strike prices are continually listed by derivatives exchanges in accordance with trading developments. Consequently, there are always sufficient tradable strike prices available.

Contract period
The Expiration date specifies the duration or due date of the transaction. Internationally, the third Friday of each month is the last trading day for derivatives at

exchanges, also referred to as the "settlement day". The third Friday of a quarter-end month is also referred to as "final settlement day". Both options and future contracts expire on this day.

Place & time of transaction

These details depend on the regulations valid at the particular exchange. They indicate where the derivative will be traded. Exchange trading times enable supply and demand to meet, and thus ensure orderly and continuous trading. This is true for both floor trading and computer-based trading.

Quality of the underlying

The quality of the underlying is particularly important for commodity-based derivatives, as there can be several variations in the qualities of the same commodity. It specifies precisely what merchandise will be delivered and received (e.g., sugar No. 11). The same is true for company stock, in which the contract specifies what kind of stock (equity stock or preferred stock) will be delivered. These specifications help to avoid mistakes or misunderstandings.

If the elements of the contract are not standardized they need to be negotiated individually. Individual contracts cannot be traded on derivatives exhanges, for it is highly unlikely that a third party will look for precisely the same specifications. It is a bilateral, individually agreed on derivative transaction governed by a customized contract.

Standardization of derivative transactions can also produce disadvantages. For instance, an investor may not be able to precisely hedge his positions in regards to quantity and duration (e.g., due to a predefined contract quantity). In this case, an OTC transaction which is tailored individually to the investors' preferences, will be the better choice.

1.4 What functions do derivative exchanges fulfill?

In order for derivatives exchanges to develop, the existence of well-organized and flourishing cash markets is essential. The exchange then provides the organizational framework in which trade in the derivatives listed can be set up and pursued.

As mentioned initially, the chief motive for the establishment of derivatives exchanges was the reallocation of risk. Derivatives exchanges offer participants a means to hedge against unwanted price shifts in the cash market. Risks are transferred from hedgers wishing to protect themselves from risk, to speculators who actively embrace risk. The latter are indispensable to ensure continuous trading at the derivatives exchange, and thus enable it to run smoothly. They take on existing risks without bringing on new risks.

In addition, derivatives exchanges generate additional price information, revealing price trends in the spot markets. This permits more efficient and effective decisions, for prices of derivatives markets carry more information than prices in spot markets. This facilitates faster and more proactive trading at the derivatives markets as well as the spot markets.

Due to the relatively low transaction costs and speedy execution, even large positions can be traded efficiently and rapidly, with the capacity to move enormous sums in a matter of minutes. Entire markets can be traded in one single transaction, e.g., with an index future. Moreover, to open a deal on a derivatives exchange investors do not have to raise the entire amount underlying that deal. All they need to provide is a depository amount, or the so-called margin. Its purpose is to ascertain contractants' solvency. When options are purchased ("long options") the premium paid is only a fraction of the corresponding contract value. This enables investors to trade even large sums with limited capital expenditure. Another major advantage of derivatives exchanges is the possibility to profit from a prices decrease. While investors in spot markets can only bet on an appreciation, derivatives markets enable them to place their bets on a downturn. This way they can make money even as stock prices fall. Derivatives exchanges provide the necessary financial instruments to pursue these strategies.

1.5 Who are the market participants at derivative exchanges?

There are several different types of market participants at derivative exchanges. According to their basic approach, they are grouped in 4 categories: hedger, speculator, arbitrageur, and spreader.

Hedger

The hedger's motive is to safeguard existing positions. He can be considered the true raison d'être of derivatives exchanges. The hedger is risk averse, and protects himself against price risks by actively transferring them to other market participants. Hedging allows him to better plan and calculate, e.g., his gains from a spot position. The result is a classic risk transfer. As we have explained before, transferring price risks were originally the idea behind every derivative transaction.

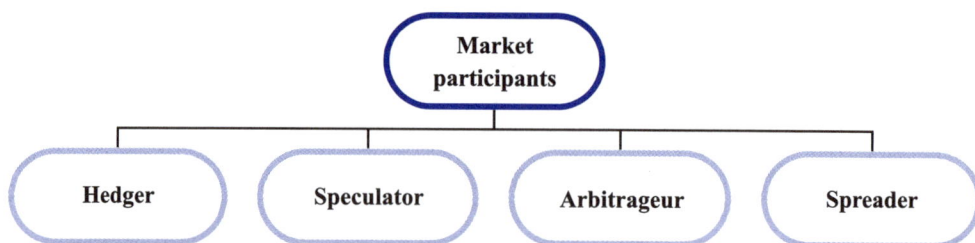

Figure 1.3: Market participants at the derivatives exchange

Speculator
The speculator is the natural antagonist of the hedger. His trading activities are driven by his hopes to close a transaction with a gain. In return, the speculator actively takes on risk, and through his positions creates the necessary liquidity in the markets. He actively embraces risk in anticipation of a profit.

Arbitrageur
The arbitrator engages in arbitrage by taking advantage of different price levels for a given asset and profits from that price difference. This takes place with zero risk, for contracts are purchased and sold simultaneously. With these activities, the arbitrator also contributes to fluent trading in addition to the contribution to fair market prices. Most arbitrators are banks and brokers. The arbitrage opportunity does however disapear in the course of events because through the very act of arbitraging, price differences for the respective trading objects are leveled out.

Spreader
An investor that targets spreads attempts to make a profit by taking advantage of price differences. He buys a contract which he deems low-priced, and sells a contract he considers high-priced. The simultaneous opening and close-out of positions results in a price difference. The spreader can maximally profit from this price difference.

1.6   How are derivative exchanges organized?

A derivatives exchange can be organized as both a floor-trading or an electronic exchange. The traditional form is floor trading, and is performed on the "floor" by **open outcry** or hand signals. By contrast, at electronic exchanges such as Eurex, trading is pursued silently and anonymously through the data system. All trading participants communicate through data lines. This facilitates smooth supra-regional and international trading since all participants have access to the same market and price information at exactly the same time. Entering orders via the trading screen makes for extremely fast processing. Orders are processed 100 percent automatically. Liquidity is additionally ensured through active Market Making.

1.7 Understanding derivative exchanges and markets – what do we need to know?

Investors
We will briefly explain the term investors due to the the frequency of the term in this book. Our definition of an investor is someone who engages in derivatives and securities transactions. He can be both, a private (retail) investor or a professional (institutional) investor. He can even sell something he does not possess (short selling), or conclude any kind of derivatives transaction without any restricitions in terms of size or admission. Thus, in our definition an investor has unlimited financial means at his disposal, which he can use at any time and anywhere he desires. Furthermore, we think of the investor as combining experience with skill, and therefore is versatile in using any kind of financial instrument.

Derivative
We should also define the term "derivative". The word originated from the Latin term "derivare" (to derive). It is a financial instrument derived from another, "underlying" instrument (such as a Company share).

The development of a derivative is always linked to the development of the underlying. The underlying in turn is hardly affected by investments in derivatives, since when we invest in derivatives we anticipate a change in the price of the underlying asset. Only very seldom is the underlying itself an essential element of an investors' strategy. In other words, it is the origin and basis, but not the object of an investment. It can turn into an investment if the derivative instrument is exercised. In this case, the derivative itself ceases to exist and is replaced by the underlying asset, which now becomes the basis of the transaction.

Hedging

Hedging is an action to secure investments already made or which are planned, but remain to be carried out. Through hedging transactions, investors protect themselves from adverse market developments and and provide a safer basis for their strategies. The element of protection is always the focal point.

Also, hedging always involves an expenditure. The hedger is a risk averse investor; an investor that places great value on predictability. Through his operations he transfers risk to another party, and thus disposes of that risk. In exchange for that he is prepared to pay a monetary compensation to the risk-accepting party.

Speculation

At this point we would like to expand a bit on the subject of speculation. With speculative positions the situation is very different. The term originated from the Latin "speculare" (to look or glance). Speculation is always a short-term commitment aimed at generating profit. However this calls for a more precise differentiation, as speculation may also be designed to be medium or even long-term. In these cases, however, we tend to speak of strategic investments or deliberate speculation on future developments.

The act of committing to investments in order to realize a profit accounts for most of the liquidity in derivatives markets. We would therefore be justified in saying that speculation is the driver behind all orders. Only if someone is ready to take a risk will there be a transaction. A speculator knows what risks he is taking on, and usually has a good understanding of these risks. According to our definition, speculation is the act of generating returns while accepting the risks involved. Thus, a speculator takes on risks (which are often generated by the economy as a whole) and attempts to derive a legitimate profit from his risk-taking. Speculators are very important for national economies, for without risk-taking investors our economic system would not endure. One might even say that speculation is the motor of our economy.

Dividends and interest

At this point let us take a brief look at interest rates and dividends, as they can directly or indirectly influence transactions with financial derivatives.

Dividends

Dividends are considered a means for corporations to distribute their profits, and directly influence the asset underlying a derivative transaction. Dividends affect the derivative transaction itself. A part of the company's profits is paid out to its shareholders, which decreases the company's equity. This in turn decreases the price of the underlying asset, and also changes the price of the respective derivative.

Closing date

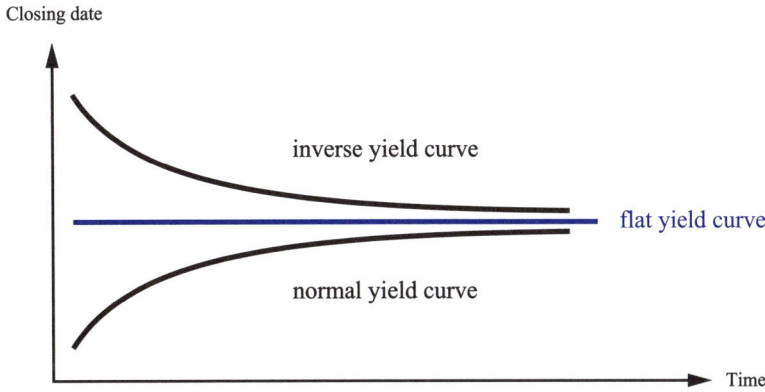

Figure 1.4: Interest structure curves

Interest

Looking at interest rates, we immediately notice that there are different levels for different Expiration dates. By plotting these interest rates in a graph we obtain the interest-structure or interest-rate curves for each Expiration date. It is important to determine the probability of a change in the interest structure, and the extent of the expected change. We differentiate between three typical interest structure curves:

- **Flat interest curve:** There is no difference between the periods. Interest rates follow a flat curve.
- **Normal interest curve:** Interest rates rise as the maturity grow longer. Interest structure curves with this shape are typical of a gradual economic upturn.
- **Inverse interest structure curve:** Interest rates decrease as the Expiration dates extend. An inverse curve is often found during economic recession and in times of deflationary tendencies. Inflation is expected to go down. Money market rates are high, capital market rates are lower. The central bank has taken action to reduce the money supply.

The difference between long-end and short-end interest rates is referred to as term spread. The term spreads for the Euro and the U.S. Dollar are calculated with the following formulas:

Term spread euro

$$S_{eur} \left(\frac{10}{1} \right) = i_{10} - i_1$$

$S_{eur} =$ Spread EUR interest rate

Term spread USD

$$S_{usd}\left(\frac{30}{0,5}\right) = i_{30} - i_{0,5}$$

S_{usd} = Spread USD yields

As a basic rule, the interest curve goes up when the term spread is positive and the economic upturn can be expected to continue. Likewise, a negative term spread indicates recession tendencies.

Note on the U.S. situation:
In the United States it is customary to specify yields (returns) rather than interest rates; therefore the curve is referred to as the yield curve.

1.8 "Bursa Mater et Magistra": How can reasonable trading behaviour at derivatives exchange be described?

This title, phrased a bit provocatively, is intended to stimulate readers' thoughts on this title, phrased a bit provocatively, is intended to stimulate readers' thoughts on the occurences at exchanges. The first and very important factor when using the instruments and strategies described here is to be very clear about what volume you are trading and what responsibility you bear with your position book. While trading 1,000 futures contracts is not a problem, you should always be aware that these 1,000 contracts can represent an enormous value, for instance in the case of the Euro Bund Future (FGBL) is 100,000,000 Euro. Another important factor you need to understand is that the derivatives exchange is not there for people to get rich quickly. Rather it represents a platform created by humans which offers opportunities to accomplish that goal. It takes deliberate action and persistence to have lasting success in derivatives markets. Errors and mistakes must be recognized and eliminated, vanity and delusion can result in dramatic losses. The basic rule of thumb is that five small strategies are preferable to one great strategy. It can be very dangerous to let yourself be blinded by all the money and the rapid succession of events.

   That is what we mean by "bursa – mater et magistra". The exchange is a good place to learn, and with the right strategy you will be in good hands. Errors are permitted but must be corrected – if you do not take that principle to heart you will fail. For it is true what they say about the exchange, and specifically about the derivatives exchange: Trading is all about emotions and expectations. It is imperative to understand which direction trends are pointing, and to correct previous decisions that have proved to be wrong. The only difference between a good investor and a bad one is that the good investor corrects earlier mistakes and quickly moves on to a new strategy. If you wildly chase a dream you will never be able to get hold of it. If however you approach that dream deliberately and step by step, it will come true for you at some point.

Summary:
Derivative deals have existed since antiquity, and are not an invention of our era. In their present form, derivative transactions emerged around 1975. There are two basic types: unconditional derivatives (futures and forwards) and conditional derivatives, or options. The derivatives contracts traded at modern derivatives exchanges are standardized, thus guaranteeing smooth trading processes.
At a derivatives exchange we find speculators, hedgers, spreaders and arbitrageurs as market participants. They encounter one another in electronic and floor trading. Active market making secures smooth trading. A possible motive for derivatives trading is a desire to protect oneself, to speculate, or to do combination trading. The origin of derivatives exchanges was the desire to transfer risk: it is passed on from the hedger to the speculator.
Derivatives traded outside the exchange are called forwards or OTC options.

2 Set-up and structure of derivatives exchanges – the Eurex case study

This chapter deals with the following questions:
1. How do electronic exchanges work?
2. What is the Market Maker principle?
3. How is trading carried out at Eurex?
4. What derivatives can be traded?
5. What does the term "clearing" mean?
6. What kinds of order specifications exist?
7. Which settlement days exist?

2.1 How do electronic exchanges work?

Eurex is a prime example of a fully computerized exchange. It originated from a merger of DTB (Deutsche Terminbörse – German Derivatives Exchange) and SOFFEX in 1998. Of these, the DTB (founded in 1988 as a holding company) had already specialized in electronic trade. Before the DTB's time, derivative trading had almost been non-existent in the Germany due to a lack of corresponding regulations, and so the new exchange initially struggled with some difficulties. But soon the benefits of derivatives trading were widely recognized and the DTB was able to hold its own amidst the competition from European and U.S. exchanges. The most outstanding feature of the young exchange is its innovative structure featuring a high degree of transparency, functionality and security. Transactions are effected silently and rapidly via the central processor: A software application immediately assigns each incoming order to another, existing order. If orders cannot be executed immediately, the central processor transmits them to the central order book. As soon as execution is possible, the system automatically initiates the so-called matching process (execution and assignment of orders). New orders are assigned according to time/price priority, which means that the first order that can be executed will be traded. If more orders become executable they will be processed according to their time of entry ("first come, first serve").

A very important aspect is the system's security. Eurex has introduced three security levels:

- The first is technical security, starting with Eurex's centerpiece, the central processor. The central processor exists to prevent a complete shutdown. Should the first processor fail, the second one – which is connected in parallel – will immediately take over. Also, all processing and communication lines are redundant. In addition, there are multiple back-ups of all data and orders.
- The second security level ensures market security. Processes are permanently monitored and examined for possible signs of manipulation.
- The third security level concerns participants' safety. For each participant, Eurex defines an appropriate right of access. This ensures that only authorized staff can enter orders at a trading screen. In addition, Eurex also controls its staff's access to data sources. This ensures that only in-house trading and clearing data can be accessed. Any attempted access by third parties is refused. With this system and set of regulations, Eurex is one of the world's leading derivatives exchanges.

2.2   What is the market-maker principle?

Eurex has introduced the Market-Making principle in order to support continuous trading in all products. Market Makers are institutions which continually or on demand, provide binding prices for the product series they offer. The **bid-ask prices** listed are called **quotes.** In quoting, the Market Maker must observe a contract quantity limit set by Eurex, as well as a predefined margin. In addition, the Market Maker must answer at least half (depending on his market-making status, up to 85 percent) of the **quote requests** received within one minute, and keep these quotes open for 10 seconds. Only then has the requesting partner a change to respond to these quotes by placing an order. After having answered 150 requests within one day, a Market Maker can refuse or ignore further requests. This Market-Making scheme is referred to as **Regular Market Making**. It exists for product series trading less fluently, and refers to placing a **quote on request**. Often market making is also referred to as "market support". For without the Market Makers, it would often be impossible to trade products, in particular rare ones. If a trading participant has placed an order for a product for which no quote has been entered in the system, the system automatically issues a bid for quotes. The order is then either executed or captured in the central order book.

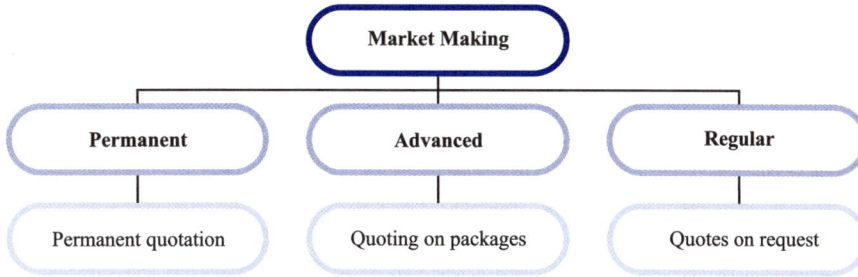

Figure 2.1: Types of Market Making

Permanent Market Making is available for options (at certain strike prices which are "at the money"). Permanent Market Makers **permanently** maintain quotes for their respective products. **This permanent quotation ensures fluent and rapid trading.** As such, Permanent Market Making is of utmost importance, as without it rapid and consequent trading would not be possible. Quoting on packages of products (stock options, index options, and options on fixed-income futures) are referred to as **Advanced Market Making.** Again, quotes are **permanently** posted so that execution is ensured. Contrary to Permanent Market Making, quotes are not restricted to individual series but refer to product packages defined by the exchange, and which may entail different products.

2.3 How is trading carried out at Eurex?

Trade at Eurex is structured in various phases, to include the following sections:

Pre-trading phase
In this phase, all trading participants can enter, modify, or cancel orders. There is no trading activity.

Opening phase
Trade at Eurex begins with an opening auction. First, a balanced order book is created. Balancing entails the determination of opening quotations and possibly the respective first deals. Prices determined are based on the price level at which the largest order volume can be executed. Existing orders are matched to the extent possible. Trading sets in once a balance has been established.

Trading period

During the trading period, open orders and quotes are permanently compared. All orders and quotes submitted during the trading period, which are better or equal to existing order and quotes on the opposite side of the order book, are immediately matched. If an order cannot be matched it will be transmitted to the central order book. Order execution is reported back in real-time. Both orders and quotes can permanently be entered, modified, or deleted.

Closing auction

In this phase, the order book is once again balanced. All open orders and quotes are consolidated and carried out as far as possible. The Closing Auction ends for a given product once the netting process for all futures contracts based on this product has been concluded.

The Closing Auction ends without setting a final closing price quote under the following conditions:

- There are not market orders for certain futures contracts, and thus not possible to pair limited orders and quotes
- There are market orders which cannot be executed

If there are not market orders for certain futures contracts and it is not possible to pair limited orders and quotes, or if there are market orders which cannot be executed, the Closing Auction ends without setting a final quotation (settlement prices).

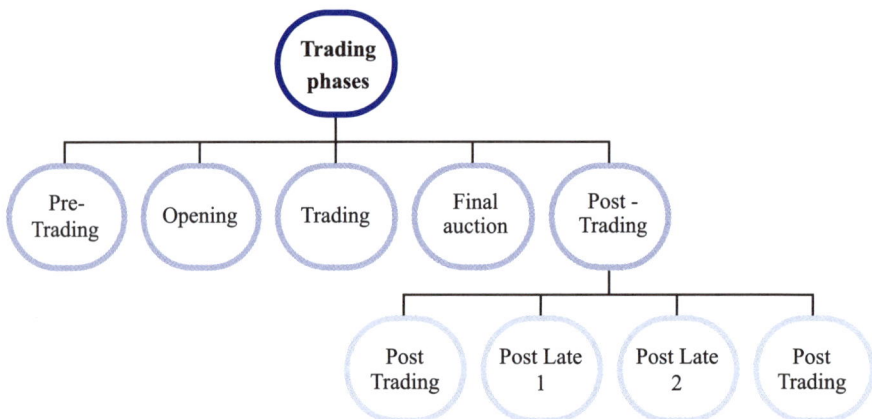

Figure 2.2: Trading phases at Eurex

Post-trading phase

This phase is divided in four sub-phases:
- **Post-trading full**: In this phase, orders can be entered, modified, or deleted.
- **Post late 1:** Orders for OTC products cannot be entered.
- **Post late 2:** The Post Late 2 period exclusively applies to interest rate options on the last trading day.
- **Post trading restricted:** During this period, only data retrieval is possible. Orders for the following trading day can be entered but will not be executed until the next day.

After these phases, batch processing (the processing of all contracts traded) starts and data queries are no longer possible. The system is updated and prepared for the following trading day.

Theoretically, trading could go on around the clock. Actually, system maintenance would only take a matter of minutes. Even so, Eurex has resolved to maintain fixed trading hours; whereas GLOBEX, the electronic trading system of the CME in Chicago, operates 23 hours per day, going offline for maintenance and updating only.

2.4 What products can be traded at Eurex?

In principle, derivative contracts can be traded on any product. We will name the most common and add a few examples.
- Indices
  - DAX®
  - Dow Jones EURO STOXX 50®
  - S&P 500
- Company shares
  - Commerzbank AG
  - ThyssenKrupp AG
- Bonds / interest rate products
  - Euro Bund Future (FGBL)
  - 30 year Treasury Future (T-Bond)
- Commodities
  - Oil
  - Gold
  - Frozen Concentrated Orange Juice (FCOJ)

These are just a few examples out of many. Contract specifications for Eurex products have been summarized in the appendix.

2.5 What does the term "clearing" mean?

Clearing is an essential activity behind each and every order. It includes the processing, back-up, and settlement (in terms of both payment and volumes) of the transactions concluded. At Eurex, clearing is performed by the Eurex Clearing AG.

Trading participants authorized to trade on the Eurex platform are distinguished by their clearing status, which is sub-divided into the following three levels:

General clearing member
This license is granted to banks with a minimum of € 25 million of trading capital. They are authorized to perform transactions on behalf of their customers or of other trading participants that do not have clearing licenses.

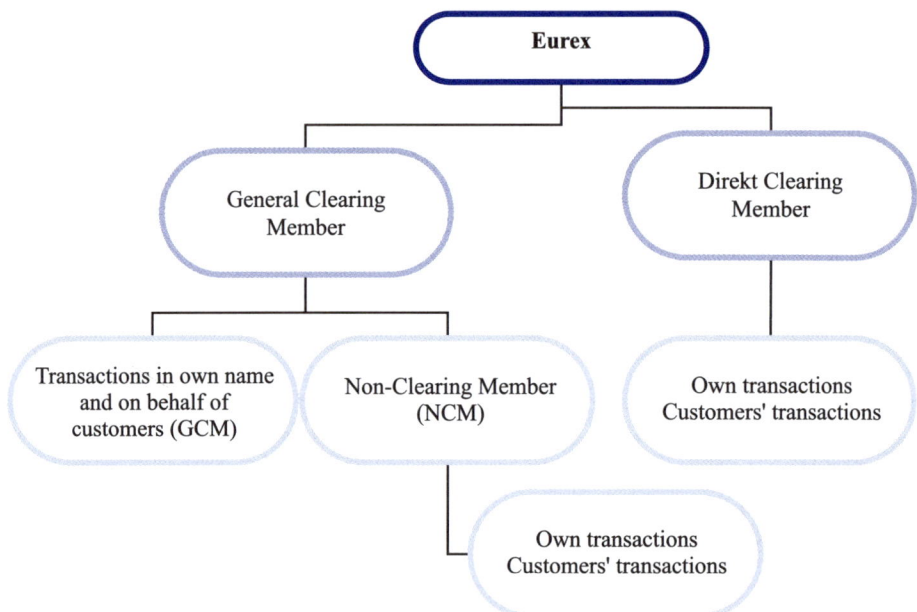

Figure 2.3: Eurex trading members

Direct clearing member
Banks with a minimum of €12.5 million in trading capital can obtain this type of license. It authorizes them to conclude transactions in their own name and on behalf of their customers.

Non-clearing member (NCM)
NCMs do not perform any clearing activities. However this does not mean that they have no access at all to Eurex-based trade. They can choose to participate through a bank with a general clearing license. This requires a formal agreement with the General Clearing Member. These agreements represent a separate legal relationship, as only clearing members can be contracting parties to Eurex Clearing AG.

2.6 What categories of order specifications exist?

When placing orders in the derivatives market, the following terms must be given:
- What kind of derivatives will be traded?
  - Options or futures?
  - If options: Call or put?
- Do you intend to buy or sell?
  - Long or short?
- How many contracts? What underlying asset?
- What month and year of expiration?
- Strike price, if applicable (for options)
- Execution limit, if applicable (or lowest/best bid = market order)
- Validity of order, if applicable (only today (Good-For-Day – GFD), until cancellation (Good-Till-Canceled – GTC) or until a certain date (Good-Till-Date – GTD))
- Which trading place?
- Are there any particular characteristics?
- Covered or uncovered?
- Is it a combination trade?
- Opening or close-out?
- Possibly further order details.

Orders can be posted **with or without restrictions.** Unrestricted orders are referred to as market orders, and are executed immediately if possible. Restricted orders – such as, for instance, limit orders – can take a while longer to process, as they can only be executed at or above limit. If an order cannot be executed right away it will be entered into the Eurex order book. The same is true for partial execution: The remaining parts are also entered into the order book.

Restrictions
- **Limit order:** This means that a certain price limit must be reached for the order to be executed. The order may only be executed at or above the price stipulated, whereas a market order is traded at the next available price.
- **Stop order (STP):** This is a future order which can be executed once a specified price is reached. In other words, it must be purchased above or sold below the current price. This type of order restriction is usually applied for system orders which are posted based on technical analyses. It enables investors to define safety points for themselves, enabling them to either prevent losses or make sure they will enter an upward market at precisely the chart point they favor.
- **Fill and Kill (FAK):** Orders with this designation must be executed without delay, possibly broken down in partial orders. Parts not executed will be canceled.
- **Fill or Kill (FOK):** Orders of this type must be immediately executed in their entirety, otherwise they will be canceled. Partial execution is excluded.
- **Spread order:** A spread order trades the complete spread within one order. Sale and purchase results are simultaneously indicated (in aggregated form).
- **Immediate or Cancel order (IOC):** This order is to be executed immediately; partial execution is also permissible. Parts not executed will be canceled. This

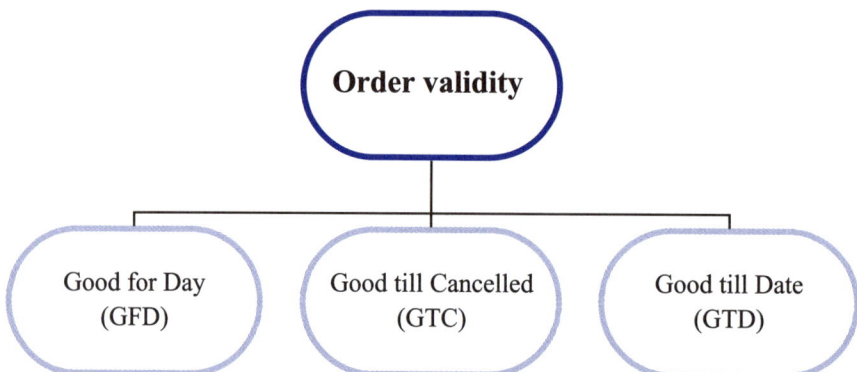

Figure 2.4: Different kinds of order validity

type of order is tradable at Eurex for futures combination orders and for options.

Another order detail that can be defined beforehand is validity. We distinguish between orders valid on the same day only (**Good for Day; GFD**), orders valid until a certain date (**Good till Date; GTD**) and orders valid until cancellation (**Good till Cancelled; GTC**).

Order execution

In order to avert unwanted price volatility, Eurex has defined a maximum range for futures within which unlimited orders are possible. This is to protect the investor (the party placing the order) from unwanted price moves.

Order execution (matching) is done according to **price/time priority.** Orders which cannot be executed immediately (or only in part) are entered into Eurex's electronic order book and executed as soon as they can be matched. Partial execution is possible at any time (except for orders with respective restrictions). Due to being a computerized exchange, the speed of execution at Eurex is very high. Immediately after execution, the system reports back on the contracts traded (underlying assets), the execution price, and the quantity traded.

Further order types

At other derivatives exchanges, there are additional and very different order types. For instance, a **Market-if-Touched order** becomes valid when the price indicated is traded. Therefore the order turns into a market order. A **Not-Held order** or **Take-Time order** allows the broker a certain amount of discretion in its execution. If the broker believes that the order can be executed more favorably at a later point in time he is free to include it into his order book and execute it whenever he deems appropriate. In this instance, legal recourse is excluded.

A **Cancel-Former** order always stipulates a former order to be canceled, whereas a **One-Cancels-the Other** order entails various combinations. Whenever an order is executed another order, which has been posted simultaneously (i.e., in combination), will be canceled. Last but not least, there are orders to be executed at the very end or start of the trading period. The orders are only valid for that period, and are referred to as market-opening or market-closing orders.

It is of utmost importance for investors to understand all of these order specifications – no matter which type of order they ultimately choose, depending on their particular situation. At the same time, it is important to understand which order types one's bank or broker is offering, for not all of them offer the whole range. Finally, investors should always make sure that the order they are about to place really makes sense. Unreasonable orders (or orders that do not match the market) should be refrained from and most bankers and brokers will refuse to take them.

If an underlying stock is suspended in the primary market, all derivative orders based on it will usually be canceled. After reintroduction of the underlying instrument these orders will have to be placed again.

2.7   What expiration dates are used by Eurex?

Option series expire on the third Friday of each month, and index futures expire on the third Friday of the last month of the quarter (both rules are commonly practiced internationally). The last trading day for fixed-income futures is two trading days before delivery day (delivery day = 10th day of month of expiration). The last trading day for options on fixed-income futures is six market days before the first calendar day of the option's month of expiration. Weekly options expire on the first, second, third, forth and fifth Friday.

Summary:
Eurex is one of the world's leading derivative exchanges, and originated from the merger of DTB and SOFFEX in 1998. Eurex is a fully computerized exchange, versus a call-out exchange. Active Market Making ensures liquidity and rapid trading. The range of products at Eurex is very diverse, and is continually expanding and adapting to market developments. The security system is organized on several levels. Trading participants can apply for different kinds of membership status. Trading at Eurex features speedy, fair, and cost-efficient processing, as well as fair pricing for the options and futures series offered.

3 Options – Conditional derivatives

This chapter deals with the following questions:
1. What are options, and what is the difference between call and put options?
2. Where do options differ?
3. What are weekly options?
4. When does it make sense to trade in weekly options?
5. What are Low Exercise Price Options?

3.1 What are options and how do call options and put options differ?

In essence, options are bilateral agreements which are valid for limited time period and involve a right of choice. As these contracts are standardized, they can be traded on the derivatives exchange. The word "option" originated from the Latin "optio", meaning "free will" or "free choice". The investor has a right of choice. As mentioned before, options where the details of the contract have been defined individually are referred to as OTC options. The contracting parties negotiate them directly, the exchange is not used as intermediary. Options always involve an asymmetric distribution of risk.

There are two basic types of options: call options (involving an option to buy) and put options (involving an option to sell).

Call options
A call option (buying option) provides its buyer (referred to as Long) with the right but not the obligation to purchase a certain quantity (contract size) of an underlying or instrument within a certain period of time (maturity) or by certain date (last trading day), and at a price defined upon contract conclusion (strike price).

Example:

> An investor wishes to invest in stock from company X. Based on his analysis; he expects the stock to appreciate. Instead of investing in it directly he purchases call options. Thanks to the lower amount in liquid funds required, he can purchase much more options than he could purchase stock. Should the stock price increase as expected, the investor will benefit even more as a result of the leverage effect.

Put options

A put option (selling option) provides its buyer (long) with the right but not the obligation to sell a certain quantity (contract size) of an underlying within a certain period of time (maturity) or by a certain date (last trading day), and at a price defined beforehand (strike price).

Example:

> An investor carries stock of company Y in his portfolio. He expects stock prices to go down but is not entirely sure. To secure his position, he purchases put options on the Y stock. Thus, if the stock price goes down he will be able to compensate for his losses. As the puts purchased will lose value if the stock appreciates, our investor will take a loss in his options position, but if that increase is higher than his losses are worth they will be offset. Conversely, if the investor sold his stock immediately he would not be able to benefit from a possible price increase. In short, the purchase of put options enables him to generate at least some profit from his investment, which he could not do if he sold his stock right away.

The counterparty to the purchaser (long position) is the seller (also referred to as writer of the option or short position). He has no right of choice but depends

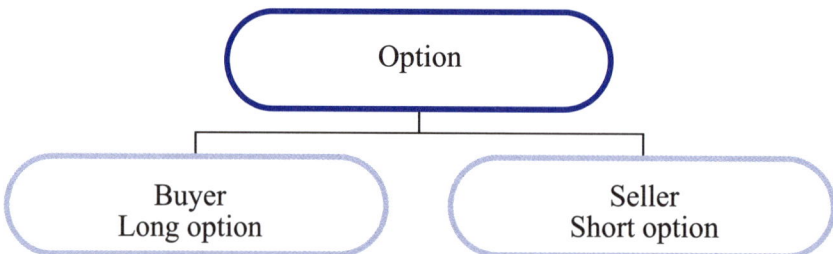

Figure 3.1: Options and parties involved

on the buyer's decision. In return for that he receives a premium from the buyer. Thus, he has entered into an obligation (since he has no right of choice) to sell (call option) or buy (put option) the predefined quantity of the underlying security at the time and price agreed, if or when the option is exercised.

Table 3-1: Rights and obligations with options

	Right	Obligation
Buyer	Exercise of option	Payment of premium
Seller	Receiving premium	Delivery or receipt

3.2 What types of options do exist?

Type of option

We have previously learned that options can be divided into call and put options.

Another distinguishing criterion is the way they are exercised. Options that can be exercised throughout their maturity are referred to as American-style options, and most of them are based on individual securities. Options which can only be exercised at the end of their maturity (i.e., on the respective last trading day) are called European-style option. This type is mainly found in index options.

Of course, options also differ in what commodity or security (e.g., stock) they refer to. The technical term used here is "underlying": The underlying is the trading object which a derivative is based on. Underlying assets can be shares, indices, commodities or even other derivatives.

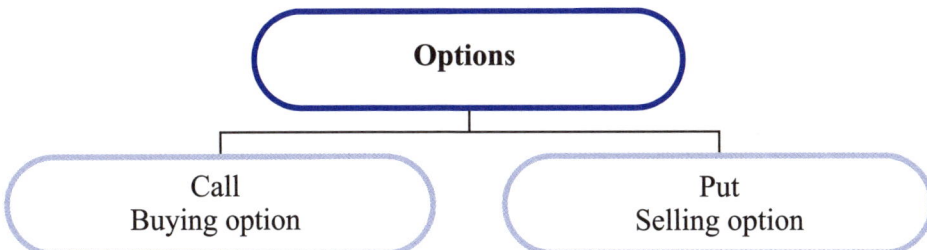

Figure 3.2: Types of options

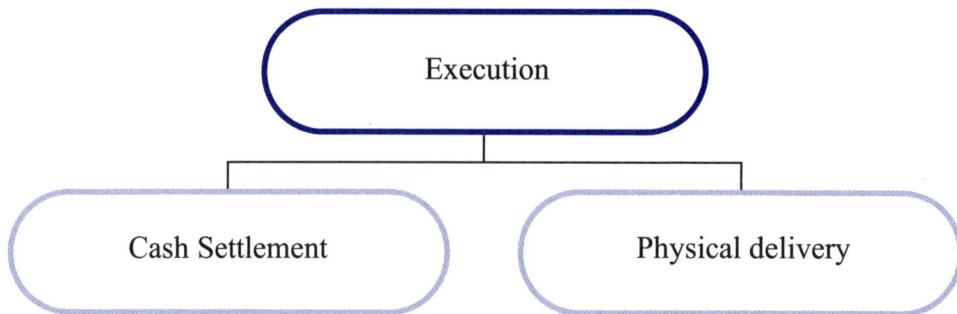

Figure 3.3: Different ways of executing an option

A final difference consists in how option contracts are settled – i.e., in cash or by physical delivery of the underlying asset. Cash settlement is used whenever physical delivery is impossible (as, for instance, with index options): In that case the difference between the underlying and the strike price is paid in cash. If an underlying must be delivered physically (as in the case of equity options), delivery is coordinated by the clearing house.

3.3 Options trading

Contract
Having talked about contracts several times now, we probably owe you a precise definition. A contract is a minimum-quantity derivative transaction. For example, a traditional equity option comprises 100 shares. Premiums for index options are given as index points, which must be multiplied with a certani figure – the index multiplier – to determine the actual amount. The multiplier is calculated separately for each index. For instance, for the German Stock Index (DAX®) it is 5 Euros per point, for the Dow Jones Euro STOXX 50® it is 10 Euros per point. Multipliers are published by derivative exchanges and can be looked up in their trading regulations. A contract is the minimum unit tradable for a derivative instrument, and thus includes a certain quantity. The word "contract" originates from 15th century officialese for a binding agreement (Latin: contractus).

Premium payment and receipt
The premium (from the Latin praemium = gain or advantage) to be paid or received for an option must be paid immediately upon conclusion of the deal. It

must be made available to the short investor without delay. Thus, the long investor is faced with liquidity expenditure, and the short investor with a liquidity gain
on that same day. This mode of payment applies for all traditional options.

Modes of execution
An order is entered into post-processing when an option is actively exercised. For
this purpose, clearing participants with the respective Short positions are identi-
fied and assigned an execution at random. On the following day, customers are
informed and processing is initiated. Active execution is called "exercise", passive
execution (by the short investor) is called "assignment". Hence, the assignment is
an order for delivery or receipt resulting from the exercise.

In practical terms this means that if a long call is exercised, the short-call investor must deliver the underlying asset. Delivery is coordinated by the clearing
house. If a long put is exercised, the exercising party delivers the underlying to
the writer who is obliged to accept it. After exercise the option ceases to exist:
The contract is fulfilled and therefore expires. Reviving the original option right
is not possible. Investors can only replace it by a new transaction at the exchange,
i.e., by entering into a new contract and committing to a new transaction.

Special situations when exercising options
In view of the particularities of dividend payments, Eurex has decided not to
permit options to be exercised on the day of shareholder meetings. It used to be
possible formerly, combined with a cancellation of dividends, however the complexity of the process caused Eurex to cease offering this type of transaction.
Should the shareholders' meeting take place on the last trading day, the respective
options can only be traded until (and including) the day before.

Option products
Option strategies could be based on any underlying and implemented accordingly. In practice, they are usually based on liquid and common stock of large
and medium indices, as well as selected exotic options. As far as index options
are concerned, they are also listed for trade according to their market liquidity
and demand. For instance, ETFs (Exchange-Traded Funds) are available, among
others for DAX®-30 equities. It is important to understand what derivatives the
trading broker or bank is offering. For every derivative trade, security of clearing must be ascertained. Only then can secure settlement be guaranteed for all
parties, and this is why banks and brokers only offer contracts they are able to
process.

Oftentimes the same contracts are traded on different exchanges. Investors
should therefore keep an eye on their liquidity and processing. In most cases it
is recommendable to process contracts on their home exchange where liquidity

is highest. The respective contract specifications are laid down in the exchanges' regulations, and must be viewed *before* initiating the first transaction to avoid bad surprises at a later point. Also, investors should think about a possible settlement or exit strategy before closing the deal.

3.4 What are weekly options?

Outside the ordinary expiration cycle (3rd Friday of the month) Eurex has been offering weekly options since April 24, 2006. These options can expire on the first, second, or fourth Friday of the month. As such, they complement Eurex's range of option maturity within one expiration cycle. There are also options that expire on the fifth Friday of a month. Should there be no fifth Friday in the month in question, the expiration date is moved to the next fifth Friday.

3.4.1 When does it make sense to trade in weekly options?

Weekly options make sense whenever investors wish to cover the interval between two "regular" expiration dates; for instance, during the periods when quarterly reports are published. Many institutional investors also use this type of option to keep flexible. Prior to their introduction to the exchange, weekly options were only traded OTC. Since the series only run for a very short time, weekly options have a high gamma exposure – that is, the option price responds very dynamically to changes in the underlying asset. Both speculation and hedging strategies can thus be managed very tightly. For instance, speculation strategies can be set up shortly before companies publish their latest numbers. The same is true for hedging transactions if a negative development is anticipated.

Currently, weekly options are available for DAX®, Dow Jones Euro STOXX 50® and SMI® companies. Contract specifications are the same as for "normal", "long" series.

3.5 What are Low-Exercise-Price Options?

Low Exercise Price Options (LEPOs) are options with an exercise price close to zero (hence their other name, "zero-strike options"). The value of these options changes in parallel with that of the underlying asset, due to being deep In the Money. LEPOs are used, for example, to create "structured products". The advantage compared to a direct investment is that you can build up short positions without needing to physically borrow the shares. This means that these instruments are also available to investors who are unwilling or unable to engage in security loan transactions. The daily settlement price is determined using the binominal model by Cox Ross Rubinstein. If necessary, dividend payments, current interest rates and other payments will be taken into account.

3.6   Closing out a derivative position

Whenever an investor wishes to disengage from his derivative transactions, he can do this at any point during their maturity by closing open contracts. Close-out is affected by an offsetting deal which eliminates all rights and obligations from the original contract.

Table 3-1: Opening and close-out

Opening	Close-out
Long call	Short call
Short call	Long call
Long put	Short put
Short put	Long put

Example:
>An investor holds 100 open short put contracts on stock of company X. He wishes to dispose of that risk. He closes the 100 open short put contracts by transacting an offsetting deal in which he purchases 100 long put contracts with identical contract details. The spread between purchase and sale price is his gain or loss.
>Short put 100 X contracts = € 15,000
>Long put 100 X contracts = € 10,000

In this example, our investor realizes a profit of € 5,000.

If an investor has purchased a long option and wishes to close this position he sells the option. If he has originally sold the option, he will need to buy it back in order to close his position.

In practice, closing orders are annotated accordingly.

3.7 Roll-over

A roll-over enables an investor to extend his position beyond the last trading day. He closes out the position and simultaneously reopens it with expiration on a later date. In the course of such a roll-over, it is also possible to change the strike price and/or number of contracts. If no additional expenditure accrues for the investor, there is a premium-neutral roll-over. The roll-over extends an investor's position beyond the original contract maturity. By adjusting the number of contracts and/or the strike price, the investor can adapt his options position to current market developments.

Example:
> Investor A holds 100 open contracts on the X future. Since he assumes the X index to continue rising, he wishes to extend his position beyond the original expiration date. He sells the 100 contracts and simultaneously acquires 100 new contracts with a later expiration date. This way he has rolled over his position to the new expiration date.

Summary:
Options can be traded on the exchange or over the counter (OTC). American-style options can be exercised throughout their maturity; European-style options can only be exercised at term end. Settlement can be done either in cash or by physical delivery. An investor wishing to close his position prematurely and dispose of all rights and obligations can conclude a closing or offsetting deal. Alternatively, option positions can be extended or "rolled over".

4 The pricing of options

This chapter deals with the following questions:
1. How are option prices determined in theory?
2. What value drivers influence option prices?
3. What do the so-called Greeks mean?
4. What is the put-call parity?
5. How are option prices determined under the Black-Scholes model?
6. How are option prices determined under the binominal model?

4.1 How are option prices determined in theory?

On derivative exchanges, options are traded at prices which we call premiums, and which can be determined by theoretical means. Before we deal with this complex subject matter, let us first have a look at the basics of option pricing.

Intrinsic value

The price of an option consists of two basic components: its **intrinsic value** and its **time value**.

Put in simple terms, the intrinsic value is the positive difference between the strike price and the price of the underlying asset.

A call option has an intrinsic value if the price of the underlying is higher than the strike price of the option.

Example:
> Underlying asset: € 30
> Strike price: € 28
> Intrinsic value: € 2

A put option has an intrinsic value if the price of the underlying is lower than the strike price of the option.

Example:
  Underlying: € 30
  Strike price: € 32
  Intrinsic value: € 2

Hence the three pricing possibilities: An option can be **at-the-money (ATM), in-the-money (ITM),** or **out-of-the-money (OTM).**

Table 4-1: Possibilities for option pricing

	In the money	At the money	Out of the money
Call	Price of underlying > strike price	Price of underlying = strike price	Price of underlying < strike price
Put	Price of underlying < strike price	Price of underlying = strike price	Price of underlying > strike price

The real value of an option at the end of its maturity is also called "intrinsic value".

The intrinsic value can be equal to zero, but can never be negative.

Since out-of-the-money options have a value, there is another very important factor for option pricing: the time value.

Time value

If there was no time value, only in-the-money options would have a price which would be exactly equal to the in-the-money amount. Thus, the time value is the difference between the intrinsic value of an option and its premium **(time value = option premium – intrinsic value).** Another noteworthy point is that the time value increases with an option's remaining maturity, owing to its very function. The longer the option's remaining maturity, the greater the chance that it will end up in the money, therfore having a real (intrinsic) value on its last trading day.

  Likewise, an option's time value decreases with its remaining maturity. This decrease is not linear but exponential, and is also due to the function of the time

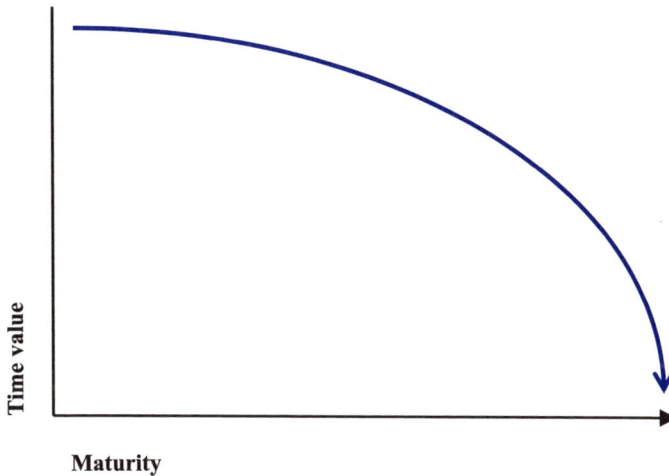

Figure 4.1: Time value function

value. The longer there is a chance that the option will end up in the money, the higher its time value – and vice versa. This is because the chance that an option ends up generating a profit decreases exponentially toward its last trading day, while the risk of worthless expiration increases at the same rate.

For all these reasons, the following rule of thumb should be observed:

> Options with a short remaining term should be sold because their time value is rapidly decreasing, and options with a long remaining term should be purchased.

As was explained before, out-of-the-money options have no intrinsic value. We should add here that options that are deep in the money have almost zero additional time value, as the function of that time value – expressing the probability that the option may end up in the money – has already been fulfilled.

Premature exercise of options

The price mechanism described shows that it is often not a very good idea to exercise an option long before its expiration since you will lose plenty of time value. Let us elaborate using an example:

> **10 long-call options on the X share**
> Strike price: € 50
> Share price: € 50

Option premium: € 7.50

Maturity: 3 months

If this options was exercised, the time value of € 2.50 (€ 7.50 option price – € 5 in-the-money amount / intrinsic value = € 2.50 time value) would be lost. We would be able to sell the shares for € 50, but take a loss of € 2.50 in time value.

If an investor assumes the price of the underlying to fall and therefore wishes to realize his profit he will be well advised to close his options position. This enables him to realize both the time value and the intrinsic value of the option.

Short speculation in options always refers to the time value, which is often expressed as an extra part of the option premium.

4.2 What value drivers influence option prices?

Price of the underlying asset

The price of the underlying is a major driver as the option premium changes along with it. A call option increases in value if the underlying appreciates, and decreases in value if its price drops. Conversely, a put option will increase in value when the underlying becomes cheaper, and vice versa.

This mechanism follows from the basic set-up of both options; the right to purchase a good becomes more expensive if the good appreciates in value and the right to sell it becomes more expensive when it drops in price.

This also explains why a derivative (an instrument derived from a basic investment structure) is continually dependent on the price of the underlying. Consequently, changes in the price of the underlying will always incur changes in the price of the derivative.

Volatility

Volatility (from the Latin *volare* – to fly) is a statistical figure used to measure the intensity of fluctuation of the price of an underlying within a given period of time (aggregated risk). Note that volatility indicates the extent of fluctuations only – not their direction. With a **historical volatility** of 10 and a mean value of 100, the underlying fluctuates between 90 and 110. Volatility is calculated based on the standard deviation (s), which is the square root of the **average mean-squared deviation** of an underlying. The standard deviation expresses how much the individual returns of a period fluctuate around the mean value. The squared standard deviation s_2 is also referred to as variance. The standard deviation is more adequate, even though the variance is easier to determine.

Formula:
$$\sigma = \sqrt{\frac{1}{n} \times \sum_{i=1}^{n} (r_i - \mu)^2}$$

We can safely assume that two thirds of all future market prices will be within this volatility range, which enables us to estimate the intensity of fluctuation and the risk associated with it. In most cases, a sound estimation of the risk is immensely important.

Volatility can be visualized using the Gaussian bell curve:

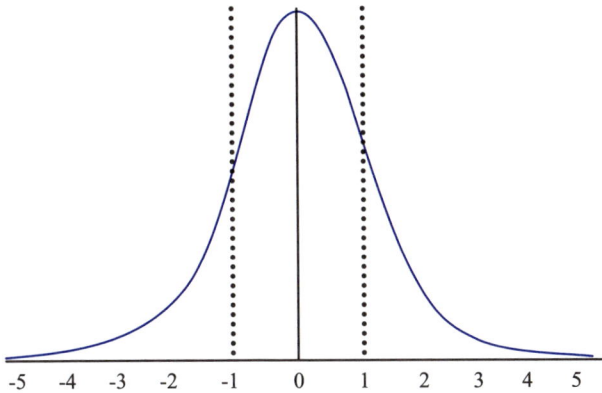

Figure 4.2: Gaussian bell curve

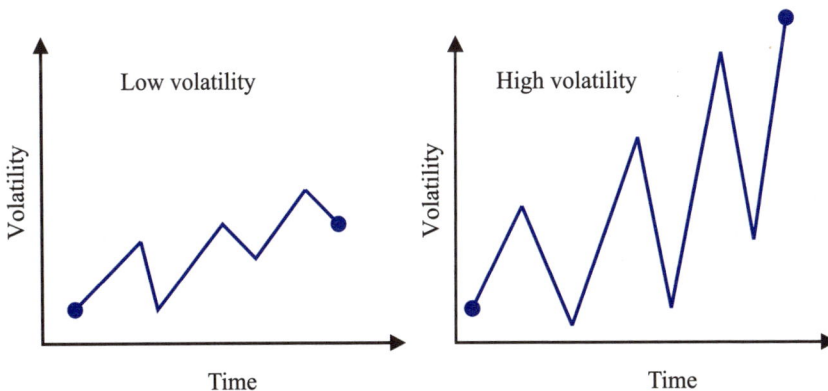

Figure 4.3: Low and high volatility

The time value of an option is very much subject to volatility. Based on principle, the greater the volatility, the higher the option's time value. Option prices rise as volatility increases, and drop as it decreases.

Another term frequently used is **implied volatility.** We will go into more detail about that at a later point in this chapter. For now we will briefly explain the term. Implied volatility is the volatility resulting from options' current market prices. It reflects the volatility expected by trading participants with regard to the underlying asset's future development. Implied volatility can be quite different from the historical volatility based on statistics. Another term for it is "traded volatility". This volatility, which is "perceived" and thus paid (or asked) by the trading participants, is an important component of option pricing and in general of premiums paid. Implied volatility can be derived from the Black-Scholes formula by iteration.

Market interest rate

An increase in market interest rates leads to a price increase for call options, and a decrease for put options. This function compensates for the market interest advantage or disadvantage of different types of options. A potential disadvantage from investing in options, as compared with a direct investment or order in the underlying asset, is compensated.

Dividend payouts

Dividend payouts affect the price of the underlying asset both **directly** and **indirectly.** Their direct influence works to decrease the price of calls and increase the price of puts, at least in the case of American-style options. With European-style options, expected dividends are already taken account of in the premium. In this context it is important to mention that the indices underlying index options can differ. On the one hand we have performance indices, where dividends paid out are assumed to be re-invested in the index, and on the other there are price indices, where dividend payouts are counted as losses which cause the index to drop. This differentiation is important because it directly affects option pricing.

Remaining maturity

As mentioned before, an option's remaining term is another major value driver. The price-decreasing effect increases as time approaches the option's expiration date. The option's time value decreases exponentially as the probability of it ending up in the money decreases. Consequently, the influence of the option's time value increases with the decrease of its remaining term.

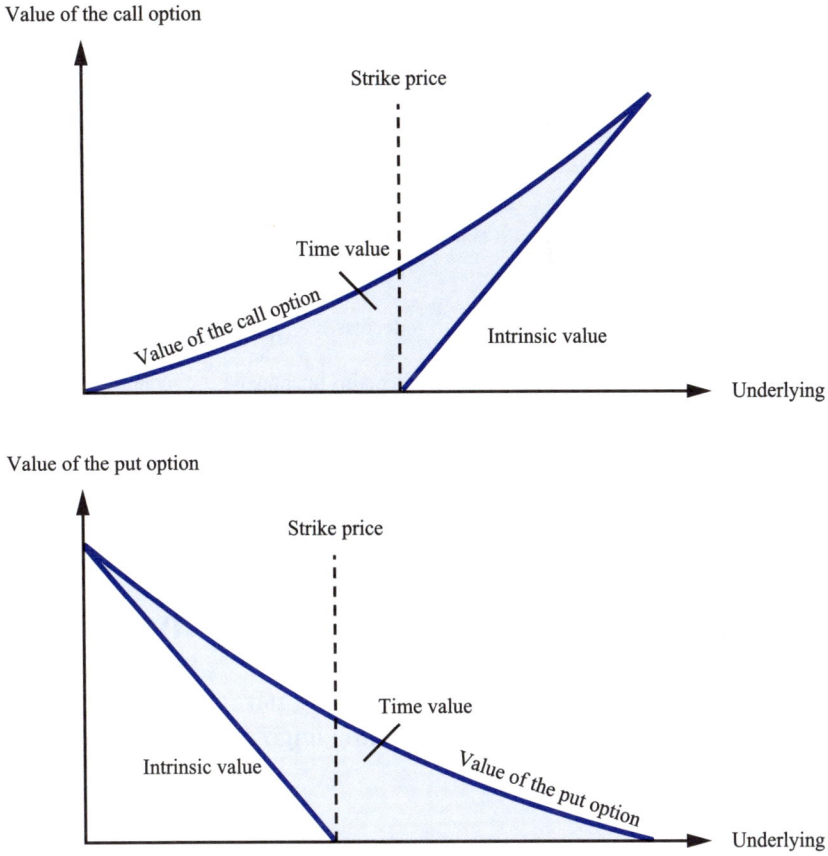

Figure 4.4: Visualization of an option's time value (call and put)

Table 4-2: Overview of parameters driving the option price

Parameter		Option price Call	Option price Put
Underlying	increases	increases	decreases
	decreases	decreases	increases
Volatility	increases	increases	increases
	decreases	decreases	decreases

Table 4-2: (*continued*) Overview of parameters driving the option price

Parameter		Option price Call	Option price Put
Remaining maturity	decreases	decreases	decreases
Market interest rate	increases	increases	decreases
	decreases	decreases	increases
Dividend payout **American-style** **European-style**		decreases remains unchanged	increases remains unchanged

4.3   What do the so-called Greeks mean?

To express how much a change in an influencing parameter affects the option price, we use sensitivity factors which in trading lingo are referred to as "Greeks" (due to the Greek letters used).

Delta

The Delta of an investment measures the extent to which the price of the under-lying influences the option premium, specifically: which way the premium moves if the price of the underlying changes by one unit. Thus, the Delta expresses the direct price influence of the underlying on the option.

The algebraic signs of the different Delta positions are as follows:

Table 4-3: Algebraic signs for call and put Delta

	Long	Short
Call	+	–
Put	–	+

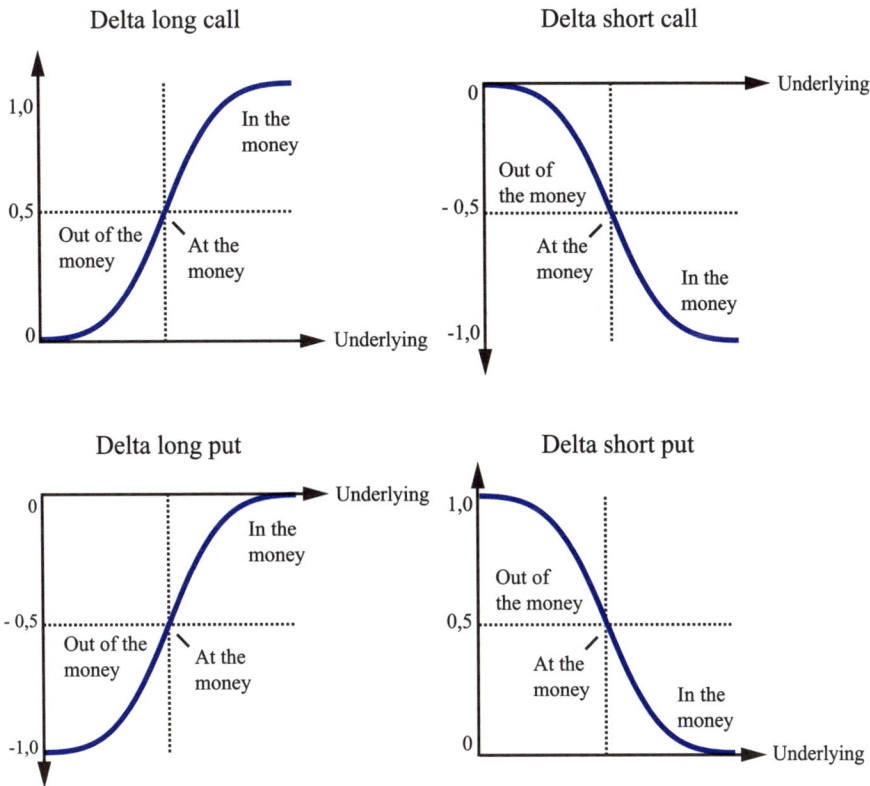

Figure 4.5: Delta function

Table 4-4: Delta values

Delta of a...	Out of the money	At the money	In the money
Long call / short put	Approx. 0 to 0.5	Approx. 0.5	Approx. 0.5 to 1
Long put / short call	Approx. 0 to –0.5	Approx. –0.5	Approx. 0.5 to –1

Gamma

Whereas the Delta indicates the change in the option price, the gamma expresses how much the Delta of an option will change if the price of the underlying changes by one unit. We could say that the gamma is the "Delta of the Delta": It is the second (mathematical) derivative of the option price and the first (mathematical) derivative of the Delta. The gamma measures the increase of the Delta.

Rho

This Greek indicates how much the value of an option will change if the interest rate changes by one percentage point.

> **Rho is always positive for a long call and a short put.**
> **Rho is always negative for a long put and a short call.**

Theta

The Theta of an option expresses how much time value an option loses every day if the price and other conditions of the underlying remain unchanged. Sensitivity is strongest for at-the-money options with a short term.

If the Theta of an option is 0.25, this means that in theory the option loses € 0.25 in value "overnight".

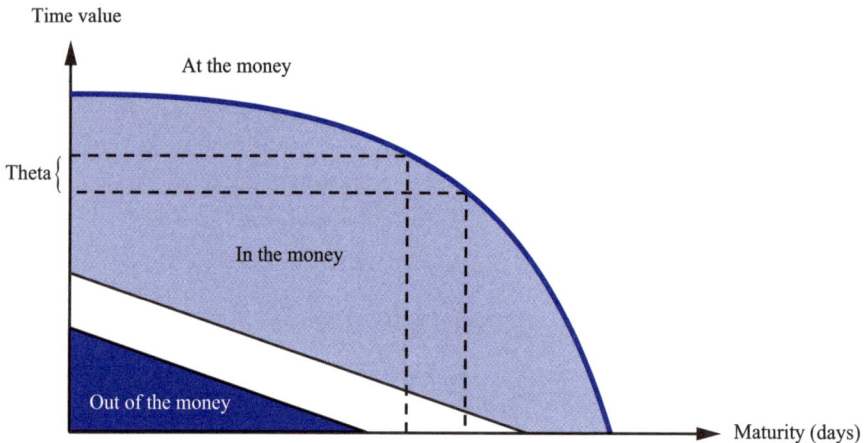

Figure 4.6: The Theta function

Vega

The Vega of an option expresses how a change in volatility by one percentage will influence the option price.

Example:

If the Vega of an option is 1.7 and volatility is 25 percent, this means that – ceteris paribus – an increase or decrease in volatility by 1 percent (to 26 percent or a 24 percent, respectively) will increase or decrease the value of the option 1.7-fold. Consequently, Vega decreases along with the option's remaining maturity.

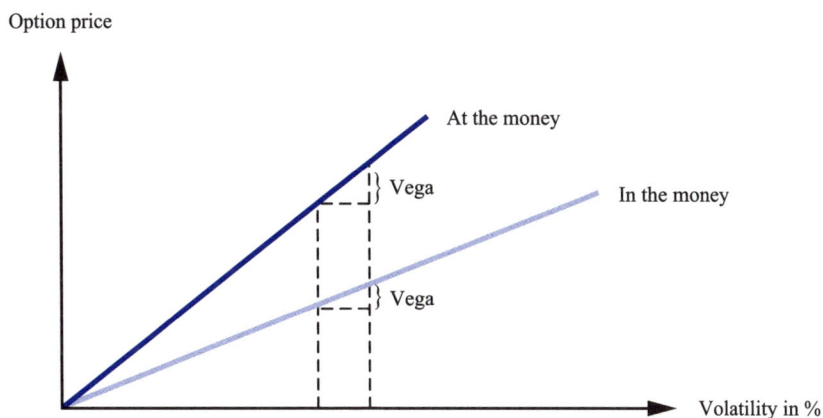

Figure 4.7: Visualization of the Vega function

In this section, we have elaborated on issues of a primarily practical nature.

Let us now turn to the classic option pricing models. In view of their complex nature we have decided to discuss them in relatively simple terms, focusing on two models: the formula of log-normal distribution developed by Black and Scholes and the binominal model developed by Cox, Ross and Rubinstein.

Table 4-5: Overview of algebraic signs for Greeks

	Delta	Gamma	Vega	Theta	Rho
Long call	positive	positive	positive	negative	positive
Short call	negative	negative	negative	positive	negative
Long put	negative	positive	positive	negative	negative
Short put	positive	negative	negative	positive	positive

4.4 What is the put-call parity all about?

The price of a put option can be derived from the price of a call option. To calculate this, we use the following formula which is also called a put-call-parity equation:

$$C = (S - E) + \left(E \times \left(\frac{r}{1+r} \right) \right) + V$$

Where:
C = call price
$S - E$ = intrinsic value
$(E \times (r/(1+r)))$ = opportunity cost of the writer
V = insurance premium
E = strike price

We assume the value of V (the insurance premium) to equal the price of a **put option**. This is logical since the put price can be considered a kind of insurance. The price of a put option can be derived from the above formula by simple transformation. This is what we refer to as call-put parity. If we can determine the price of a call option, the parity equation allows us to determine the put price as well.

By conversion we get:

$$C = S - E \times \frac{1}{(1+r)^t} + P$$

Where:
t = annualized remaining maturity
P = put price

Thus, if we can set the price of a position it is also possible to determine a mathematically fair price for the counter-position.

4.5 How are option prices determined under the Black-Scholes model?

In 1973, Fischer Black and Myron Scholes published a relatively simple model for the theoretical determination of option prices. We should mention that Robert C. Merton was involved as well but preferred to have his findings published separately. In 1997, Merton and Scholes were awarded the Nobel Prize in Economics for this model (Fischer Black had died in 1995). It has gained great popularity since thanks to its simplicity, although it is based on very restrictive assumptions.

Assumptions of the Black-Scholes model:
- The option is of the European type
- There are no dividend payouts on the underlying share throughout the option's maturity
- There is no transaction cost
- The interest rates for risk-free investments is known and constant, and identical for the debit and the credit side
- Capital markets are efficient, meaning that stock prices develop at random and there is no arbitrage
- Share returns are distributed log-normally
- No taxes are being payed

Based on these assumptions, Black and Scholes have developed this formula:

$$c = S_0 N(d_1) - Ke^{-rT} N(d_2)$$

$$p = Ke^{-rT} N(-d_2) - S_0 N(-d_1)$$

$$d_1 = \frac{\ln(S_0 / K) + (r + \sigma^2 / 2)T}{\sigma\sqrt{T}}$$

$$d_2 = d_1 - \sigma\sqrt{T}$$

Where:
S_0 = price of the underlying share

K = strike price of the call option
ln = natural logarithm
e = basis of natural logarithm = 2.7128
r = risk-free interest rate
$N(d)$ = cumulative normal distribution of d
v = volatility
t = remaining maturity of call

In the first part of the equation we see the number of shares required to form a risk-free portfolio of shares and call options. Thus, we derive the Delta at this point.

If we now assume arbitrage to be excluded, and if we apply the Itô Lemma, then we can derive the Black-Scholes differential equation based on the same assumptions as listed above.

$$\frac{\partial V}{\partial t} + rS\frac{\partial V}{\partial S} + \frac{1}{2}\sigma^2 S^2 \frac{\partial^2 V}{\partial S^2} = rV$$

Where:
V is the value of the option.

The problems of this model are:
1. Black and Scholes assume constant volatility, which as a glance at market prices will quickly reveal is unrealistic. The change of values does not follow a Gaussian normal distribution but, as shown by Benoît Mandelbrot, is distributed exponentially and interdependent. Thus, deflections can be much greater than assumed under the standard model.
2. The equation is only valid for European-style options.

4.6 How are option prices determined under the Binominal model?

The Binominal model is another method to determine a fair option price. It is used to value the option when the price of the underlying changes. The Cox-Ross-Rubinstein model is a logical extension of the Black-Scholes model, and one of the option pricing models most frequently used. On principle, the binominal model distinguishes between recombinant and non-recombinant trees, of which the non-recombinant ones are immensely important for path-independent options.

Basic prerequisites: We assume perfect markets in which there are no transactions costs, taxes, or conditions for inclusion. Revenues from naked sales are immediately available and instruments can be arbitrarily divided. There is only one interest rate for money borrowed or lent out. For any interval considered, we know both that the price changes and what the risk-free interest rate is. It is further assumed that we are dealing with growth strategies only, and arbitrage profits are not possible.

The initial assumption under the binominal model is that the price of an underlying can either go up (u) or go down (d) by x units.

This permits the following derivation:

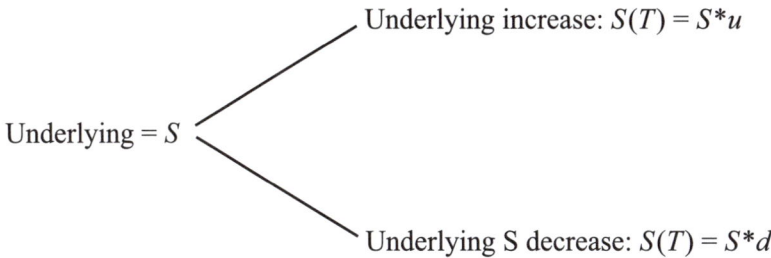

Underlying increase: $S(T) = S*u$

Underlying $= S$

Underlying S decrease: $S(T) = S*d$

Where:
$S =$ price of the underlying share
$u =$ rate of increase
$d =$ rate of decrease

We derive the values for C_u and C_d. Evaluation is based on the assumption of an arbitrage-free market. In the next step, we will form risk-free portfolios from delta long positions in the underlying asset and short positions in call options.

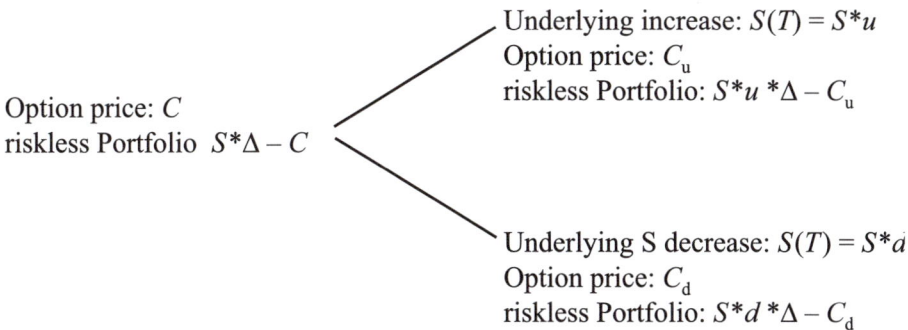

Underlying increase: $S(T) = S*u$
Option price: C_u
riskless Portfolio: $S*u *\Delta - C_u$

Option price: C
riskless Portfolio $S*\Delta - C$

Underlying S decrease: $S(T) = S*d$
Option price: C_d
riskless Portfolio: $S*d *\Delta - C_d$

The portfolio weight is determined as follows:

$$S \cdot u \cdot \Delta - C_u = S \cdot d \cdot \Delta - C_d \Leftrightarrow$$

$$\Delta = \frac{C_u - C_d}{S \cdot u - S \cdot d}$$

The value of the risk-free portfolio, discounted down, is equal to the portfolio value at a time $t = 0$.

$$(S \cdot u \cdot \Delta - C_u)e^{-rT} \text{ with } \Delta = \frac{C_u \quad C_d}{S \cdot u - S \cdot d} \rightarrow$$

$$S \cdot \Delta - C = (S \cdot u \cdot \Delta - C_u)e^{-rT} \rightarrow$$

Call at time $0 =$

$$C = S \cdot \Delta - (S \cdot u \cdot \Delta - C_u)e^{-rT} = S \cdot \frac{C_u - C_d}{S \cdot u - S \cdot d} - (S \cdot u \cdot \frac{C_u - C_d}{S \cdot u - S \cdot d} - C_u)e^{-rT}$$

By rearranging these equations we get:

$$C = S \cdot \frac{C_u - C_d}{S \cdot u - S \cdot d} - (S \cdot u \cdot \frac{C_u - C_d}{S \cdot u - S \cdot d} - C_u)e^{-rT} =$$

$$= \frac{pCu - (1-p)C_d}{e^{rT}} \quad \text{with} \quad p = \frac{e^{rT} - d}{u - d}$$

The option price is considered the discounted expected value, and determined with this formula:

$$C = \frac{pC_u - (1-p)C_d}{e^{rT}} = \frac{E^P[C(T)]}{e^{rT}} \quad \text{with} \quad p = \frac{e^{rT} - d}{u - d}$$

We realize that to evaluate options we need to determine the discounted cash-flows, whereby p in the above equation is interpreted to be the risk-neutral probability.

This reveals that the calculation only uses an implied probability, rather than the actual one, as expressed by the parameters d and u in our initial consideration.

Therefore the expected value of a stock for the time T can be determined as follows:

$$E[S_T] = p \cdot S \cdot u + (1-p) \cdot S \cdot d \quad \text{with} \quad p = \frac{e^{rT} - d}{u - d} \leftrightarrow$$

$$E[S_T] = p \cdot S \cdot (u-d) + S \cdot d = \frac{e^{rT} - d}{u - d} S \cdot (u-d) + S \cdot d$$

$$= e^{rT} \cdot S - d \cdot S + S \cdot d = S e^{rT}$$

Risk-free probability (**p**) is equal to the risk-free interest rate (**p**).

This model can now be transferred to a two-period or multiple-period model as required. This allows for the possibility to simulate and determine the theoretical change in option prices when the given basic intentions emerge.

4.7 Tradable option prices

Let us go back to practice once more.

The quotes which are posted on derivative exchanges and based on which the respective instruments can be traded, are usually posted by Market Makers. However, since there are also thinly traded (and thus not very actively managed) contracts it is sometimes necessary to apply limit orders, in particular in cases where no quotes are available. Only for very liquid option series is it recommendable to post a market order. In tight markets (with not very liquid series), or if contract series are not actively managed, it is absolutely imperative to set a limit. In addition, investors have the right to ask for a quote. This should always be done if no quotes have been posted. We strongly caution against unguarded forays! Especially in case of a roll-over they can result in dramatic premium shifts and unwanted losses.

Summary:
Option prices usually consist of two components: the intrinsic value and the time value. The intrinsic value of an option corresponds to the amount by which exercising the option would be better than trading the underlying stock at its current quote. If an option does not have an intrinsic value it consists of the time value only. Hence, options can be either "at the money", "in the money", or "out of the money". The time value of an option is the amount paid for the chance that the option will end up in the money. As this chance decreases exponentially toward the end of the option's maturity, so does the time value. The two option pricing models most widely used are the Black-Scholes model and the binominal model by Cox, Ross, and Rubinstein.

5 Strategies involving options

This chapter deals with the following questions:
1. What are the four basic strategies in options trading all about?
   What strategy is behind the basic position 1 – long call?
   What strategy is behind the basic position 2 – short call?
   What strategy is behind the basic position 3 – long put?
   What strategy is behind the basic position 4 – short put?
2. How to hedge with options
3. What option combinations are common?
4. How to build up a strategy in options trading?
5. What significance does the market opinion have?

5.1 What are the four basic options trading strategies all about?

In options trading, there are four basic strategies which provide the foundation for all other strategies, and therefore need to be well understood by investors:

- **Long call:** An investor taking a long call position is convinced that the price of the underlying will go up. He purchases the right to buy that underlying (by virtue of his owning the call). If his expectation comes true the call option will increase in value. Of course the investor could also decide to buy the underlying financial instrument, but to this end he would have to raise considerably more funds. In other words, by using a call option the investor can leverage the capital he invests. His downside potential is limited to the premium paid, while he has a chance to benefit from unlimited appreciation of the underlying. As he is not obliged to provide subsequent payments, he only bears the original risk inherent in premium payment.
- **Short call** An investor going short a call option counts on constant or slightly decreasing share prices and attempts to generate additional revenues from that decrease. He sells call options and can generate a maximum profit to the amount of the premium received. The risk involved is that he may be obliged to deliver the underlying at the strike price. However this risk can be minimized if the call writer owns that asset at the time of the transaction. This position is

referred to as a "covered option", as the obligation to deliver can be met out of one's own "inventory" and losses in excess of that are excluded. However, the investor still risks a loss. For example, if the price of the underlying asset rises beyond the strike price plus the premium, he will no longer be able to partake of the resulting profits.

• **Long put:** An investor in a long put position counts on a price drop for the underlying asset. By buying the option, he either attempts to hedge against this price drop or speculate on it. Again, the risk of a loss is limited to the option premium paid. Profits are unlimited only in theory, as any investment can drop to zero at maximum, which in fact does represent a limit.

• **Short put:** An investor writing a put option (= short put position) counts on constant or slightly increasing security prices. He attempts to benefit from that price increase and actively takes on the risk involved. In exchange for that he receives the option premium, which also represents his maximum gain. By contrast, his loss is unlimited in theory as he might be forced to purchase the underlying. However we should not leave unmentioned that company share can never drop below zero even if the company in question goes bankrupt. Consequently, even in a worst-case scenario the risk is limited to a calculable value.

In the following sections we will outline these four strategies in greater detail.

Basic assumptions: We shall assume that the underlying instrument is a company share. Any fees and costs possibly accruing shall be left out of consideration.

5.1.1 What is the strategy behind basic position 1 – long call?

An investor buying a long call acquires the right but not the obligation to purchase the underlying stock in the course of, or at the end of, of the option's maturity. For this right he pays a price to the contracting party (the call writer) in the form of the option's premium. The holder of the short call is obliged to deliver the stock if and when requested by the long call position.

Example:

     Long call on X stock
     Strike price € 50
     Expiration date: September
     Option premium € 3.

In our example, the option buyer has the right to buy the X stock at € 50 through-out the entire term of the option (that is, by the third Friday in September at the latest). He has purchased that right by paying a premium of € 3 to the seller im-mediately upon conclusion of the transaction.

If the price of the X stock rises beyond the strike price (which in our example is € 50) the buyer of the option (long) will exert his right and exercise the option. The seller (short) will have to deliver the stocks at € 50 apiece.

Break-even point of this strategy
The break-even point is € 53: Since the holder of this option has initially paid € 3 in exchange for the right to buy the stocks at € 50 apiece, these € 3 must be ac-counted for in the equation.

Scenario analysis:
- **The stock trades below € 50:** The buyer of the call option realizes his maximum loss on the option's expiration date. The option expires worthless.
- **The stock trades between € 50 and € 53:** The holder of the call option realizes a limited loss. The option's value on its expiration date corresponds to its intrin-sic value, as it is in the money.
- **The stock trades above € 53:** The holder of the option has reached the profit zone. On its expiration date, the option is worth more than when the transac-tion was concluded.

As we have seen, the underlying must exceed the break-even point for a long call in order for the buyer to realize a profit when exercising the option.

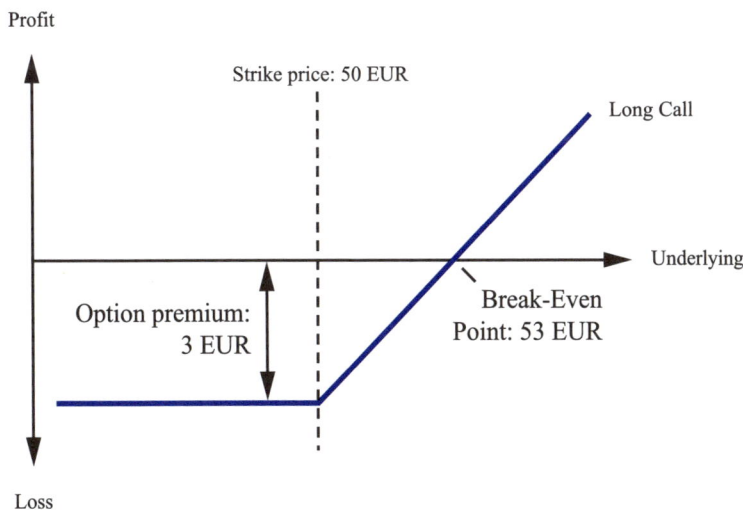

Figure 5.1: Profit and loss scenario for a long call position

5 Strategies involving options

5.1.2 What is the strategy behind basic position 2 – short call?

In our above example the investor purchased a call option. Now let us assume he sells that option, using the same example once more:

> Short call on X stock
> Strike price € 50
> Expiration date: September
> Option premium € 3.

As seller of the call on the X stock our investor has received a premium of € 3. This makes him the option writer, that is, he will have to deliver the stock at the buyer's request.

At this point we must distinguish between two different basic settings. In one setting, the investor holds a short call position on stock he owns ("covered call"), and in the other he holds an uncovered ("naked") short call position. **Naked call writing** is the selling of call options without holding the underlying asset. This position is much more speculative than **covered call writing,** where the writer is also the holder of the underlying asset.

Let us first consider our example for the naked call writing scenario:

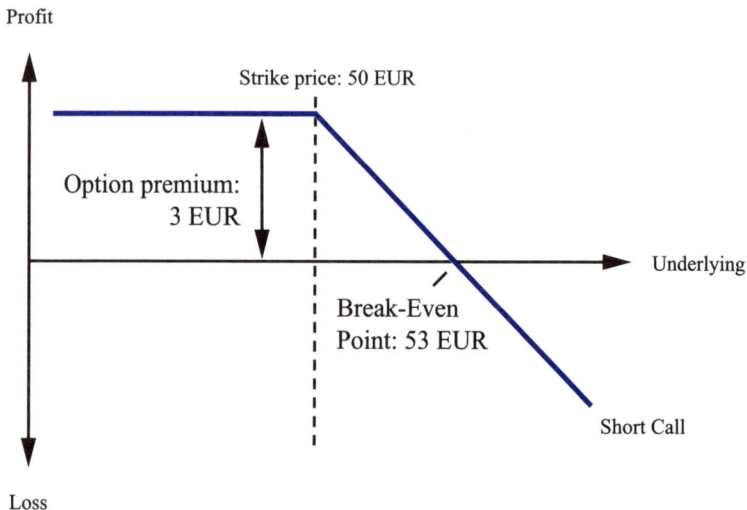

Figure 5.2: Profit and loss scenario for a short call position (naked call writing).

Here, the profit and loss situation is exactly opposite to the long position.

Scenario analysis:
- **The stock trades below the strike price of € 50:** The short call investor achieves his maximum profit. He has received the full premium, and the option expires worthless.
- **The stock trades between € 50 and € 53:** Our short call investor achieves a smaller gain. As the long investor exercises his call option, the short investor must deliver the underlying shares. To do that, he needs to purchase them in the market first. (Remember we are talking about naked call writing.) The difference between the option premium received and the expenditure to purchase the stock, minus the strike price, is his gain.
- **The stock trades above the break-even point of € 53.** The investor takes a loss. He is obliged to deliver the shares at the strike price agreed. His loss is determined as follows: (Purchase price – strike price) – option premium.

Note: The risk of a loss with a short call strategy is unlimited in upward markets!

The conservative variant of a short call position is the **covered call writing** (CCW). Here, the investor sells call options on assets he holds. If the options are exercised the short investor can deliver from his own portfolio. CCW is a strategy aimed at increasing returns, as primarily passive assets generate additional returns through premium payment. The risk is limited to the profit not achieved. If the underlying rises above the strike price the CCW investor must deliver, and can no longer benefit from further increases. Should the overall position (spot instruments and derivatives) drop below € 47 (€ 50 strike – € 3 premium) the investor realizes an overall loss, as he holds both the derivative instrument and the underlying asset. Conversely, potential price drops in the spot market position are compensated by the revenues from the derivatives transaction.

Example of a CCW investment:
Our investor has the following shares in his portfolio:

10,000 shares of X Corporation; purchase price € 30, current market price € 48

10,000 shares of Y Corporation; purchase price € 50, current market price € 51

5,000 shares of V Corporation; purchase price € 35, current market price USD 34

5,000 shares of C Corporation; purchase price CHF 28, current market price CHF 75.

All assets are passive, and the investor only uses them to obtain dividends.

Strategy: During the period in which no dividends are paid out our investor writes a covered call, ensuring that the call options are out of the money. With the premiums received he achieves a positive cash-flow. If the options are exercised by the counterparty, our investor's risk is limited as he is already in possession of the underlying shares. Thanks to the premiums received as an extraordinary profit, the investor has hedged against slight decreases in the market price.

5.1.3 What is the strategy behind basic position 3 – long put?

A long put investor has acquired the right but not the obligation to sell the underlying assets to the put option seller (short put) during or at the end of the option's maturity. He pays a premium to the writer in return for the writer's actively taking on the risk involved. In other words, the long put investor has acquired the right to become a seller of stock by exercising his option.

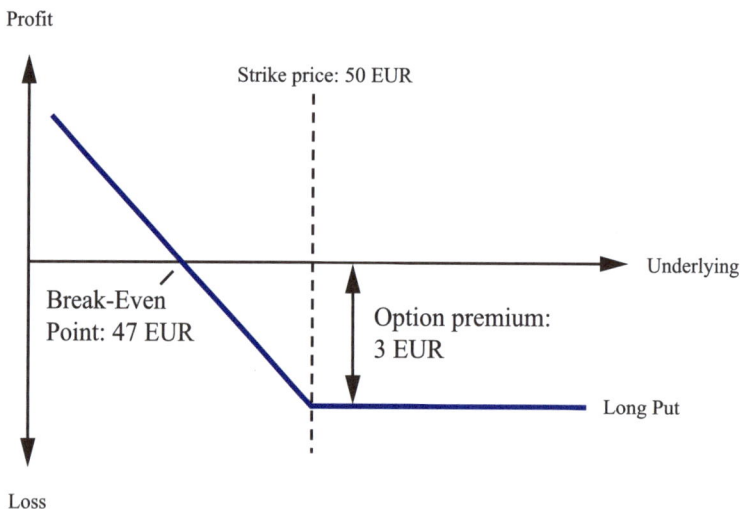

Figure 5.3: Profit and loss scenario for a long put position

Let us explain based on our above example:

> Long put on the X stock
> Strike price € 50
> Option premium € 3
> Maturity September.

The long put investor holds the right to sell the X stock to the short put investor by September. This right cost him € 3, which have been paid to the short put investor when the deal was closed. At the same time, the strike price per share has been set at € 50.

The break-even point of a long put is the market price beyond which the share must drop, for the buyer to realize a profit by exercising the option.

Sale at:	€ 50
Premium:	€ 3 (already paid)
Break-even point:	€ 47

Scenario analysis:
- **The stock trades below € 47:** The long put investor realizes his maximum profit.
- **The stock trades between € 50 and € 47:** The investor realizes a limited loss, as on its Last Trading Day the option is only worth the in-the-money portion.
- **The stock price rises, contrary to the investor's expectations:** The investor takes his maximum loss. Although limited to the option premium paid, this must be considered a complete loss.

This strategy is suitable for both a hedging strategy and speculation on a drop in market prices. If long puts are used for hedging purposes the option premium paid corresponds to the insurance premium paid for the option maturity.

5.1.4 What is the strategy behind basic position 4 – short put?

The counter-position to what we have just described is the short put. A short put investor has agreed to buy the underlying on a certain date (or within a certain period) and at a certain price, for which he receives the option premium. This is also his maximum profit. His potential loss however is the entire purchase price (at strike), since he is obliged to purchase the shares (with a maximum possible price drop to zero).

In our example, the short put investor will have to buy the shares for € 50 apiece when the option is exercised. Since he has already received € 3, his actual issue price is € 47. If the share price drops below € 47, the short put investor realizes a loss.

Scenario analysis:
- **The stock trades below € 47:** The short put investor takes a loss.
- **The stock trades between € 47 and € 50:** The short put position realizes a limited profit.
- **The stock trades above € 50:** The investor keeps the option premium received, which means that he realizes his maximum profit.

This strategy is very risky if prices are falling. Investors face potentially high losses while possible gains are limited to the option premium.

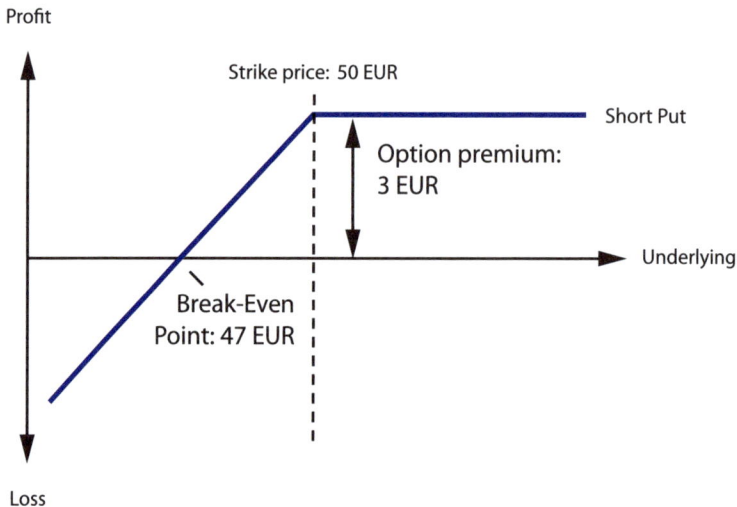

Figure 5.4: Profit and loss scenario for a short put position

Table 5-1: Overview of four basic positions

	Basic assumption	**Deal specifics**
Long call	Price of underlying will go up	Must pay premium, can possibly buy underlying asset
Short call	Price of underlying will remain constant or drop slightly	Receives writer's premium and must possibly deliver
Long put	Price of underlying will go down	Must pay premium, can possibly sell underlying asset
Short put	Price of underlying will remain constant or go up slightly	Receives writer's premium and must possibly buy underlying asset

Table 5-2: Overview of 4 basic positions and their assumptions

Position	**Market price of underlying**	**Volatility**	**Effect on time value**
Long call	↑	↑	–
Short call	↓	↓	+
Long put	↓	↑	–
Short put	↑	↓	+

5.2   How to hedge with options

One of the most fundamental notions in options trading is the hedging of present or future positions. The simplest hedging approach is to take a short underlying position. It means that the investor sells the part of his position that he wishes to hedge. This is easy but often not very effective. It makes more sense to hedge a portfolio with derivative instruments.

To hedge with options you always need a hedge ratio, which indicates how many options will be needed to hedge the position in question. In calculating the hedge ratio t makes perfect sense to use the Delta of the option, as it expresses the extent to which the option value will change due to fluctuations in the underlying price.

Calculating the hedge ratio:

$$\text{\# of contracts} = \frac{\text{Number of shares}}{\text{Contract size}} \times \frac{1}{\text{delta of option}}$$

Example:

Our investor has 10,000 shares of V Corporation in his portfolio. He wishes to hedge them at € 40. For this purpose he chooses a put option with a strike price of € 40 and a Delta of −0.50.

Number of contracts = 10,000 / (−0.50)

Number of contracts = −200

The investor thus needs 200 contracts (the sign does not matter) to hedge the position. In the event that the price of the V share drops, the hedge position will compensate for his loss. However, our investor will have to keep adjusting his hedge whenever the Delta of the options changes. For example, with a Delta of −0.60 he will only have to hold 167 contracts. This strategy is very expensive, as it requires constant adjustment to the changes in the Delta.

Alternatively, our investor could employ a protective put strategy, buying put options in the same amount as the underlying stock in his portfolio. In effect he would carry out a 1:1 hedge which, however, would tie up considerable funds.

Another protection approach is the **β hedge.** In this strategy, the **β** of the portfolio is used. It is a portfolio protection strategy based on an index option. This type of hedging is very common, as the β factor can be determined for any portfolio.

Hedge ratio for a β hedge: The number of contracts is determined using the following formula:

$$\text{\# of contracts} = \frac{\text{Equivalent of the Portfolio}}{\left(\text{Index level} \times \text{contract size of index option}\right)} \times \beta - portfolio$$

5.3 What option combinations are common?

At the beginning of this chapter we have explained that all option combinations are based on the four basic positions. In this section we shall briefly explain the most common combinations (or combos, as they are called by traders).

Straddle

A straddle is the simultaneous purchase or sale of an identical number of calls and puts for the same underlying instrument, with the same expiration date and at the same strike price. The important thing, as you can see, is the degree of volatility rather than the direction in which prices fluctuate.

Long straddle

An investor building a long straddle position assumes both a major market price change for the underlying and an increase in volatility. In what direction the market price will move does not matter, as the investor has positioned himself on both sides. Such a strategy combines unlimited profit potential with a loss potential limited to the option premium paid.

Construction of a long straddle: The simultaneous purchase of a call (long call) and a put (long put) with identical maturity and strike prices results in a long straddle.

Example:

Long call, X share, strike € 50, expiration September, option premium € 2.

Long put, X share, strike € 50, expiration September, option premium € 1.80.

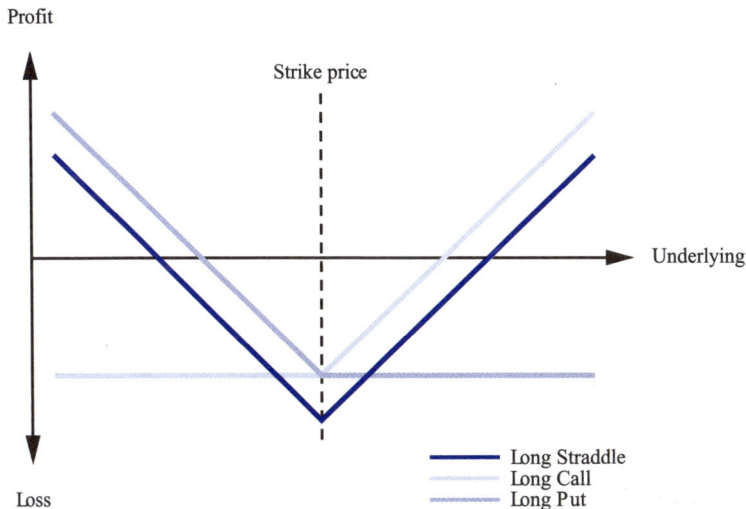

Figure 5.5: Profit and loss scenario for a long straddle

The total premium expenditure under this strategy is € 3.80; its break-even point is € 53.80 or 46.20. As we can see from this example, the premium must be considered in its entirety when calculating gains and losses. As long as the underlying price is between both break-even points the investor is in the zone of limited or full loss. He reaches the zone of unlimited profit once the underlying price exceeds or drops below one of the two break-even points. The investor profits from increasing volatility because it results in price increases for long options. Therefore this strategy is also referred to as positive volatility strategy.

Short straddle
A short straddle is the exact opposite of a long straddle. The investor assumes the price of the underlying to remain close to the strike price.

Example:
Short call, X share, strike € 50, expiration September, option premium € 2.
Short put, X share, strike € 50, expiration September, option premium € 1.80.

As the total premium expenditure under this strategy is € 3.80, its break-even points are € 52 and 48.20. The investor realizes losses if the underlying price fluctuates more, and profits with lesser volatility. The loss potential of this strategy is unlimited. It is therefore considered a risk strategy, as the risk is contrasted with limited proceeds from the premiums.

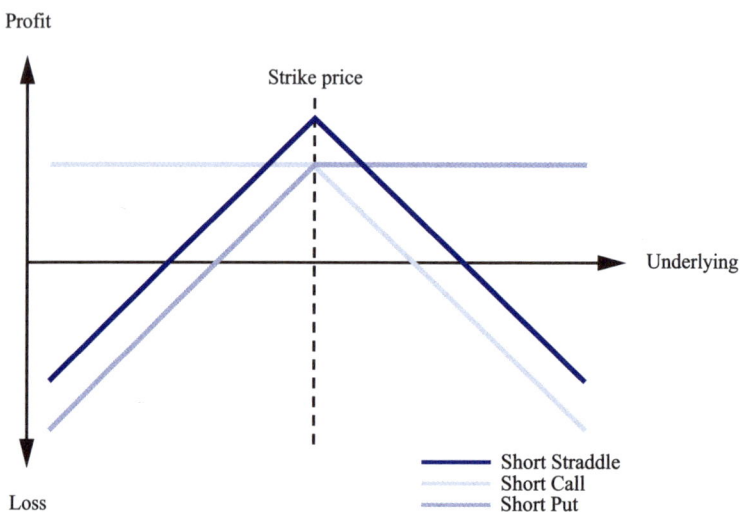

Figure 5.6: Profit and loss scenario for a short straddle

Strangle

A Strangle is the simultaneous sale or purchase of an identical number of put and call options on the same underlying and with the same expiration date, but different strike prices. Thus, this strategy differs from the straddle only to the extent that the calls and puts have different strike prices. (Another definition of the Strangle can be the purchase or sale of calls and puts with the same strike price, but different maturity).

Long strangle

On principle, a long strangle strategy follows the same basic considerations as a long straddle. The only difference is that market price fluctuations are assumed to be greater.

Example:

Long call, X share, strike € 40, expiration September, option premium € 1.
Long call, X share, strike € 36, expiration September, option premium € 0.80.

Break-even points of this strategy are at € 41.80 and 34.20. Between the two there is a relatively wide margin for losses. If the underlying price ends up between the two points the investor will take a loss. However if it passes one of the two points potential profits are unlimited. By contrast, the loss is limited to the premium paid when closing the deal.

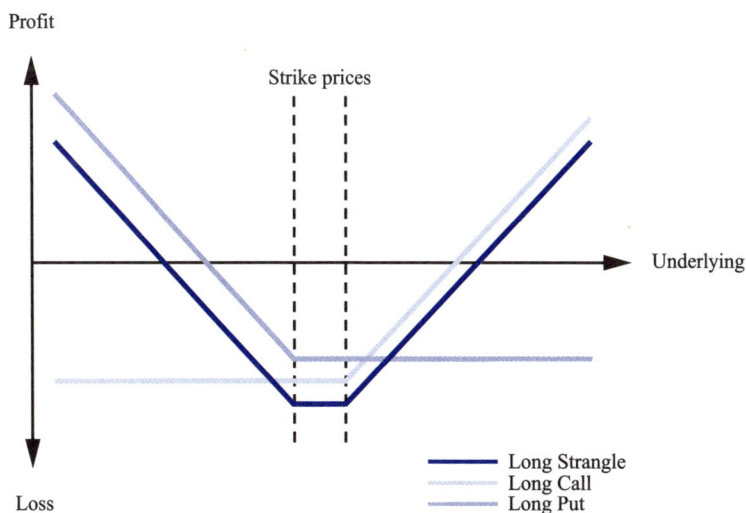

Figure 5.7: Profit and loss scenario for a long strangle

Short strangle

A short strangle is the exact opposite of a long strangle. Its advantage vis-à-vis the short straddle is that the broader corridor of options involves greater opportunities. Maximum proceeds are limited to the premium received, while potential losses are unlimited.

Example:

Short call, X share, strike € 40, expiration September, option premium € 1.
Short put, X share, strike € 36, expiration September, option premium € 0.80.

Break-even points under this strategy are at € 41.80 and 34.20.
Note that rapid market price increases or decreases can equally drive this strategy into the loss zone. It is therefore advisable to clarify beforehand when and how the position will have to be closed in a worst-case scenario.

Spreads

A spread is the simultaneous purchase and sale of options of the same type, but with differing strike prices and/or expiration dates.

In trading lingo, spreads based on call options are called **bull spreads** while spreads built on put options are referred to as **bear spreads**.

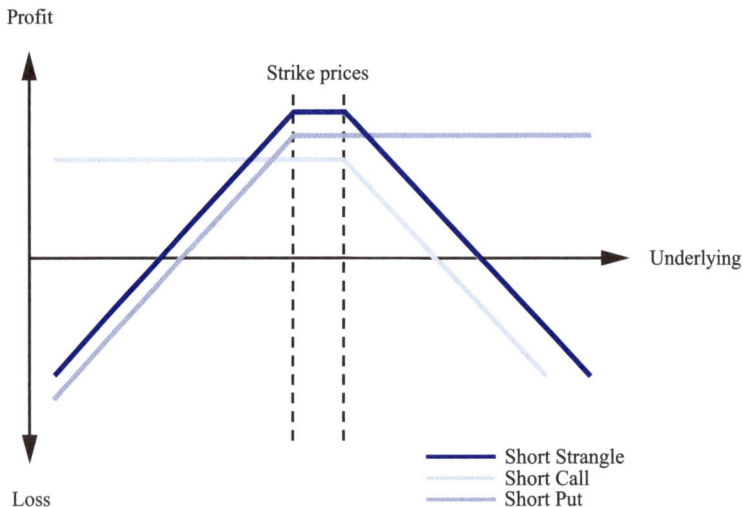

Figure 5.8: Profit and loss scenario for a short strangle

If the investor faces a net premium expenditure for constructing the spread, then we refer to it as a **debit spread**. Conversely, the **credit spread** (or sold spread) provides the investor with a net premium credit.

Let us clarify based on two examples:
Debit bull spread: This involves the purchase of a call option and the sale of a call option with a higher strike price.

Example:

        Purchase of a call option on the X share
        Strike price € 40
        Expiration in September
        Option premium € 1.50

        Sale of a call option on the X share
        Strike price € 50
        Expiration in September
        Option premium € 0.50

The resulting net expenditure is € 1.

Investors pursuing this strategy realize their maximum possible gain if on the expiration date the underlying share is listed at or above the higher strike price. It equals the difference between both strike prices minus the difference in option premiums. Maximum loss occurs when the security drops below the lesser of the two strike prices and both options expire worthless.

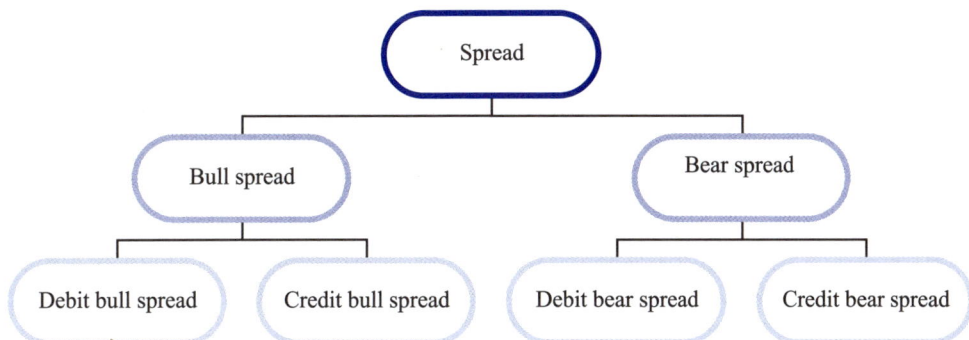

Figure 5.9: Basic spread types

Credit bear spread: The investor assumes the market to essentially move sideways with a slight upward bias. However, for the event of a market drop his strategy comprises a long put position. The investor goes short a higher put and buys a lower long put. Due to the short put, which protects against a higher strike price, he receives more in premium payments than he paid for the long put. The result is a net premium income, which represents his maximum profit. The maximum loss is the difference between both strike prices minus the net premium.

Example:
> Sale of a put option on the X share
> Strike price € 50
> Expiration in September
> Option premium € 3
>
> Purchase of a put option on the X share
> Strike price € 45
> Expiration in September
> Option premium € 1

The result is a net premium income of € 2.
The maximum value is € 3.
Now the individual amounts must be given a name.
(50−45 = 5; 5−2 = 3).

Table 5-4: Strategies for a positive market attitude

Market expectation	Option position	Potential profit	Potential loss
Strong increase	**Long call** + Call 30	unlimited	Maximum: Premium paid
Slight increase	**Purchase bull spread** + call 30 − call 35	Maximum: Difference in strike prices minus net premium expenditure	Maximum: Net premium expenditure
Slight increase	**Short put** − put 30	Maximum: premium paid	Almost unlimited

Table 5-5: Strategies for a neutral market attitude

Market expectation	Option position	Potential profit	Potential loss
Sideways move	**Sale of bear spread** + put 36 − put 40	Maximum: Net premium proceeds	Maximum: Difference in strike prices minus net premium proceeds
Sideways move	**Sale of bull spread** + call 40 − call 36	Maximum: Net premium proceeds	Maximum: Difference in strike prices minus net premium proceeds

Table 5-6: Strategies for a negative market attitude

Market expectation	Option position	Potential profit	Potential loss
Slight decrease	**Short call** − Call 40	Maximum: premium received	unlimited
Slight decrease	**Purchase of bear spread** + put 36 − put 32	Maximum: Difference in strike prices minus net premium expenditure	Maximum: Net premium expenditure
Strong decrease	**Long put** + put 36	Almost unlimited	Maximum: premium paid

Table 5-7: Strategies for a volatile market attitude

Market expectation	Option position	Maximum profit	Potential loss
Strong fluctuation	**Long straddle** + put 36 + put 36	Almost unlimited	Limited to premium paid
Very high fluctuation	**Long strangle** + call 38 + put 34	Almost unlimited	Limited to premium paid
Fluctuating around strike prices	**Short straddle** − Call 36 − put 36	Maximum: premium received	Almost unlimited
Fluctuating between strike prices	**Short strangle** − Call 38 − put 34	Maximum: premium received	Almost unlimited

5.4   How to set up a strategy for options trading

It is advisable to develop strategies that build on each other. If it is a new venture, you should also make sure you retain sufficient liquidity for later operations. This is generally a very important factor only if an investor has enough liquid resources can he expand and manage his strategies appropriately. In this context, note that it is always better to open fewer positions but manage existing positions expertly and consistently.

Another important aspect to consider is that external factors such as volatility can be important value drivers where you can deliberately achieve an advantage. For instance, you may set up a volatility-based strategy in addition to your speculative positions. While these enhancements may be of overall insignificance to your portfolio, they do contribute to your returns and can usually be traded quickly and at low cost. Thus, there is another opportunity for you to add to your account balance. You can add both option strategies with risk-decreasing effects and complementary options which you only hold for a short period (intraday).

In our opinion, a portfolio needs to be structured in three groups:

Group I: Long-term strategic deals. This includes positions which you enter over the long term based on strategic considerations. They form the core holding of your portfolio and may include both hedging and combination strategies.

Group II: Speculative positions. This group places the traditional, derivatives-based bets on certain market movements. The only purpose of these positions is speculation.

Group III: Ultra-short speculation. These speculative positions are often traded intraday. For longer-term speculation they are extended by a maximum of three days, with smooth transitions to Group II. Investments from this group are made, for instance, ahead of companies publishing their results or on days with extraordinary market movement.

Beware, however, of letting investments of Group II turn into Group I investments! The original purpose behind an investment – even if not successful – should be maintained!

Examples:
       Group I:
       Index-based futures, futures on interest rate derivatives, options on bond futures, etc.

Group II:
Investments such as options on indices, options on share portfolios, short put options, etc.
Group III:
This group includes very short-term futures, foreign-exchange futures, option positions on a particular security, etc.

In the above example, the investor attempts to take advantage of as many opportunities as possible. To do this, he needs the following:
• Sufficient liquidity
• Sufficient information
• Sufficient market attitude

Liquidity and information are usually available. The most sensitive component is the market attitude, which should ideally be correct.

5.5 What is the significance of market opinion?

In our view, every investor needs to take his own perspective on the market, evaluate it, and decide on his investments accordingly. Second-hand opinions often bring negative results.

Every investor should form his own opinion and decide independently what he does and does not wish to do. Consequently, it is indispensable that a new option investor is acquainted with the instruments available. Only investors who really understand the instruments available can make prudent decisions. At the same time, they develop an intuition (a "feel") for opportunities and risks, and can relate them to their investments.

In this regard the two large investor groups are very different. On the one hand we have the institutional (professional) investors commanding liquidity and expertise – on the other a number of private investors who, while they may also be capable of acquiring the expertise, frequently lack in liquidity or do not want to put it on the line.

On principle, both groups should receive the same kind of advice. However, private investors should have access to more detailed information on the risks involved, their extent and particular consequences. While the same strategies may be advisable to them, they will often find them to be of no use as they lack the liquid resources required.

Over the past few years, there has been an increasing trend among private investors toward securitized derivatives. The reasons derive from the fact that the
products are easy to explain, easy to understand, and easy to use for investments
of different sizes. We should add that securitized derivatives are also available to
professional or institutional investors, but often make little sense for that group
due to size and cost considerations. In our own experience, the more common
practice is for private individuals to purchase securitized derivatives from institutional investors, while the latter show a greater tendency toward traditional
derivative instruments, either on derivatives exchanges or OTC.

Summary:
In options trading there are four basic strategies:
Long call – absolutely positive
Short call – stagnation, slight decrease
Long put – absolutely negative
Short put – stagnation, slight increase
Along with the so-called combination strategies, such as straddle, stran-
gle, spreads, etc. With combinations, different opportunity and risk pro-
files can be covered; however, it is important for investors to stay on top
of things at all times.
Due to the premium payments and the two value components (time
value and intrinsic value) options involve an asymmetrical risk distribution.

6 Futures – unconditional derivative instruments

This chapter deals with the following questions:
1. What are futures and forwards?
2. How do futures work?
3. What is the difference between an index future and a bond future?
4. What is the DAX Future?
5. What is the Euro Bund Future?

6.1 What are futures?

Classical derivatives date back to the beginning of underlying trade. As early as in the 16th century derivative transactions on rice were concluded in Japan. The first financial futures were traded in August 1977 in Chicago, based on the 30-year U.S. Treasury Bond (T-Bond). Today there is a multitude of futures based on very different underlying assets. Index-based futures and interest rate futures, as well as commodity futures, are widely used and represent an essential component of futures markets.

What is the difference between a future and a forward? The answer is simple: A future is a contract which, due to its standardized elements, can be traded on the exchange. With its particular characteristics it is easily transferable to a third party. A forward is the exact opposite, where a customized contract exists be-

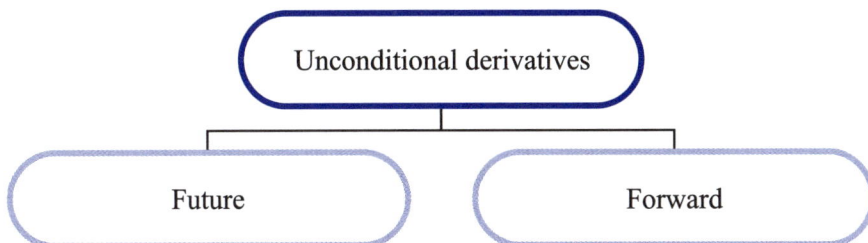

Unconditional derivatives

Future

Forward

Figure 6.1: Unconditional derivatives

tween two parties, usually a bank and its client. As such, it cannot be transferred to a third party as easily.

Both instruments count among what we call unconditional derivatives; that is, they comprise contractual obligations which must be met by all means. By concluding the contract both parties commit to meeting their respective obligations. The underlying intention of a forwards investor is to hedge against risks or speculate on a medium-term market movement. Due to the limited tradability of forwards, they are not suitable for short-term or "real" speculation but are generally used to hedge another transaction and the resulting payment flows.

As this book focuses on the trading and design of exchange-traded derivatives, the following sections will deal with futures only.

> By definition, a future is a derivative instrument comprising an obligation to purchase (long) or deliver (short) a certain underlying at a predefined price, at a fixed date, and in a particular (also predefined) quality and quantity. There is no right of choice. The transaction must be completed.

6.2 Futures markets

Futures can be based on a range of underlying classes, of which the following are most common:

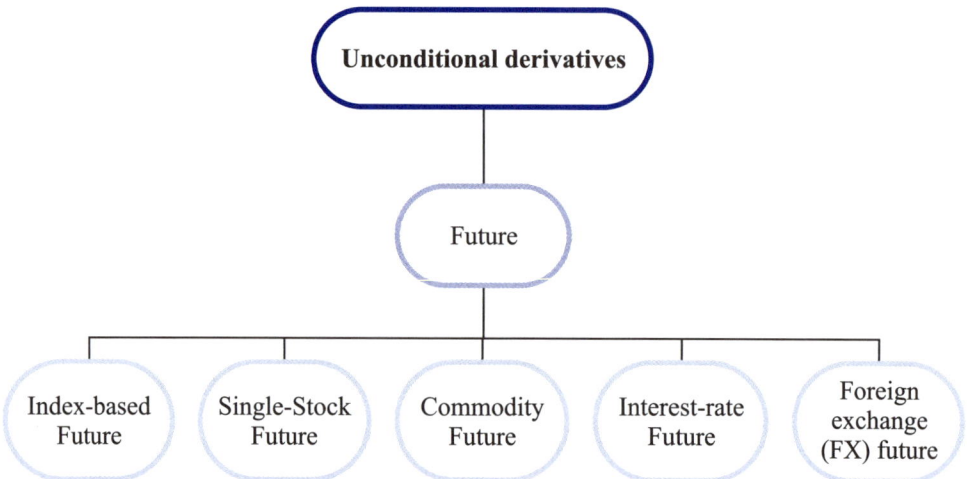

Figure 6.2: Most common types of futures

6.3   Futures trading

In order to trade in a futures contract, an investor needs a certain amount of money, which represents a part of the actual contract value and is referred to as **initial margin**. Its purpose is to protect the investor from his close-out risks until the next exchange trading day and it must be paid by both the buyer and the seller.

During the time an investor holds a futures contract in his position book, profits and losses are adjusted on a daily basis. The respective payments are referred to as variation margin. For more information on margins see Chapter 17.

A futures investor can choose between two basic strategies:
- He buys a future ("goes long") if he counts on an upward trend.
- He sells a future ("goes short") if he speculates on a downward trend.

As mentioned before, an investor in a long future expects an upward trend for the underlying asset. Due to the limited liquidity (initial margin) required for the investment he achieves the leverage intended. He realizes a profit if the underlying price – and with it, the price of the future – goes up, and enters the loss zone only in case of a price drop. As mentioned initially, the profits or losses realized are adjusted at market close by means of a cash entry. Hence, an investment of this kind is to be recommended when prices are rising or the trend is intact.

By contrast, an investor should only invest in a short future if he expects the underlying price to go down. In analogy to the above, the short future will only reach the loss zone if the underlying goes up.

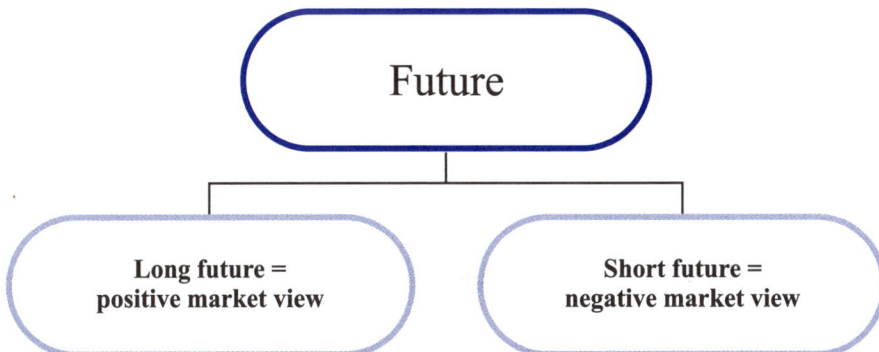

Figure 6.3: Possible market opinions of a futures investor

Futures are traded in the same manner as options, and can also be opened and closed through offsetting positions. This type of unconditional derivative is widely used by professional investors, as it offers the possibility to trade the entire market rapidly and at limited cost.

Table 6-1: Opening and closing of positions in futures

Opening	BUY FUTURE (long)
Closing	SELL FUTURE (short)
Opening	SELL FUTURE (short)
Closing	BUY FUTURE (long)

6.3.1 Delivery

There are two ways to deliver on future. One is the traditional physical delivery, which is used for example with the Euro Bund future. The other is cash settlement through payment/ receipt of the difference between settlement price and futures price. This variant is used when dealing in index-based futures, for example where physical delivery of the underlying is not feasible.

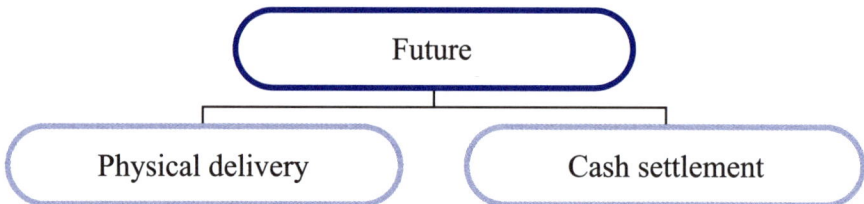

Figure 6.4: Settlement modes for futures

6.4 Index-based futures

There are numerous futures based on indices. We will now outline a few practical examples for the DAX® index based future (FDAX®). To do so, a few prerequisites are needed. When dealing in index-based futures it is always important to clearly understand the underlying: Is it a performance or a price index? How many shares are included in the index? How is the index calculated? What is the index multiplier, what are the trading times to be observed? Only after knowing the answers to these questions should an investor start trading in the index-based future in question.

Let us elaborate for the DAX® index-based future.

The underlying instrument here is the DAX® performance index of Deutsche Börse AG which comprises 30 shares. Each of them is selected based on a set of rules defined by Deutsche Börse AG (including free-float, size, etc.). Adjustments to the index are carried out at defined points in time, or whenever basic conditions change. The weighting of the different shares is adjusted on a quarterly basis.

Since the DAX® is a performance index, dividends are factored in as reinvestment. This is in contrast to the Dow Jones Industrial Average, which is a share price index. Adjustment for dividends paid is done on the ex-day using an adjustment factor.

Another basic piece of information concerns the settlement mode. Since indices cannot be delivered physically, settlement will be made in cash for the difference in amount. In practice, most of the futures contracts are closed before their expiration date.

A future based on the DAX® (FDAX®) is worth € 25 per index point. Consequently, if the FDAX® goes up one point the amount of € 25 is credited to the long investor's and debited to the short investor's account. This process is called **Mark to Market**. Entries are affected every day until the position is exercised or closed, which ensures that all accounts are balanced when the exchange closes. The following day, the daily profit-and-loss statement in the position book again starts at zero.

Investments in futures have a leveraging effect, as they enable investors to commit to considerable investments by putting up a limited margin. This way, investors can achieve the same effect as a classic cash investor while requiring much less liquidity.

With index-based futures, the difference is stated in points, which are then converted into the respective currency by using an index multiplier (€ 25 for the FDAX®; 1 point = € 25).

Example:

An investor buys (goes long) 10 DAX® Futures contracts at 6,700 points. At the end of the day the FDAX® is quoted at 6,650 points. The investor's loss is 50 points. With the index multiplier being € 25 per point, this translates into a loss of € 1,250 per contract. In this example, our investor's loss resulting from all 10 contracts amounts to € 12,500.

Let us briefly put the amounts traded into relation.

In our example, 10 FDAX® contracts are equivalent to an amount of € 1.675,000 (10 × 25 × 6,700 points), whereas the investor only pays an initial margin of currently 410 points per contract, which totals € 102,500 (410 × 10 × 25). In other words, with his capital investment of € 102,500 he controls a total amount of € 1,675,000!

Table 6-2: Index-based futures frequently traded

Index	Future
DAX®	DAX® Future (FDAX®)
Standard & Poor's	S&P 500 Future
Dow Jones Industrial Average	Dow Jones Industrial Future
FTSE	FTSE Future
Dow Jones Euro STOXX 50®	Dow Jones EURO STOXX 50® Future
…	…

Table 6-3: Underlying market opinion of futures investors

Futures position	Basic assumption
Long future	Upward markets
Short future	Downward markets

6.5 Interest-rate futures

The picture looks very different for instruments for which transactions are settled physically, such as the Euro.Bund Futures (FGBL). This future is based on a synthetic federal bond with a nominal coupon of 6 percent and a remaining maturity of 8.5 to 10.5 years. As the federal bond is of a fictitious nature it can comprise a basket of bonds which can be used for delivery when the future reaches its maturity date. However, as these bonds do not match the 1:1 ratio assumed, they will need to be calculated using a conversion factor. With this factor, the different coupons and terms can be harmonized in line with standard contract specifications for the Euro-Bund Futures. Note that in practice most futures contracts are not actually delivered physically as they are closed out or rolled over prior to maturity.

Trade in interest rate futures, such as the Euro-Bund Futures or the 30 Year Treasury Bond Futures (T-Bond) is both very intense and highly liquid. Using different kinds of futures (based on bonds with different terms) investors can benefit from changes in the interest rate market, as well as from imbalances and shifts in the interest structure curve. For instance, an investor assuming increasing interest rates (long-term end) will sell contracts on the Euro-Bund Future. This way he can cover both ends of the interest structure curve and, through effective valuation modeling; invest in interest-rate derivatives even as the interest structure curve is shifting.

This is true even for operations exceeding one's own currency region. In addition, the Euro Bund Futures (EUR) and the T-Bond Futures (USD) can be combined. Should the investor assume that interest rates will go down in the U.S. and go up in Europe, he can buy the T-Bond Futures and simultaneously sell the Euro-Bund Futures. By combining this with an FX Future, he can expect higher returns.

Table 6-4: Maturity structure for different futures

Futures	Maturity of underlying instrument (years)
Euro Schatz Futures (€)	1.75–2.25, federal bonds
Euro Bobl Futures (€)	4.5–5.5, federal bonds
Euro Bund Futures (€)	8.5–10.5, federal bonds
Euro Buxl® Futures (€)	24.0–35.0, federal bonds
CONF Futures (CHF)	8.0–13.0, Swiss Confederation
T-Bill Futures (USD)	Three-month U.S. treasury bills
10 Year U.S. Treasury Note Futures (USD)	10-year U.S. government bonds
30 Year U.S. Treasury Note Futuers (USD	30-year U.S. government bonds

Table 6-5: Basic intentions in the bond futures trade

Futures position	Basic assumption	Settlement
Long future	Falling interest rates; rising bond prices	Must buy bonds
Short future	Rising interest rates; falling bond prices	Must sell bonds

6.6 Foreign-currency futures

Foreign-currency (FX) futures are offered by CME in Chicago, among others. Here, investors can trade in fixed currency pairs, such as € / USD. One contract is worth € 125,000. An investor can either buy a future (go long) because he assumes the Euro to rise versus the dollar, or sell the future (go short) because he assumes the opposite. The same obviously applies for other currency pairings. Due to the rapid and liquid trade, these futures are also useful for short-term speculative purposes, not only for medium or long-term investments. A possible increase in returns can be achieved by short-term and complementary deals in an active derivatives book.

Table 6-6: Conceivable FX Futures

€	USD
€	CHF
€	YEN
GBP	USD
AUD	USD
...	...

Derivative exchanges offer almost any currency pair, as far as reasonable and necessary. As settlement is usually physical, the futures are usually closed prematurely.

6.7 Commodity futures

Trading in Commodity Futures is a very important and exciting component of derivatives markets. Commodity futures are also the origin of derivative exchanges. Today they are no longer used for hedging purposes only, but frequently also for speculation. In Germany commodity futures are not very common, as is quite obvious from the fact that the major commodity futures exchanges are located in the U.S.

   At these exchanges, the following types of products can be traded:

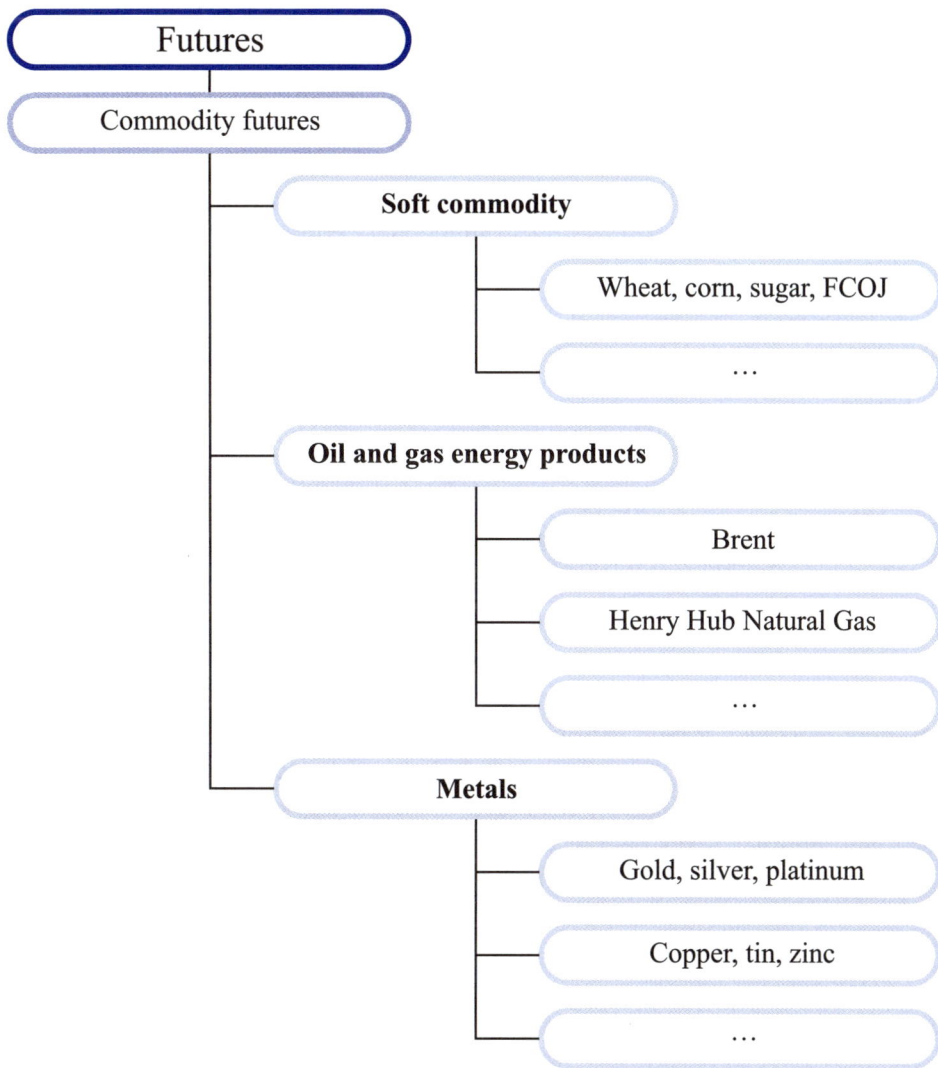

Figure 6.5: Product categories at U.S. commodity futures exchanges

Again, it is important to distinguish whether futures are settled in cash or physically. Usually both variants are available. For speculative purposes, it is preferable to choose cash settlement and exclude physical delivery from the start.

6.8   Single-Stock futures

In addition to what we have described above, there is another kind of futures where the underlying is an individual company share. At Eurex, for example, Single-Stock Futures are traded for all Dow Jones EURO STOXX-50® companies. As for traditional index-based futures, the investor can speculate on rising or falling prices of the underlying security. Thus, Single Stock Futures complement the range of security-based futures.

Table 6-7: Basic intentions of investors in Single-Stock Futures

Futures position	Basic assumption
Long future	Rising share price
Short future	Falling share price

6.9   The market for futures trading

As futures and options investors should be able to form a sound assessment of the market, we will now examine the so-called open interest, which indicates how many contracts are open: Each contract counts only once as for each short position there must be a long position. Hence, the open interest rises when two market participants initiate a new deal, and declines when two participants close out a deal. By contrast, it remains unchanged when one market participant closes out a deal and another takes his place. By putting the open interest into relation to sales and market prices, you can draw certain conclusions regarding the state of the market.

Table 6-8: Open interest and state of the market

Open interest	Prices	Sales	State of the market
↑	↑	↑	↑
↓	↑	↓	↓
↑	↓	↑	↓
↓	↓	↓	↑

Trading on a derivatives exchange is anonymous, which means that the two contracting parties do not know each other – and do not have to know each other – in order to enter into business relations. Rather, the exchange works as a central counterparty, which excludes the risks of transactions not being fulfilled and ensures orderly processing.

Summary:
A future is an unconditional derivative instrument, which means that the transaction must be carried through. Futures are differentiated according to their mode of settlement, which can be either physical or in cash (by payment of the difference amount). Futures can be based on a range of underlying assets, of which the most common are indices, interest rates, commodities, foreign exchange, and individual securities. In a traditional futures transaction, an investor can either express a positive market opinion (go long) or a negative market opinion (go short). Since futures count among to the Delta 1 instruments, meaning that they act according to the respective cash positions, the investor participates 1:1 in their performance.

7 Pricing of futures

This chapter deals with the following questions:
1. How is the price of a future determined?
2. How is the price of an interest rate future determined?
3. What is a CTD bond?
4. What does "final settlement" mean?
5. What expiration dates are common for futures?

7.1 Future pricing – how is it done?

Prices of futures are easier to determine than those of options.

An investor has two possibilities; in one instance he can either buy a portfolio consisting of the assets underlying the future. In another instance he can buy the future itself. If the investor chooses the portfolio he will need to buy the underlying assets in accordance with their weighting within the future, and hold them for exactly the same length of time as the corresponding futures position. The purchase of securities incurs an expenditure, in return for which the investor receives the respective yield. If future contracts are priced proceeding from these assumptions and if we assume an arbitrage-free environment, both variants should generate the same result. Thus, the price of a future is determined by the following formula:

Theoretical future price = underlying + (financing cost − lost yields)

$$Future\ Preis = C_t + \left[C_t \times r_c \times \left(\frac{T-t}{360} \right) - d_{t,T} \right]$$

Where:
C_t = Underlying instrument (e.g., index level)
r_c = Money market interest rate (percent, current/360)
t = Valuta of spot market positions
T = Fulfillment day of a future
$T-t$ = Remaining term of a future
$d_{t,T}$ = Dividend payment expected for the period t to T

Net financing costs, as result from the difference between financing cost and lost profits, are referred to as **cost of carry** (CoC) or **basis.**

$$\text{Basis} = \text{future price} - \text{spot price}$$

The cost of carry (CoC) can be positive or negative. It is positive if returns are higher than financing costs, and negative if the financing costs exceed the returns.

With the last trading day for the future drawing closer, the basis shrinks. On the last trading day the spot price equals the derivative price. This phenomenon is referred to as basis convergence. Due to the decreasing financing cost and the returns on the investment, the basis equals zero on the day of expiration. The spot price (price of the cash investment) and the future price are now the same.

Table 7-1: Futures basis

The spot price is...	The future price is...	The basis is...
... lower than the future price	... higher than the spot price	negative
... higher than the future price	... lower than the spot price	positive

As we see, determining the future price is not very complicated. It is done by simply taking the price of the cash instrument (underlying), adding the holding cost in the derivatives market, and deducting the profits which could have been generated if the underlying instrument had been purchased directly rather than via the future. We also see that volatility has no effect on futures pricing.

7.2 Pricing of interest rate futures

The interest structure curve strongly affects the pricing of interest rate futures. Short-term interest rates affect the refinancing of an investment in a bond, while longer-term interest rates affect the coupon and thus the investment income. Consequently, with a normal interest curve the income is higher than the financing cost, and the derivatives price can have a positive basis because the spot price is higher. From this context it is easy to see that the future price decreases as the term of the future increases. The opposite is true for an inverse interest structure curve. In this case, the basis of the future is negative and its financing cost exceeds its holding cost. As a result, the future price increases over its maturity. The following is an overview of the three possible interest structure curves:

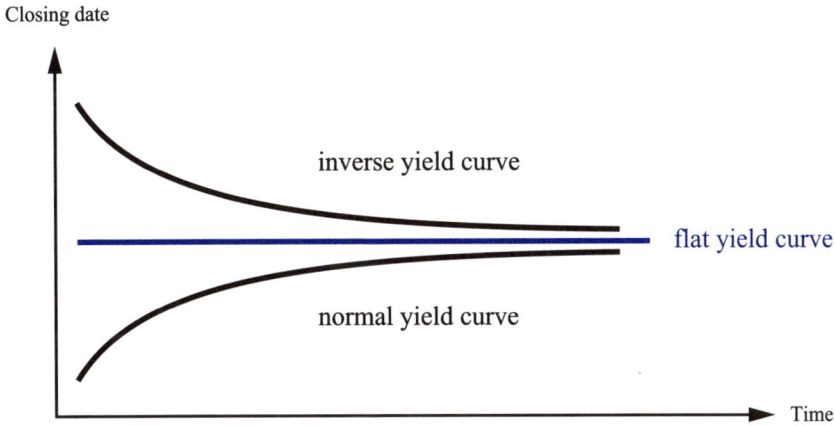

Figure 7.1: Interest structure curves

Fair value of an interest rate future

$$F = \left(\frac{U}{P}\right) - Z + C$$

Where:
F = future price
U = cash position
P = price factor
Z = coupon yield
C = financing cost of cash position

By means of transformation we get:

$$\left(\frac{U}{P}\right) - F = Z - C$$

Where:
F = future price
U = cash position
P = price factor
Z = coupon yields
C = financing cost of cash position

The fair value is reached when the theoretical equals the actual basis. In other words, the fair value corresponds to the price of the underlying instrument plus financing cost, minus the coupon yields accrued in the course of the holding phase.

The price factor only takes on its full significance on the maturity date. It is applied to determine the final settlement price.

Final settlement price = Settlement price of future × nominal × price factor + interests accured

7.3 What is a CTD bond?

A CTD (cheapest-to-deliver) bond is the bond that generates the greatest profit or smallest loss when delivered (on the futures contract). It is ultimately used for delivery, and represents the best variant from a synthetic standpoint. The price of the CTD bond is determined using a conversion factor (W_{pys} / W_{syn}). This factor is used to adjust for different bond terms (regarding coupons, maturity, etc.). After calculating all delivery options, the cheapest-to-deliver bond is selected and delivered.

However it is important to note that most investors do not wish to deliver/accept the underlying asset, and therefore close or roll over their futures contract prior to maturity. A market participant wishing to hold his futures positions until final settlement must specify which bond he will deliver (notification day = last trading day). Delivery is made on the second exchange trading day after settlement day. It is carried out via the clearing house (as for stock options).

7.4 What does "final settlement" mean?

The price determined on a future's settlement day is called final settlement price. The futures contact is settled, or delivered on, at that price. Before closure of the transaction the parties agree on either physical or cash settlement (which is then included in the contract specifications). An investor should always take this information into account. To avert unwanted obligations it is definitely advisable to close prematurely and avoid a potential delivery. If an investor, due to his basic market opinion, wishes to extend the transaction beyond its original maturity date he can always opt for a roll-over; i.e., close the original position and open a new one with a later maturity date.

7.5 What are common maturity dates for futures?

Usually, there is a minimum of three different maturity dates for futures. For instance, Eurex offers futures on the Dow Jones EURO STOXX 50® for the next three quarter-end months. Each exchange has its own set of regulations specifying which futures maturity dates are available for the different products. For index-based futures, the following three quarter-end dates are usually offered.

Table 7-2: Overview of possible futures series, using the Dow Jones EURO STOXX 50® Future as an example

1st possibility	March	June	September
2nd possibility	June	September	December
3rd possibility	September	December	March
4th possibility	December	March	June

If an investor decides to trade in a future extending beyond the next maturity date, he needs to take into account the possible negative development of his financing cost – that is, they could be higher (for a long future) or lower (for a short future). The same problem could result for roll-over positions in futures. In cases like these, losses incurred by existing price differences are referred to as roll-over

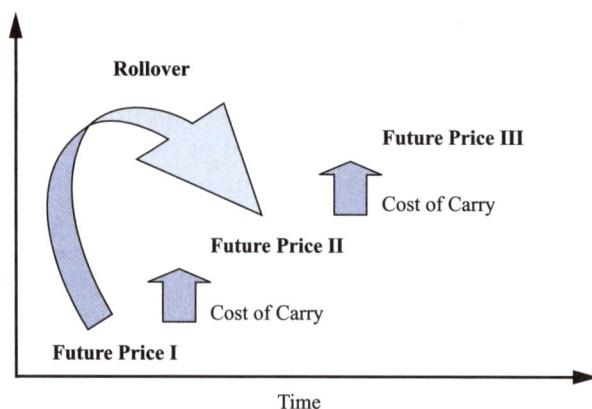

Figure 7.2: Roll-over loss

losses. Unfortunately, such losses cannot be avoided, as they result from pricing and are independent of the strategy employed. The following diagram shows a roll-over loss (subsequent futures will be more expensive to buy).

Summary:
In this chapter we have dealt with the net financing cost and its effects on futures pricing: It can cause either a price increase or a decrease, and accordingly, we speak of a positive or negative basis.
Basis convergence refers to a situation where on settlement day the future price equals the spot price. Also, we have reviewed the two delivery modes – physical and cash settlement.

Future price – cash price + cost of carry

Cost of carry = financing cost – lost yields

$$\text{Future Price} = C_t + \left(C_t \times r_c \times \left(\frac{T-t}{360} \right) - d_{t,T} \right)$$

8 Strategies involving futures

This chapter deals with the following questions:
1. What strategies are possible in futures?
2. How are these strategies set up?

As with all derivatives transactions, with futures the investor's main intentions are:
- Speculation,
- Hedging, or
- Arbitrage.

However there are more reasons why futures markets are important for the overall market. One of these reasons is leverage. As relatively little capital is required, the investment gains leverage – that is, the investor can engage in a major investment with limited expenditure. Another advantage is that the investor can do this not only from the buyer's (long) but also from the seller's side (short). A third advantage is the certainty that transactions will be filled. The solvency risk is minimized (as the contracting party is the exchange's clearing house). This also ensures rapid tradability and liquidation of old positions. Finally there are cost-efficient and rapid transactions covering a broad spectrum and variety of tradable instruments. Thus, an investor is able to execute his deals rapidly and effectively.

Long futures position
The investor expects the underlying price to rise, and consequently goes long a futures position. His profit is the difference between the low purchase price and the higher selling price. However if the market prices fall, he takes a loss. The opportunity and risk profile of a long position is almost identical to that of a long position in the underlying. Due to the leverage effect, however, the results are different.

Short futures position
The investor expects the underlying price to fall, and consequently goes short a futures position. His profit is the difference between the higher selling price and the lower repurchase price of the future. If the future goes up, contrary to expectation, the investor takes a loss.

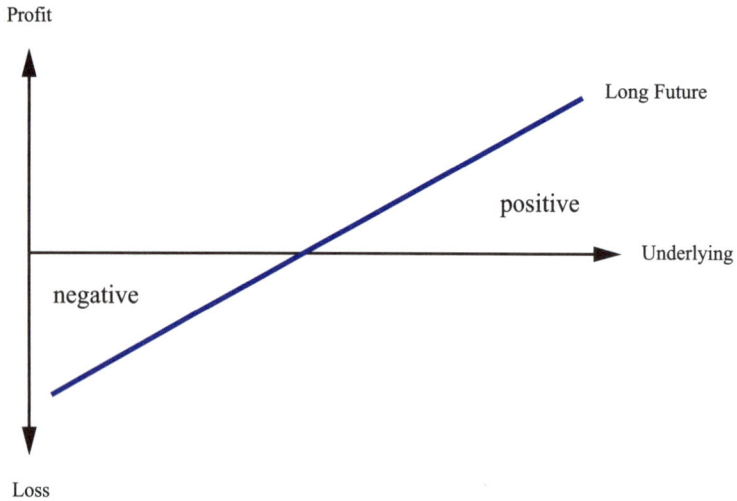

Figure 8.1: Visualization of a long futures position

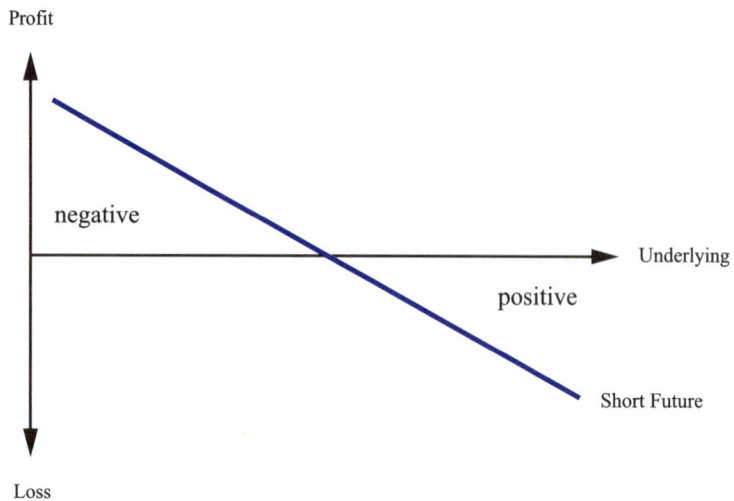

Figure 8.2: Visualization of the short future position

Both futures speculations shown can be considered basic strategies which other strategies build upon. At this point, allow us a few essential remarks; for an investment in futures, an investor must meet three basic requirements:

- High degree of liquidity
- Considerable expertise
- Detailed and comprehensive information.

Only an investor meeting these requirements should consider investing in futures. While trading in futures positions is very simple, handling them is not. Both speculative and hedging uses are commong. Hedging with a traditional futures position is quite simple, where the goal is to hedge against rising or falling market prices.

The traditional case involves hedging against falling prices. An investor fears that his portfolio will lose value, and uses a short future to protect it. Classic hedging of this kind is only possible if the portfolio and the asset underlying the future match. Since this is often not the case, the widest possible spread is sought and a hedging strategy is set up based on this future.

The first step consists in calculating the number of futures contracts needed:

$$Hedge\ Ratio = \frac{Portfolio}{Index-future-points} \times \frac{1}{index\ multiplier}$$

Example:
>An investor has a portfolio worth € 1 million. He wishes to hedge it against a price drop. As the securities in his portfolio are most comparable to the Dow Jones EURO STOXX 50®, the investor decides to use the Dow Jones EURO STOXX 50Future® (FESX) to hedge the portfolio. First he calculates the hedge ratio:
>**(Portfolio / Dow Jones EURO STOXX 50®) / Index Multiplier = X**
>**x = (1 million / 4,450) / € 10**
>**x = 22.47**
>The investor needs to sell 23 Dow Jones EURO STOXX 50 futures® contracts to hedge his portfolio.

Hedging against higher market prices may sound misleading at first, but is indeed worth considering. Let us assume our investor expects a considerable stream of funds in six months' time but due to the current state of the market an investment seems unfavorable at present. In this situation the investor will attempt to hedge the current price level although he will make his investment only six months later. This type of hedging is appropriate in particular if the investor expects to have regular liquid funds at his disposal in the future. Thus, he synthetically effects his investment which he will be able to pay in six months. Contrary to hedging against a price drop, in this case the investor buys a future to hedge against rising prices.

In both cases the investor fears that market prices in the cash market will change to his disadvantage. With the two strategies described, he locks in his opening or closing price for the investment.

As explained in the previous chapter, the price of a future comprises spot market costs and the cost of carry. This results in a price difference between futures on the same underlying but with different expiration dates, which is referred to as time spread. It results from the difference in net financing cost for differing remaining maturity. By contrast, expectations regarding the underlying price and its development during this period have no effect.

Investors can take advantage of this spread and invest on it.

Purchase of a spread
The futures investor purchases the nearer contract and sells the farther out contract.

Example:
> Purchase of X index expiring in March
> Sale of X index expiring in December
> Sale of spread.

The futures investor sells the nearer contract and purchases the farther out contract.

Example:
> Sale of X index expiring in March
> Purchase of X index expiring in December.

When should you choose which strategy?

Principally, we must distinguish between futures on stock price indices and futures on performance indices. Also, we must consider the price trends for both, the index and the net financing cost.

Table 8-1: Spreads

Type of index	Rising prices	Falling prices
Performance index	Sale of a spread	Purchase of a spread
Price index cost of carry > 0	Sale of a spread	Purchase of a spread
Price index cost of carry < 0	Purchase of a spread	Sale of a spread

This shows that with performance indices, a strategic decision can only be derived from the price trend. The longer a future's remaining maturity, the higher its market price (negative basis). If the underlying price goes up, so does the basis. Since this concept equally applies to both contracts the spread increases proportionally. The exact opposite is true for falling prices: The spread futures investor takes a loss.

By contrast, in the case of performance indices the investor must focus on the net financing cost: If the basis of the future is positive, the investor should do the opposite as compared to a performance-index based futures position.

Intermarket spread

An inter-market spread means that an investor buys and sells the same contracts at two different exchanges. This way he takes advantage of the price differences at the two trading places.

Example:

> Purchase of X index at exchange A for 11,000
> Sale of X index at exchange B for 11,010.

Due to the advance of information technology this type of spread is seldom tradable today.

Inter-contract and intra-contract spread

An **inter**-contract spread means that two futures with different contract specifications are mutually traded. The investor assumes a change in basic conditions for both contracts. An **intra**-contract spread means that contracts for the same future but with differing maturity date are mutually traded. The investor assumes a change in contracts due to the difference in maturity. The following examples differentiate the two contracts:

Inter-contract spread: Euro Bund Future vs. Euro Bobl Future

Intra-contract spread: Euro Bund Future with different maturity details

For both operations, profits are generated from the sheer difference. The investor benefits from the price differences.

Example:
> Purchase of Euro Bund Future with September maturity
> Sale of Euro Bund Future with December maturity

Cash-and-carry arbitrage

The purpose of an arbitrage operation is to generate risk-free revenues based on price imbalances. These imbalances result whenever there is a difference between the future prices currently traded and the spot market price. Arbitrage gains are possible if the difference between the current basis and the theoretical basis is greater. If the future is too expensive compared to its theoretical fair value, the investor will sell it and buy the underlying asset. This is referred to as cash-and-carry arbitrage. If the opposite is the case – that is, if the future is lower-priced – the investor will buy the future and sell the underlying asset. This operation is called a reverse cash-and-carry arbitrage.

> Cash and carry → sale of futures and purchase of spot market product
> Reverse cash and carry → purchase of futures and sale
>   of spot market product

An underlying instrument, such as an index, cannot be purchased and sold as easily as a future. Consequently, an investor will construct a basket by buying all values with a beta of approximately 1. If the correlation coefficient is high the investor can emulate the index. Although this will not be a 1:1 emulation, he will achieve a parallel synthetic constant.

Example:
> We construct a Dow Jones EURO STOXX 50® basket with securities which have a beta of approximately 1 and a high correlation coefficient and trade the Dow Jones EURO STOXX 50® Future (depending on the state of the market).

The problems of such transactions are these:
- They involve transaction costs.
- Naked sales are sometimes difficult to accomplish, or incur costs.
- Bonds entail a choice on the settlement day.

Hedges

In the previous chapters we have talked about long and short hedges, and in the case of futures they equally apply. With a long hedge (purchase of a future) the investor hedges against the risk that prices will go up before his planned investment $(t + x)$, while a short hedge is used to hedge an investment already effected $(t - x)$.

A long hedge always refers to an investment that has already been approved but is yet to be made. For instance, an investor will receive € 1 million in three months and wishes to use these funds to invest in DJ Euro STOXX 50® shares. However his worry is that the index will go up before then. Hence he buys futures contracts to compensate for this possible development. As soon as he is in receipt of the liquid funds he closes out his futures contracts and purchases the securities. If the future has increased in value because the index has appreciated, the investor has compensated for that through the higher revenues from his futures contracts. If the future has decreased in value because the index has gone down, the investor has taken the same loss he would have sustained if investing in the securities from the start. In other words, with this transaction the investor locks in the original price for his investment.

With a short hedge, the investor protects his existing portfolio against price drops. He has already effected his investment in the spot market. As he expects a price decline which he cannot foretell, he hedges against this decline by selling the futures contracts. If prices actually do fall the investor will thus have compensated for the price losses in his portfolio. If they do not, the hedging strategy (opposite futures position) will incur costs which the investor will have to bear.

Beta hedge with an index-based future

Since a beta factor (β) can be determined for every portfolio, this parameter is of optimal use for hedging purposes. The beta factor expresses the sensitivity of a portfolio as compared to the overall market.

An investor will adjust the beta factor of his portfolio in line with his market expectations. If he assumes an upward market, he will carry a high share of stocks in his portfolio and build a long position in index-based futures on that basis. The opposite is true if the investor expects a downward market: He will then reduce the company shares in his portfolio and build short futures positions instead.

Risk management

When we speak of risk management it is indispensable to make very clear what kind of risk we are referring to. We distinguish between the **unsystematic** risk associated with an individual engagement and the so-called **systematic** risk, or total market risk. While the unsystematic risk can be eliminated through active management of one's securities account and diversification, the systematic risk is intrinsically present in the market, and therefore affects all investments in that market.

Table 8-2: Beta values

Value	Meaning
Beta (β) = 1	Stock behaves like market 1:1
Beta (β) > 1	Stock moves more than market
Beta (β) < 1	Stock moves less than market

Correlation coefficient (r)

One way to determine whether a single stock moves with or against the market is to calculate the correlation coefficient. It can range anywhere between −1 and +1.

Table 8-3: Correlation coefficients – values and meaning

Value	Meaning
r = +1 Maximum positive correlation	There is a positive correlation (synchronism)
r = 0 Correlation is neutral	There is no (or a random) correlation
r = −1 Maximum negative correlation	Developments run (absolutely) contrary

Beta hedge for expected downward market trend

In order to hedge a portfolio, it is necessary to determine its beta factor (β). Having done that, the investor can build a beta hedge as follows:

$$\# \: of \: futures \: contracts = -1 \times \left(\frac{value \: of \: portfolio}{(index \: level \: \times \: contract \: seize)} \right) \times \beta \: portfolio$$

Example:

An investor holds an X-index based portfolio worth € 1.5 million. The β is 1.1. The X index stands at 6,700 points; the index multiplier for X futures is € 25 per point. The investor wishes to hedge this portfolio.

$$= -1 \times (1,500,000 / (6700 \times 25)) \times 1.1$$
$$= 9,8$$

He will need to sell 10 contracts.

Whenever conditions change the investor will need to adjust his hedge.
A long hedge is built correspondingly, with contracts being purchased rather than sold.
The formula is the same:

$$\# \; of \; futures \; contracts = -1 \times \left(\frac{value \; of \; portfolio}{(index \; level \; \times \; contract \; seize)} \right) \times \beta \; portfolio$$

Why are hedges built with futures?

For one thing, transactions in futures are low-priced and transparent. For another, a strategy of this type can be implemented fast and rigorously. While it is true that positions must continually be monitored and adjusted, there are useful and time-saving technologies to do that.

At this point, allow us a few words on the transparency of futures transactions. As portfolios are never composed of home market assets only, and coverage of one's home markets is usually not sufficient, futures are an excellent instrument to cover these markets comprehensively and transparently. Transparency results from the futures pricing method as well as by the trading continuity ensured by the Market Maker. The fast and low-cost execution of orders is another important feature of futures markets. One negative factor which, however, generally only concerns customer business dealing with private investors is the size of the orders traded.

Hedging with interest-rate futures

To build a hedge against falling or rising interest rates, the following basic methods are available:

Price-factor and nominal-value method: Is used mainly to hedge the CTD.

$$hedge\ ratio = \frac{nominal\ value_{Cash}}{nominal\ value_{Future}}$$

Duration method: Is used to ensure comparability between price sensitivities with regard to the CRD.

$$hedge\ ratio = \left(\frac{nominal\ value_{spot}}{nominal\ value_{future}}\right) \times \left(\frac{duration_{spot}}{duration_{future}}\right) \times PF_{CTD}$$

PF_{CTD} = Price Factor of CTD

Basis-point-value method: Is used to determine how much the price of a bond will change if the rate of return rises or falls by one basis point. This method is applied for both, the spot market position and the CTD, and then put into proportion.

$$hedge\ ratio = \left(\frac{nominal\ value_{spot}}{nominal\ value_{future}}\right) \times \left(\frac{\Delta_{spot,\ BP}}{\Delta_{CTD,BP}}\right) \times PF_{CTD}$$

The changes in value can be derived from the rate-of-return calculation

Regression method: Is used to determine the degree of correlation between the cash and the futures market.

$$Hedge-Ratio = \frac{nominal\ value_{Cash}}{nominal\ value_{Future}} \times RC$$

RC = Regression coefficient

Cross hedge

Since a portfolio will usually include assets for which there is no matching futures contract, investors are often forced to build a so-called cross hedge. This is done by building futures positions which resemble the respective spot market instrument. In such a manner, investors can use positions with similar market trends to cover another position. This method, however, only works if prices run strictly parallel to each other. The same is true for portfolios which are not based on a uniform interest-rate environment. For these, investors need a combination of different futures.

Two sides of a coin

As we have seen, hedges offer an opportunity to model clearly and transparently the remaining risk contained in a portfolio; however, as nice and useful they may seem, they do involve certain problems. Each hedge causes costs and expenditures and keeps hedgers from benefiting from other price trends. Moreover, it is often difficult to cover complex portfolios. Investors can always try using a cross-hedge but even then is it often impossible to accomplish 100-percent protection. On the other hand, a legitimate question is whether total protection is really necessary.

Example:

Basic intention of the investor:
Based on his chart analysis, the investor considers the X index to be over-priced and completely overbought, and expects it to drop.

Portfolio:
X-index portfolio worth € 1 million.

Set-up according to basic intention:
Short X-index contracts, sold at 7,000 points.

Owing to an economic upturn, the X-index then goes up 150 points to reach 7,150 points! The investor can no longer benefit from that development, as he has sold the X-index at 7,000 points. He realizes a loss with his positions. If the index falls to that level due to market imbalances, the investor realizes a profit. But only if the X-index falls below the 7,000 point level does the investor realize a profit rather than a minor loss.

This example shows how important it is for an investor to correctly assess the market environment. If the market moves the other way the investor will suffer losses. Since futures are Delta-1 instruments, the investor immediately participates in gains and losses.

Summary:

There are two basic strategies in futures trading:

– Long future

– Short future.

The long futures investor expects the underlying price to go up, the short futures investor anticipates a downward trend. Futures can be used for both speculation and hedging purposes. By combining different futures contracts, investors can build spreads or set up combination strategies.

Hedging strategies are grouped in long and short hedges. In addition, we distinguish between dynamic and fixed hedges.

In comparison to option strategies, strategies involving futures are clearer and simpler. Among other things, this is due to the daily adjustment for gains and losses (marking to market).

9 Options on futures, synthetic structures and combinations

This chapter deals with the following questions:
1. How can options on futures best be described?
2. How are options on futures set up and structured?
3. What is the future-style method?
4. What strategies do investors pursue with options on futures?
5. What is a synthetic derivatives market position?
6. What combination and linkage transactions are used in practice?
7. What are possible motives for combination or linkage deals?

9.1 What are options on futures?

Options on futures further enhance the wide range of derivative financial instruments. By combining a conditional with an unconditional transaction, they provide a link between the two categories.

Settlement is made by physical delivery of the futures contract, which enables the investor to obtain a complete opportunity and risk profile: The options position permits the investor a favorable, asymmetrical risk distribution, since he has a right of choice without having taken on an obligation. After exercising the option, the right of choice turns into an obligation – as the futures contract counts among the unconditional derivatives.

Options on futures are particularly common with interest-rate futures. Available forms include for example options on the Euro Bund Future (OGBL) and the 30-year Treasury Bond Future (T-BOND).

9.2 How are options on futures set up and structured?

The buyer of an option on a future (such as the Euro-Bund Future) acquires the right but not the obligation to buy (call) or sell (put) that future at a price defined upon conclusion of the transaction. In the event that the option is exercised, it is settled physically by delivery of the future: The options investor turns into a futures investor. In other words, the original options position (conditional contract) is replaced by a futures position (unconditional contract).

9.3 What is the future-style method?

When trading options on futures, the option premium is not paid when the position is opened but in the course of the option term (in analogy to the variation margin postings), i.e. through daily profit and loss settlement. Another important aspect to consider is that short-term interest rates affect option pricing. Whenever they go up, premiums are reduced on both the call and the put side, the reason being that the premium represents the present value of the profit expected on maturity date. Consequently, a rise in interest rates will cause a decrease in present value (and with it, in option prices).

Options positions are evaluated every evening, based on the settlement prices, and settled under the future-style margining system. The procedure is similar as in the case of futures. The buyer of an option benefits from higher option prices, the seller achieves a profit if prices fall.

Options consist usually of the American type. Premature exercise is not recommendable in general, as the time value will be lost. The expiration date of these options differs from the "normal" expiration date, so that the holder of a short position can decide and respond appropriately. In most cases the options are settled by delivering the nearest corresponding futures contract.

Options on futures correspond to the following futures positions, and are delivered as follows:

Table 9-1: Overview of options on futures

Options contract	Future
Long call	Long future
Short call	Short future
Long put	Short future
Short put	Long future

9.4 What strategies do investors pursue with options on futures?

To investors holding option positions, we recommend including the corresponding futures to their position book. By deliberately adding options on futures, investors can pursue both expansion and hedging strategies.

As such, an investor in short futures can build additional positions based on short options on futures, and will realize additional profits from premiums received. Should the options expire worthless, the investor will have received the premium without having built further futures positions. If, however, the position ends up in the money this will generate further futures positions and support an active management of the positions book.

Example:
A futures investor has sold the Euro-Bund Future (FGBL) at 116. His attitude towards the Bund Future is negative; he is convinced that interest rates will go up. Therefore he wishes to expand his position. As he cannot be absolutely sure, our investor decides to expand his position with options rather than additional futures.
Original portfolio:
100 contracts, short FGBL, price 116.
He expands as follows:
25 contracts, short call, strike price 116
25 contracts, short call, strike price 116.50
25 contracts, short call, strike price 117.

With these positions the investor can collect premiums, and he will become a short futures investor only if the underlying asset hits the strike price and the other side (long call) exercises the option. Thus, our investor is in a position to diversify his risk. Even if the future decreases in value (as strike prices are not reached) the investor can profit from the premium received, as well as the 100 short futures opened before. His futures positions are expanded to include options if contrary to expectations, the futures price rises. The advantage of this approach is that the investor can reduce his initial price by the premium he receives.

If the investor's attitude toward the future is only somewhat negative (i.e., to a certain lower limit) – for instance, 114.50 – he can also take offsetting positions, i.e., sell short puts with strike prices of 114.50 and 114.00 In the event of delivery, these short puts can be considered to be close-out positions, as they represent an offsetting deal (admittedly without a close-out designation but with the same effect).

In that case the investor will draw a profit of 114.50 or 114.00 from his short futures position. The calls he has sold expire; his short puts provide a counter-position. Thanks to the two short positions and the premiums gained, the investor can increase his profits. Let us break down this strategy by its opportunity-and-risk profile.

Position book: FGBL trades at 115.50.

Table 9-2: Strategies with options on futures

Number of contracts	Type of contract	Strike price	Strategy
100	Short future	116	Origin
25	Short call	116	Expand futures position
25	Short call	116.50	Expand futures position
25	Short call	117	Expand futures position
50	Short put	114.50	Cap futures position
50	Short put	114	Cap futures position

The cap defines the respective offsetting position to the original futures positions described above.

The basic profile is simple: The short futures position will generate a profit if the future price falls, and we achieve the intended revenue. Conversely, we will realize a loss if the future price rises.

Through the first expansion with short calls on futures we round off our strategy indirectly, in that we purchase the futures once the strike price is reached. While at first glance the premium seems to increase our gain, it does involve the risk of expanding our existing position. In order to hedge against that risk we sell puts with a strike price of 114.50 and 114.00 respectively. This enables us to opt out of our original strategy once the strike prices are reached; that is, we have a cap of 114 and 114.50. This way we complete our strategy and build another risk buffer with the premium received.

What scenarios are conceivable for this strategy? We expand our short futures position by exercising the call option ($\rightarrow$ puts expire), thus achieving the position we originally wanted to expand. Another possible approach is to exercise the puts ($\rightarrow$ calls expire) and close the futures positions. A third scenario would be for both types of options to expire worthless since the future price has not moved significantly. In short, by expanding the simple futures strategy we have set up a strategy that is both feasible to plan and a very complex combination. In practice, this type of linkage and combination trades happens thousands of times every day, and counts among the standard trading strategies.

Another common approach is the combination of two different futures contracts covering, for example, different durations. This enables an investor to take advantage of the changes in the interest rate curve. Note, however, that such strategies are only recommendable to investors with considerable liquid funds at hand. In addition to raising the margin, they need to be able to perform the daily profit-and-loss settlement. Moreover, customers need comprehensive know-how about opportunities and risks, as well as an overall strategy.

Finally, when pursuing such strategies it is advisable to work with both break-even points and limits. In particular for positions that require continual monitoring, a mutual limits strategy should be in place.

9.5 What is a synthetic derivatives market position?

The derivatives market positions described so far can also be emulated synthetically, thus modeling the opportunity-and-risk profile.

Together with the different individual positions, we thus achieve a new overall position which should be viewed as a whole. Closing out only one side of the position should be avoided.

Below is an overview of the possible combinations for synthetic derivatives positions.

Table 9-3: Possible combinations

Synthetic form of...	Combination of...		
	Call option	**Put option**	**Future**
Long call		Long	Long
Short call		Short	Short
Long put	Long		Short
Short put	Short		Long

Synthetic form of...	Combination of...		
	Call option	**Put option**	**Future**
Long future	Long	Short	
Short future	Short	Long	

By combining the individual derivative instruments, we obtain the extended opportunity- and-risk profile of an expanded derivative transaction. This enables investors to use the individual components to create a new, complex opportunity-and-risk structure. Combinations of this kind should only be constructed by experienced investors.

9.6 What combination and linkage deals are used in business practice?

In practice, we often find combinations of options (straddle, strangle, etc.) and securitized derivatives (such as long calls on discount certificates[1]). However it is important to note that the more complex the combination, more confusion and difficulty to survey will result in regards to the resulting opportunity-and-risk profile.

---

1 Securitized derivative on an individual security or index

Therefore it is indispensable to maintain close scrutiny of the position and ensure tradability of one's assets at all times. The greatest risk of these strategies lies in their complexity, as linkages cannot be recognized at a glance and must be documented separately. Rigorous documentation, including recommendations for possible approaches, are therefore of prime importance.

9.7 What are possible motives for combination or linkage deals?

Combinations and linkages can result from two basic intentions:

- Speculation and
- Hedging.

In case of speculation the investor will attempt to enhance his return by combining his portfolio's collateral with an additional instrument. This is advisable, for instance, in sideways markets.

The motive for hedging is usually that the investor's position has not performed according to his expectations. So he sets up a hedge, combining it with a derivatives transaction. Should he succeed he can specify a fixed, predetermined target price; otherwise he must accept the resulting loss.

Both forms of combination trade are generally used in linkage deals with securitized derivatives (such as discount certificates). The basic intention of an investor expanding his securitized derivatives position is to create an additional opportunity profile. In return for that he takes on an additional but controllable risk. He expands the standard conditions of the securitized derivative instrument (as specified by the issuer) through the derivatives position he sets up. Both strategies together form his overall position. Positions like these should only be set up by investors that are intimately familiar with exchange trading, as they must be able to correctly assess their transactions not only in traditional but also in securitized derivatives.

Example:

Our investor holds a discount certificate on the X-index. The cap has been set at 7,000 points, the index currently stands at 6,900 points. The discount certificated based on the X-index trades at € 67.50. Our investor believes that the cap of 7,000 points will be reached and that the X-index will remain below 7,400 points during the maturity of the certificate. He therefore sells additional call options with a strike price of 7,400 points. With the premium received he can immediately increase his profit.

Scenario 1: The index exceeds 7,000 points but remains below 7,400 points. The investor's expectations have come true and he can realize his maximum profit.

Scenario 2: The index remains below 7,000 points. The investor realizes his full profit from the call options sold, but only a reduced profit from the discount certificates, since the cap was not reached.

Scenario 3: The index exceeds 7,400 points. Our investor enjoys the full profit from his discount certificates but takes a loss from his short-call options, buffered by the premium received. Should the index appreciate further, he is well advised to promptly close the position, as potential losses from the short call are unlimited.

As explained before, the resulting combination must be considered within his total position. Only if we take this view can we appreciate the entire range of opportunities and risks.

Combinations are also possible with other securitized derivatives. In this case the securitized derivative has another function, which must be taken into account accordingly.

Summary:
In addition to the traditional types of options and futures, options on futures are another derivative instrument to complement the product portfolio. Options on futures differ from classic derivatives in that premiums are paid "future-style": Payment extends over the entire maturity of the instrument, similar to variation margin entries for futures positions.

In this chapter we also talked about synthetic derivatives positions. They are set up by combining two derivatives positions, resulting in the opportunity-and-risk profile of a third position. For instance, by combining two different types of options, investors can emulate the opportunity-and-risk profile of a futures position.

10 Foreign currency derivatives

This chapter deals with the following questions:
1. What are the basics of foreign currency trading?
2. What are foreign currency derivatives?
3. What are foreign currency options?
4. What are foreign currency futures?

10.1 A history of foreign currency trading

After gold convertibility was suspended in 1971 and currencies were allowed to float freely, trading in foreign currency derivatives began to increase. One reason was that investors became increasingly aware of the opportunities and risks of the new currency system. Also, they recognized the necessity to hedge against or speculate on unwanted devaluation.

There are two kinds of foreign-currency based derivative transactions. One is the OTC transactions executed by the banks at their FOREX trade centers, either between each other or on behalf of their customers. The other is the derivative instruments traded on derivatives exchanges. In this case the CME in Chicago holds a dominant position. Both kinds of foreign currency derivatives are in widespread use today, with OTC deals being used primarily for hedging while currency futures serve as a vehicle for speculative instincts.

10.2 Some basic information on foreign exchange trading

At this point we would like to make a brief excursion into the world of foreign exchange trading. The term foreign exchange (FX) refers to foreign currencies in book-money form. By contrast, foreign currency cash is referred to as "foreign

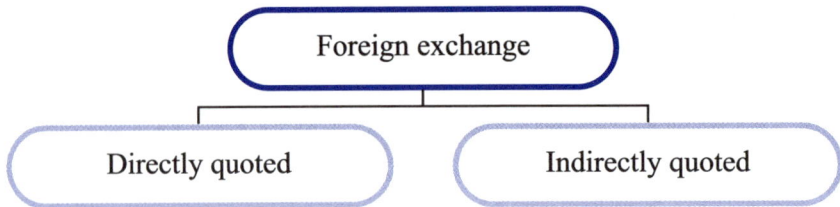

Figure 10.1: Types of quotation for foreign exchange

currency notes and coin". The term foreign exchange trade denominates the exchange of currencies. From an economist's point of view, it functions as a regulator between two economies with different currencies.

The exchange rate is defined as the price (in domestic currency) to be paid for a certain foreign currency. It is also known as direct or price quotation. The opposite is the indirect quotation, with the price of the domestic currency quoted in foreign currency.

In general, the Euro is indirectly quoted against all currencies. The only exception is the British pound (GBP), which is always quoted directly against the Euro. On principle, however, both quotations are possible since they only represent different perspectives.

While transactions in FX spot trading must be fulfilled and consummated within two business days, in FX derivatives trading there is a time gap. Fulfillment does not follow immediately after agreement between the contracting parties, but within a certain period which we shall refer to as foreign exchange derivative period.

10.2.1 Foreign exchange spot trading

In spot trading, the traded object (in this case the foreign exchange), changes hands at fixed prices, and is delivered and received within two business days after execution of the transaction. These trades where execution is immediately followed by fulfillment are carried out every day without any special considerations. They are not subject to any particular obligations, and are viewed and treated the same as any securities spot trade. Among other things, this means the investor must have the required liquid funds available to fulfill the transaction. The settlement price, which is the exchange rate of the spot transaction, is referred to a "spot rate". Trading days are all banking weekdays, except for Saturday, Sunday, and the banking holidays of the respective countries. The day of delivery is also referred to as value day.

10.2.2 Foreign exchange derivative transactions via banks

Let us first have a look at the banks' foreign exchange instruments. A bank customer can buy and/or sell forward foreign exchange, with the bank taking the counter position. These derivative operations are usually based on underlying transactions, and are used to build or expand a hedge. Most companies use this technique to hedge their import and export activities against currency risks and create a sound basis for their calculation. Depending on the specifics of the individual contract, these transactions are called OTC options or forwards. As they represent an individual contract between two parties, it is very unlikely that they can be transferred to third parties.

The basic goal of traders (often companies) is to hedge against foreign currency risks, and therefore refers to existing businesses. This means they refer to an underlying transaction, such as an import-export deal.

Only in very few cases are these transactions used for speculative purposes, although this is possible in principle.

Example:

An entrepreneur expects to receive USD 1 million in 6 months' time. He wishes to lock in the exchange rate against the Euro. To do this, he can take one of two approaches:

1. He can go short USD 1 million.
2. He can sell the USD 1 million against Euros, and then take out a 1-million-dollar loan and hold it until receipt of the payment.

Both approaches lead to the same result – which was to be expected, since otherwise risk-free arbitrage would be possible.

10.2.3 Determining the forward rate

$$Forward\ rate = spot\ rate \times \frac{1+\left(r_G \times \dfrac{T}{B_G}\right)}{1+\left(r_Q \times \dfrac{T}{B_Q}\right)}$$

Where:
T = number of days
r_G = interest rate p.a. in decimals, base currency
r_Q = interest rate p.a. in decimals, target currency
B_G = Calculation basis for base currency (360 or 365)
B_Q = Calculation basis for target currency (360 or 365)

Considering that the trading partners quote at two-way prices, we get the following formulas:

$$Forward\ rate_{bid} = spot\ rate_{bid} \times \frac{1+\left(r_{bid,\ G} \times \dfrac{T}{B_G}\right)}{1+\left(r_{ask,\ Q} \times \dfrac{T}{B_Q}\right)}$$

$$Forward\ rate_{ask} = spot\ rate_{ask} \times \frac{1+\left(r_{ask,G} \times \dfrac{T}{B_G}\right)}{1+\left(r_{bid,Q} \times \dfrac{T}{B_Q}\right)}$$

Where:
T = number of days
r_G = interest rate p.a. in decimals, base currency
r_Q = interest rate p.a. in decimals, target currency
B_G = Calculation basis for base currency (360 or 365)
B_Q = Calculation basis for target currency (360 or 365)

10.2.4 Foreign exchange derivative transactions at exchanges

The exchange has two essential functions, not only for foreign currency derivatives but also for all other derivatives. It can bring together two parties wishing to conclude a transaction, and/or ensure liquidity for the market under the Market-Maker system. Thus, the exchange functions as mediator between two parties pursuing opposite goals.

We distinguish between foreign exchange options and foreign exchange futures.

10.2.5 Overview of foreign exchange derivatives

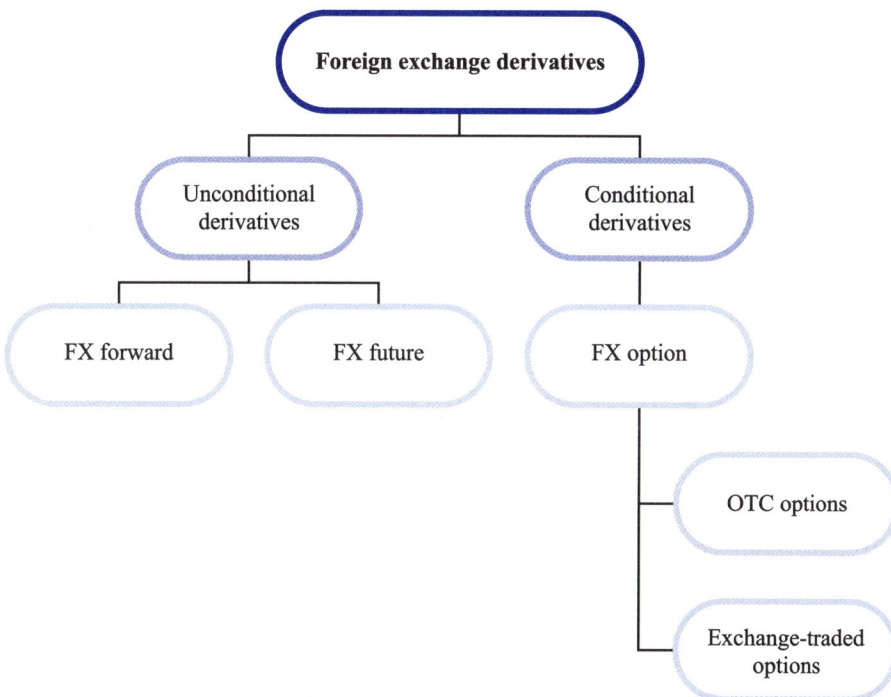

Figure 10.2: Foreign exchange derivatives

10.2.6 Cross rate

In some cases where a currency pair cannot immediately be traded against each other, a so-called cross rate must be calculated. This is the case in the Japanese yen (JPY) and the Swiss frank (CHF). First the JPY is exchanged against the Euro, then the Euro against the CHF. The resulting exchange rate is referred to as cross rate, as the currencies are traded "across". In practice, a cross rate does not present a problem since it is calculated by the banks' foreign exchange divisions, and customer accounts are adjusted accordingly.

10.2.7 Economic drivers of foreign currency pricing

- Volume of output and capital transactions
- Interest rate level
- Rates of inflation
- Economic growth
- Changes in money supply
- Trends in economic activity
- Economic policies of governments and issue banks
- Crises, conflicts, political unrest
- Lobbying by internal and external parties
- Psychological market influences, such as resignations, rumors, confirmations, announcements, elections, etc.

10.3 What are foreign currency derivatives?

The difference between the spot rate and the forward rate of foreign exchange depends on the difference in interest rates between both currencies. On principle, an investment in one currency should yield the same returns as in the second currency, and since returns are also effected by the different interest rates in the two markets these differences must be adjusted through the currency rates. This also means that risk-free investments in a foreign currency will yield the same returns as investments in the domestic currency: Currency is the convergence factor.

If the forward rate is **higher** than the spot rate, we speak of a **report**. Contrarily, a **deport** is a **discount** in the forward rate. According to the interest parity theorem, the interest rate difference between two currencies is referred to as the (interest) swap rate.

10.3.1 Swap rate

How is a swap rate calculated?

1. Determining the interest rate activity for the domestic currency

$$domestic\ interest\ rate\ activity = \left(1 + r \times \left(\frac{Duration\ (days)}{360}\right)\right)$$

Where r = Domestic interest rate

2. Determining the interest rate activity for the foreign currency

$$Foreign\ interest\ rate\ activity = \frac{1}{K_1} \times \left(1 + r_1 \times \left(\frac{duration\ (days)}{360}\right)\right) \times Forward\ rate$$

Where:
K_1 = spot rate
r_1 = Foreign interest rate

From that, we derive the following:

$$Foreign\ interest\ rate\ activity = \frac{1}{K_1} \times \left(1 + r_1 \times \left(\frac{duration\ (days)}{360}\right)\right) \times Forward\ rate$$

Where:
K_1 = spot rate
R = domestic interest rate
R_1 = foreign interest rate

Thus, the formula for the forward rate is as follows:

$$\left(1+r\times\left(\frac{Duration\ (days)}{360}\right)\right)=\frac{1}{K_1}\times\left(1+r_1\times\left(\frac{Duration\ (days)}{360}\right)\right)\times Forward\ rate$$

$$Foraward\ rate = K_1 \times \left[\frac{\left(1+r\times\left(\dfrac{Duration\ (days)}{360}\right)\right)}{\left(1+r_1\times\left(\dfrac{Duration\ (days)}{360}\right)\right)}\right]$$

Where:
K_1 = spot rate
R = domestic interest rate
R_1 = foreign interest rate

In practice, this is simplified as follows:

$$Swaprate = \frac{K_1 \times Z \times Duration\ (days)}{360}$$

Where:
K_1 = spot rate
Z = interest rate difference between currencies

According to the above, there are three conceivable interest rate differences:

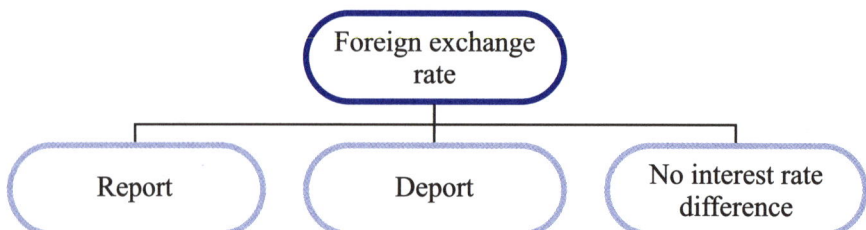

Figure 10.3: Possible interest rate differences between two currencies

Interest rate of counter-currency > interest rate of base currency = report
Interest rate of counter-currency < interest rate of base currency = deport

10.4 What are currency options?

Again we distinguish between OTC options, which are traded individually and anonymously, and traditional options as the exchange-traded and standardized form. The advantage of the former is that an investor can shape them exactly as needed. Their disadvantage is that they are useful only for that particular investor and a resale is hardly possible. Both standard and exotic options can be traded.

Like equity options, standardized currency options (as are traded, for instance, at the CME) result from the same basic intentions. A Euro/U.S. Dollar contract (CME) has been standardized at a value of € 62,500. The essential advantage of these options is their high liquidity and fast tradability at derivative exchanges.

The buyer of a currency option acquires the right but not the obligation to buy or sell a certain amount in a foreign currency on a predefined date and at a predefined price. For this right he pays an option premium to the Writer (short).

An investor buying a call option assumes an up market, an investor selling a call counts on a sideways or slightly downward market. The buyer of the put expects a down market, the seller a sideways or slightly upward market.

The buyer (long) has the right of choice (hence the term "conditional derivative") and in return pays a premium to the seller (short), who then turns into an option writer and takes on the associated risk. While the buyer can at the most lost the capital employed (via the premium), the seller in theory is exposed to an unlimited risk.

Currency options are also categorized in European-style and American-style options. The option premium is determined in the same way as has been described for equity options in Chapter 4. As with equity options, the investor can use an offsetting derivative to help dispose of the obligations entered.

Contrary to standard options, contracts on exotic options – which involve different rights – are individually agreed between the contracting parties and permit unlimited combinations.

10.5 What are currency futures?

The CME in Chicago, as one example for an exchange offering currency futures, offers a wide variety of them. These futures are standardized and highly liquid. The classic EUR/USD future (EC) has a contract value of € 125,000 and is among the contracts most frequently traded. The futures are traded around the clock (CME GLOBEX) and can be employed individually and rapidly.

Their function is comparable to that of other futures. There are two basic kinds – rising or falling – and depending on the investor's attitude, a currency future will be purchased or sold. As the settlement at maturity is made by physical delivery, many futures positions are prematurely closed out or rolled over on the last trading day.

Example:

Our investor expects the € to go up against the USD. Due to this opinion he purchases 10 €/USD futures (EC) at the CME. Should his expectations come true and the the euro has appreciated against the U.S. dollar and the dollar has depreciated against the Euro, the investor will realize a profit, and vice versa.

Although the 10 contracts have a total value of € 1,250,000, our investor only needs to raise the initial margin for this position. This way he can build a low-cost and flexible foreign currency position.

10.5.1 Possible applications

As foreign currency derivatives permit low-cost and rapid trading, they are used for both hedging and speculation. Large investors place their bets on an assumed market movement of the currency in question. In doing this it is advisable to set limits since currencies move very fast, and sometimes overnight.

Often these instruments are used to complement existing derivatives positions, such as the Euro-Bund Futures. They can, however, be also quite appealing as individual positions. In particular at times of rapid global investments, a professional management of portfolio and position books would not be possible without them.

10.5.2 Basic intentions of an investor

Just like other types of trade, trade in foreign currency derivatives is driven by three basic motives, at which we will take a brief glance now.

Hedging
Traditional hedging against currency fluctuations can result from different underlying needs – such as:
- Import-export transactions
- Securing prices for planned investments
- Protecting existing portfolios (securities, commodities, etc.)
- Securing future payment streams

Speculation
The investor speculates on an assumed change in prices at the foreign exchange markets. These speculations are independent of an underlying business, and their sole purpose is to generate additional income. However there are potential losses to consider as well. If the investor's guess is wrong and the currency rate moves the other way, he will suffer a loss that cannot be compensated by an underlying transaction.

Nevertheless these positions optimally complement speculator's position books since the combination with index-based futures and interest-rate futures provides an additional investment vehicle. The same is true for a combination with commodity futures, which can also be used for speculative purposes. We should add that currency futures are just as easily tradable as index-based futures.

Speculation on spreads or currency pairs
An investor speculating on shifts between different currency pairs relative to each other can build combinations which may partially reduce the risk profile. However at the same time there is a danger that the risk will increase exponentially if combinations are set up in series rather than offsetting each other.

Summary:
In foreign currency trading there are two types of businesses: spot transactions and derivative transactions. The latter are grouped into individual contracts between investors and banks' forexForex trading divisions, and exchange-traded derivatives (options and futures).

If a foreign currency derivative contains a price premium versus the spot price we speak of a report; a possible discount is referred to as deport. The difference between two currencies is called the swap rate.

A fast and liquid trade in foreign currency derivatives is ensured by exchange-traded currency futures. They are used for both, hedging purposes and speculation.

11 Commodity futures trading

This chapter will deal with the following questions:
1. What are commodity futures and how do they differ from commodity cash transactions?
2. Which commodities are eligible for futures trading?

11.1 Commodity futures vs. spot transactions

Commodity futures contracts differ from a traditional commodity cash (or spot) transaction in that they do not provide for delivery upon execution of the transaction, and instead delivery is deferred to some future date. Therefore it is not uncommon to enter into a futures contract when the underlying commodity is not even available and/or has not yet been produced. This type of futures contract, also referred to as the "archetype" of the futures exchange, can be considered the first trading vehicle and over time became instrumental in the establishment of futures exchanges as we know them today. The primary motive for entering into this type of transaction used to be the spreading of risk and/or the purchase of goods from faraway lands. In very simplified form, these exchanges existed already in antiquity. Today, the most important futures exchanges can be found in the USA. Among them, we will mention the CME in Chicago and the NYMEX in New York, which resulted from a merger of smaller dairy exchanges. Currently, a large portion of all commodity futures contracts are traded at the NYMEX as the world's largest futures exchange. It is considered to be the last bastion of pure capitalism. Most transactions nowadays are done with a strictly speculative mindset and the great majority of positions are closed out prematurely. By contrast, cash transactions presume delivery and acceptance in practically 100 percent of all cases.

Exchange-traded commodities are mostly bought and sold in the form of futures. Yet in principle, we will encounter both forms of derivatives, forwards (individually tailored and bilateral) as well as futures (standardized and thus tradable), with the latter guaranteeing orderly and continual trading and the possibility of a transfer to third parties. In line with the focus of this book, we will confine ourselves to futures which, in practice, take precedence over options.

Executing a commodity contract on the spot market

Delivery and acceptance of goods

Executing a commodity futures contract

Potential delivery and acceptance of goods

Close-out of position; realization of speculative gain or loss

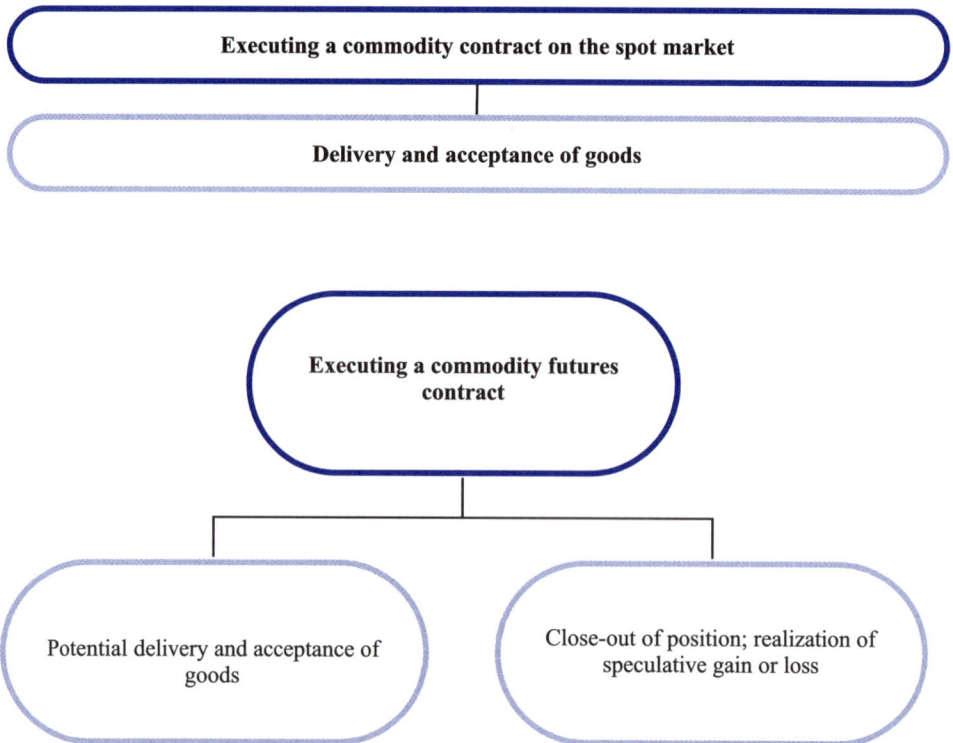

Figure 11.1: Spot market and futures contracts

11.1.1 Commodity futures

The structure of a commodity futures contract mirrors that of an index futures or bond futures contract, with all stipulations in place at the time of its execution. As with other futures, the expectation of a long futures investor is an upward market trend while an investor holding a short position hopes for a decline of the underlying commodity.

11.1.2   Opening and closing of positions and settlement

As mentioned before, a large number of commodity futures contracts are closed out prior to maturity, in line with their strictly speculative character. Simultaneously, as with an index future, an offsetting trade may release the investor from his assumed position and associated obligations. If a futures contract is not closed out prior to matutity, it must be fulfilled.

Table 11-1: Opening and closing of commodity futures

Opening	Close-out
Long future	Short future
Short future	Long future

Owing to the great variety of investor needs, there are commodity futures providing for either physical delivery or cash settlement.

Let us deal with physical delivery first. According to this scenario, goods change ownership, or are exchanged. This kind of traditional and original type of settlement is preferred, for example, by companies intending to process the acquired goods further or contemplate re-selling them (as befits the instincts of a commodity trader).

As an increasing number of speculators are entering futures trading, it has become customary – especially so over the last ten years – to offer cash settlement in addition to physical delivery. The reason is obvious: An investor purely trading on expectations of a commodity's price movement will clearly **prefer cash settlement over physical delivery** as he exclusively wishes to take advantage of market developments.

Premature close-out works exactly as it does with index futures: the spread difference is paid in cash. If the investor were to make and/or accept delivery, he is likely to encounter all sorts of difficulties since it would involve setting up the necessary and cost-intensive infrastructure, as well as buying and selling the goods, depending on the particular type of future.

Example:
> If the investor had bought a Henry Hub natural gas future and allowed delivery, he needed to transport the goods from the USA. This would be entirely impracticable and, in reality, an impossibility for most investors.

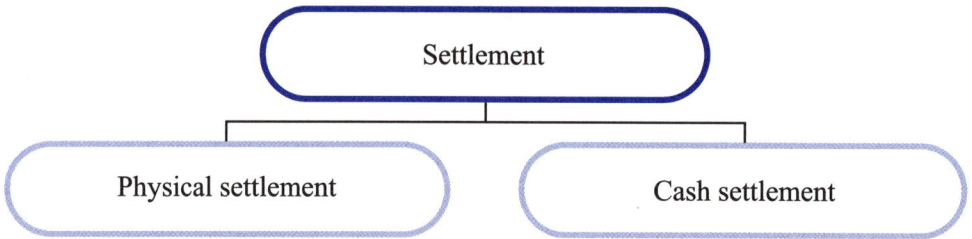

Figure 11.2: Settlement modes

11.1.3 Application of various settlement modes

Of course, overlap may occur in practice, due mainly to industrial investors' simultaneous trading in cash settlement products.

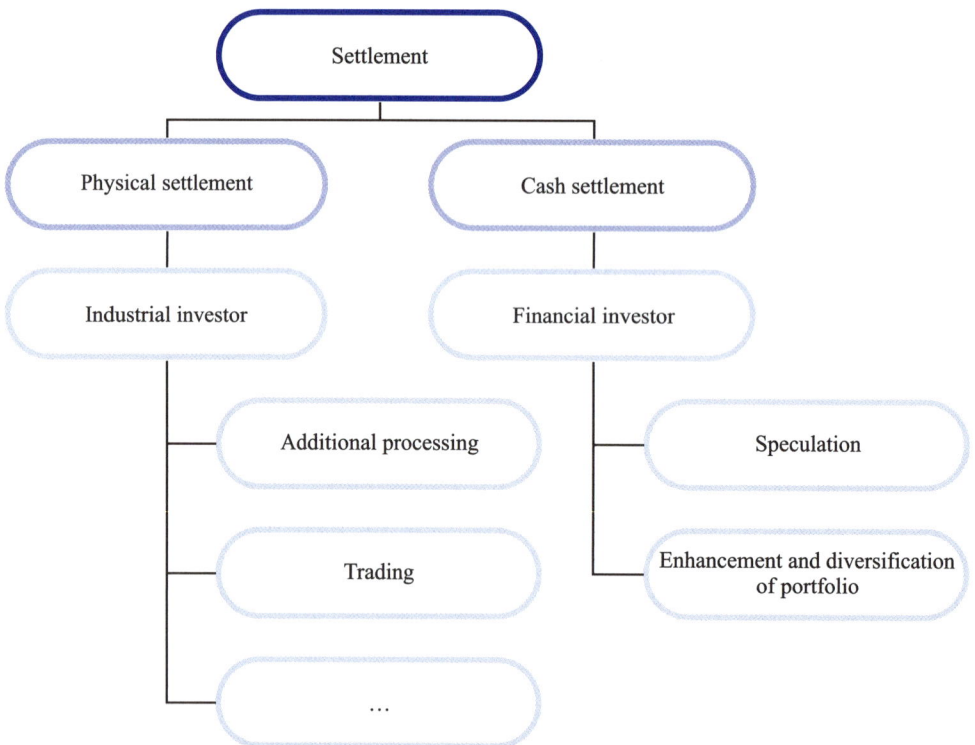

Figure 11.3: Settlement modes and application

11.2 Which commodities are eligible for futures trading?

In principle, futures contracts can be entered into for any commodity. In practice, the following commodities are the most common:

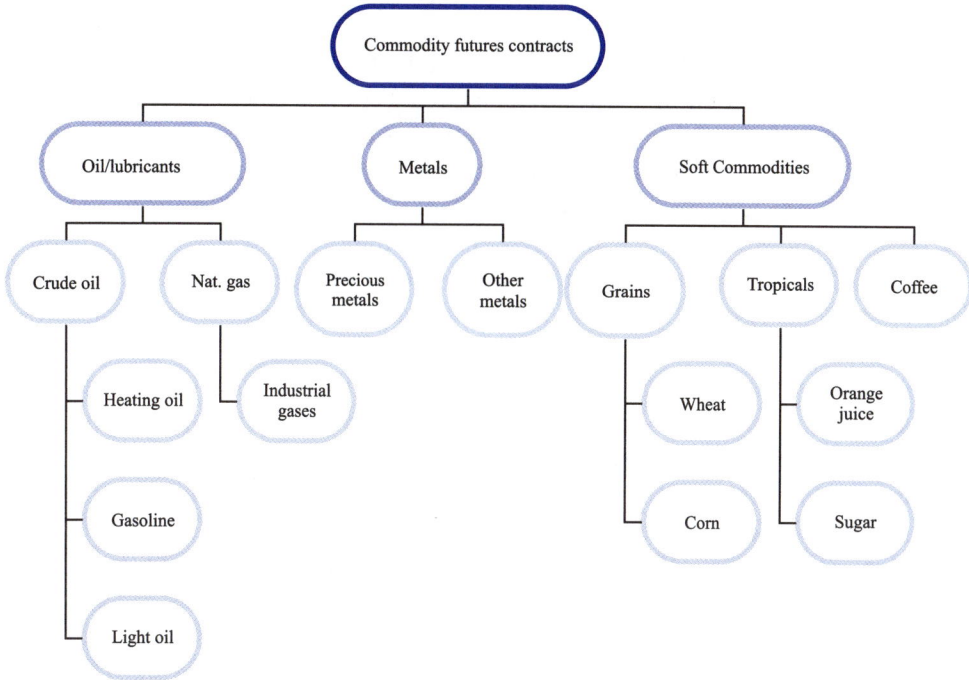

Commodity futures contracts

- Oil/lubricants
  - Crude oil
    - Heating oil
    - Gasoline
    - Light oil
  - Nat. gas
    - Industrial gases
- Metals
  - Precious metals
  - Other metals
- Soft Commodities
  - Grains
    - Wheat
    - Corn
  - Tropicals
    - Orange juice
    - Sugar
  - Coffee

Diagram 11.4: Types of commodities underlying futures trading

The above diagram shows in very simplified form the product complexes open to futures trading. One of the most heavily traded products is frozen, highly concentrated orange juice (FCOJ). At processing, the juice is reduced to a seventh of its volume under extraction of its aromatics, to be re-injected after the reduction process. The concentrate is subsequently frozen for storage. Restoration of the juice takes place by thawing the syrup and adding some water and sugar. Due to a strong world-wide demand, FCOJ has a high trading volume. One point investors should consider is that current derivatives trading refers to future years' crops; considerable price increases may therefore result from disease, environmental catastrophes or crop failure, while abundance of crops or a breakdown in consumer demand will bring lower prices.

The trading in soft commodities has increased tremendously over the past years; in particular derivatives on sugar and corn have been traded actively since both serve as feedstock for ethanol production. Even private investors are apt to invest in these complexes via other derivatives (e.g., put and call options).

11.3 Executing commodity futures contracts

In Germany, only the larger futures dealers and a few banks with relevant experience are able to trade futures on the exchanges. Very few credit institutions carry a commodity futures portfolio on their books. Most are only now in the process of establishing and building out this type of investment branch. Commodity futures contracts are only sporadically offered (mostly to institutional clients) for hedging and speculative endeavors. This situation is largely due to regulatory restrictions. Only since the new "Principle I" (issued by the Federal Office for Financial Services Regulation) came into force have banks been permitted to engage in futures trading.

Another noteworthy point is that commodity futures are mostly traded by institutions and professional investors. The market is virtually closed to private investors for reasons of insufficient liquidity in assets. Instead, they use traditional leverage products or stock certificates to participate in the trading of commodity futures. These securitized derivatives are issued by large institutions that certify the associated rights and re-package the derivative instruments into a manageable size for private investors. In the end, however, these products are similarly structured as traditional, exchange-traded derivative contracts.

A clear-cut trend is emerging here: Private investors prefer securitized derivatives (from an issuer) while professional investors strengthen and expand their positions in traditional derivatives.

11.3.1 When should an investor enter into commodity futures transactions?

While this question must be answered specifically for each individual investor, there are a number of basic prerequisites that must be met:
- An investor intent on futures trading must have sufficient liquid assets to maintain and support his positions.

- Proficiency in and knowledge of the subject matter are equally crucial, since the derivatives market is anything but a playground and a failing trade can quickly get out of hand, with mushrooming costs and unpleasant consequences.
- Thirdly, a readiness to always take the pulse of the market and have the latest information available. Taking the pulse of the market means for the investor to monitor his positions on a daily basis. The derivatives market moves at lightning speed; therefore, in addition to constant surveillance, continuous access to objective sources of information is imperative. Furthermore, the reality of different time zones may interfere, since most futures markets are located in the U.S. or elsewhere. Investors need to make sure their orders can be placed, transmitted to the trading floor and executed properly.

Those points, essential for executing a trade, are of fundamental importance and must be clearly understood.

As you may have concluded from the above, commodities futures trading is recommended for professional investors only, as only they are able to consistently garner profits. Private investors are better off with securitized derivatives.

11.4   Future developments and outlook

In the face of fast-moving and expanding markets, we perceive a great deal of opportunity in the realm of commodity futures trading. It is quite conceivable for commodity futures to grow into a strategic investment vehicle in Germany, and to be traded on the futures exchanges. Another possibility is the early introduction of commodity-based indices on which to trade futures. Since demand will determine supply, not vice versa, it should only be a matter of time before we begin to see a lively trading of commodity futures – and do so as a matter of course, as is customary in other parts of the world, foremost in the USA.

Summary:
For many investors, trading in commodity futures is exciting, yet fraught with risk. Trading in futures oftentimes serves the hedging of existing or future products, but also to place bets on price volatility in the markets. In commodity futures transactions, we distinguish between soft commodities and hard commodities (steel, iron ore, oil). For some years now, betting on commodities has expanded. These are the reasons why cash settlement contracts were devised, in addition to those providing for physical delivery

12 Pricing and influencing factors in commodity futures trading

In this chapter we will deal with the following questions:
1. How is the pricing of commodity futures determined?
2. Which factors can influence pricing and how do changes in these factors affect prices?

12.1 How are prices for commodity futures determined?

As previously shown during our discussion of index futures, the fair future price depends on the spot market instrument and the cost of carry (financing cost). Unlike in a financial futures contract, another factor to be considered is warehousing and insurance expense. Storage expense will remain out of the picture only when a product (e.g., live goods) cannot be stored. Financing costs will rise when traditional costs (as for storage) enter into the equation and they will decrease once so-called intermediate yields are realized. The latter is not quite as simple when it concerns to commodities. While a stock will yield dividends which may be booked as intermediate yield, commodities are subject to a different pricing scheme in that the so-called **convenience yield** is factored in, which may result in a rise or fall of carrying costs. If the convenience yield rises above the cost of carry, resulting in an increase, the future will trade below the current spot price or, as we call it, "with **backwardation**". By contrast, if the carrying costs exceed the convenience yield, the future becomes more expensive than the spot price: it is traded "with **contango**".

12.1.1 Prices of commodity futures

Table 12-1: Relation between cash and future price

Commodity futures			
Spot price	<	Future price	Contango
Spot price	>	Future price	Backwardation

Here, we need to distinguish as to whether the calculated convenience yield boosts or lowers financing costs. The importance of this question will be discussed in the following sections.

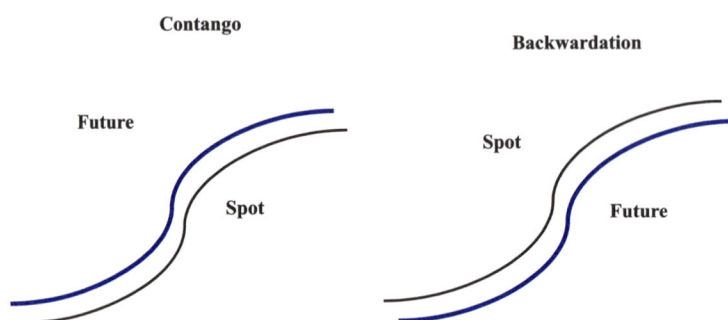

Figure 12.1: Contango and backwardation

12.1.2 How prices are determined

The convenience yield is the investor's proceeds while holding a good physically, instead of the respective derivative. With consumer goods it is not a directly quantifiable entity and instead may be derived from the future's structure. Consequently, not all futures feature a convenience yield when calculating fair value.

In the presence of a convenience yield, fair value may be calculated by use of the following formula:

$$F_0 = K_0 \times \frac{(1+i+L)^t}{(1+y)^t}$$

Where:

F_0 = Fair value
K_0 = Spot price
I = Cost of storage (net)
i = Risk-free rate of interest
y = Convenience yield
t = Maturity over years

The convenience yield can be depicted in the following equation:

$$F_0 \times (1+y)^t = (K_0 + L_0) \times (1+i)^t$$

Warehousing expenses may also be expressed as the proportional in-storage rate l, giving us:

$$F_0 \times (1+y)^t = K_0 \times (1+i+L)^t$$

The convenience yield thus defines the degree to which the equation's left side outranks its right side; it is the positive overhang of the inequality.

To phrase it in terms other than mathematical terminology, we can say that **y represents the uncertainty expected by market participants due to factors such as, for instance, crop failure.** In simple language, it indicates the real shortage of a commodity. If one assumes a bountiful supply, y will have a small value or no value at all. In case of excess supply, –y leads to discounting.

As mentioned, price calculations in commodity futures are similar to index futures:

Price of future =
price of commodity + ((financing cost + warehousing cost) − convenience yield)

Thus, the rather complex subject matter described above can be represented in a simple equation.

12.1.3 What inherent problem does a contango quotation pose?

The answer to this question lies within the subject matter itself. An investor who purchased a contango future has also paid a premium over the basic amount. The contango will cause him a loss if the spot price remains stagnant or fluctuates only minimally. If the contract is "rolled over" to the next month of the contango series, the loss potential will increase as shown in the following graphic:

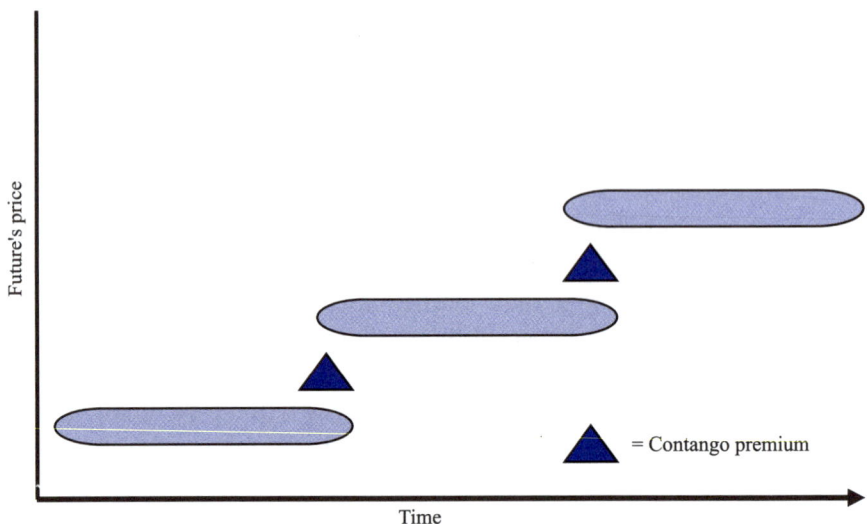

Diagram 12.2: Inherent contango problems in futures positions

In practice, a contango may lie between 15 and 20 percent within a year. Investors must be aware of the fact that only if the original contract value rises above the contango will they realize a profit. Naturally, certain market conditions may enable them to attain quicker, more efficient gains. Nonetheless, these associated facts must be taken account of in any valuation model.

The same, of course, is true for the other side of the coin: backwardation.

12.1.4 Futures trading

When trading commodity futures, investors must watch out for a few things that are of no concern in index futures.

While the trading calendar for index futures usually stretches over the next three quarter months, commodity futures feature monthly maturity (oftentimes for a period of several years) which very much benefits orderly and liquid trading. Also, the quality of the underlying instrument is specified in the contract details. For example, the light sweet crude oil future only trades sweet oil with maximally 0.42 percent sulfur content and a relative viscosity of 37 to 42 degrees API. Detailed contract specifications of this kind are vital to ensure consistency of product. This is especially important for oil with its many grades of quality; but with other commodities, too, emphasis is put on basing future contracts on uniform quality standards. In sugar, for example, we differentiate between No. 11 and No. 14.

12.1.5 Warehousing and/or storage

Another fact unique to commodities futures trading is the issue of warehousing/storage availability. Precious metals and oil are easy to store, as opposed to soft commodities and live products (cattle and hogs). In consequence, it is essential to familiarize oneself with the size of inventories and the storage facilities at hand before committing to an investment.

Right now, inventory of base metals in storage is low due to heavy demand from Asia. This opens a profit opportunity with higher prices on the horizon. A turn in trend brought on by a change in storage capacity, though, must be dealt with in a circumspect manner. If, for instance, storage facilities for coffee are wiped out by a hurricane, as happened in New Orleans, this will have a huge impact on the price levels of all futures currently traded.

12.2 How pricing is influenced by certain issues

It is obvious that commodity futures markets are apt to undergo wild price swings and will respond to outside events instantly. The following events may trigger market movement:
- Supply and demand figures
- Production data (real)
- Weather reports and climatic changes
- Natural catastrophes
- Crop failures and infestations
- Subsidy programs
- Wars, embargos and catastrophes
- Import duties
- The rate of a nation's economic growth
- Inventory buildup/depletion etc.

Those potential influences hold both risk and opportunity, and it is therefore essential for investors to be well acquainted with the subject matter. They ought to be familiar with all contributing factors pertinent to a specific future, and be able to assess their impact. Equally vital is instant access to relevant sources of information: An investor holding coffee futures, for instance, must have the latest and best information at his fingertips. This is where the gap between institutional and private investors is obvious: Institutions have exhaustive, up-to-date information within reach (because of their networking capabilities) while most private investors have to go to great lengths digging up information from sundry sources. In the next few years, we will witness a change here, as wealthy private investors will increasingly commit funds in this arena and grow into a new class of market player.

As stated above, soft goods have met with noticeably heavier demand over the last few years. This traces back, among others, to ongoing shifts in our society. For instance, at present the world experiences a boom in coffee consumption. "Coffee to go" is a universal slogan and even in the land of smiles, coffee is now enjoying great popularity – although the Chinese have long been known as tea-drinkers only. So, a "sleeping giant" enters upon the stage of international trade. Let us cite another example: sugar. What used to be a sweetening agent only has by now morphed into an important energy source. As an additive in the production of ethanol, both sugar and corn have met with skyrocketing demand.

At present, our society's demographics still show a preponderance of the young over the aging. But this is bound to change dramatically in the not-too-distant future, which will also affect our habits of consumption. Increases in individual living standards will add their share towards the demand for new products. As a consequence, the prices for these products will increase, resulting in a change of priorities: While coffee and orange juice futures were the butt of jokes in the past, investing in them is of surpassing importance. The beauty of futures markets lies in the fact that profit opportunities result from both, rising and falling prices, hence there is always an opportunity for investment. A prerequisite is to stay attuned to the prevailing trend and to invest accordingly. As plain as this may sound, to make it come true is far from easy. Because commodity futures are a straightforward, transparent instrument, profitable strategies, even for intraday trading, abound.

12.3 Gathering information

As outlined above, in commodity futures trading the availability of information is of utmost importance. Yet this poses a stumbling block for many investors. Only those with access to consistent and reliable sources of information are able to develop consistent and reliable strategies in the long term. Equally important is the proper evaluation of information – especially in commodity futures trading. Poignant and, above all, unbiased expert analysis is indispensable. After all, not many derivatives specialists will be able to interpret an expert report on a coffee crop correctly.

If you invest with a scattergun approach you are likely to fail. Rather, thorough analysis of fundamental and technical parameters is a necessary first step in setting up a viable strategy. Also, we recommend selecting instruments, the trading and clearing of which is entirely in sync with each other. At the same time, investors should never lose sight of a contract's possible exercise or assignment, and compile a benefit-(net) cost analysis early on. If a commodity futures transaction appears to be overly costly, due to its inherent complexity and specific execution, one should invariably abstain from it. The fundamental principle should be: There must be a sound ratio of risk exposure and profit potential.

Summary:
Trading in Commodity Futures is as old as the futures exchange. Investing in commodity futures is governed by different factors than are financial futures transactions. Attention must be paid to whether the commodity future is quoted as contango (higher than spot) or backwardation (lower than spot).
Another important subject is the settlement mode: We recommend choosing futures with cash settlement for speculative purposes.

13 Strategies with commodity futures and currency futures

This chapter will deal with the following questions:
1. What strategies are available in the commodity futures sector?
2. What are combinations of foreign currency and commodity futures transactions?
3. What strategies are available for trading foreign currency futures?

13.1 Common strategies in the commodity futures sector

The commodity futures exchange is looked upon as the last bastion of unvarnished capitalism. It is the place where all the things are traded that keep the world supplied. Yet, how does an investor expect to profit from those investments?

As with all other types of derivatives, we find three kinds of underlying intentions:
- Hedging
- Arbitrage
- Speculation

13.1.1 Hedging with commodity futures instruments

The basic premise for hedging a commodity trade is the existence of a commercial transaction. We either buy or sell goods. To protect these commercial transactions we enter into futures positions. The simplest of futures position can be hedged with a futures contract. If we wish to protect ourselves from rising prices in the base metals complex, we will decide to purchase a futures contract. If prices do rise as expected this purchase will compensate us for the resulting Delta. If prices stagnate the futures contract will result in a loss that must be held in check, which might well require split-second decision-making. Another possibility is to write an option (against the position) which is quite acceptable in the context of hedging strategies since raw materials prices greatly inhibit accurate cost-benefit calculations. Now, the hedge will afford us a level of predictability in looking forward. With hedging strategies, we must decide as to whether we wish to insure ongoing transactions, or lock in the price of a future transaction. In both instances, predictability is the deciding factor.

While traditional strategies with long puts or short futures are ideal for hedging a current position, long calls and long futures are required for hedging against the risk of future price increases (by compensating for them). These strategies are appropriate if an investment is contemplated down the road and the required funds are lacking at present.

13.1.2 Speculating with commodity futures instruments

An entirely different premise underlies the expectation for rising or falling commodity prices: We are not tied to a core commercial transaction, but solely bet on generating an additional stream of income. A future serves to speculate either on a bullish or bearish price trend alone, without any further objective. Our investment is exclusively geared toward a commodity's price movement.

Example:

> An investor finds the price of orange juice to be a bargain, and expects heavy crop losses due to inclement weather. As a decrease in supply suggests rising prices, our investor buys a FCOJ future. If the price trend bears out our investor's expectations he will realize a profit. Conversely, a loss will result in the event of prices declining for other reasons.

The investor, as stated, bets on price movement and accepts risk exposure, since his underlying intention is not to hedge a commercial transaction, rather his motive is pure speculation, which nonetheless should be preceded by thorough analysis.

A large portion of commodity futures contracts are of a strictly speculative nature. Most are exercised by way of cash settlement instead of physical delivery.

13.1.3 Arbitrage with commodity futures instruments

A third option is commodity arbitrage. The investor purchases a good at exchange X and simultaneously sells it at exchange Y. The resulting gap (margin) represents his profit or loss. A simultaneous trade at two exchanges limits risk on his part.

13.1.4 Spreading in commodity futures trades

The investor sets up a spread in order to profit from price differences. He will sell the seemingly overpriced contract and buy the lower-priced one. The difference in the two trades, as with any spread, is his predefined profit. The discrepancy in price movement of the two contracts allows him to pocket a profit.

These strategies are complementary to the main strategies and serve to buttress the market. In a way, they keep the market on an even keel.

Investors actively trading daily on the exchanges constantly set up new positions and close old ones. We would like to reiterate that positions are not held to maturity (i.e., expiration) but are liquidated and replaced by others.

13.2 Foreign currency and commodity futures

Combinations of currency and commodity futures are often found in trades based on a commercial transaction. Not only will they give the investor protection against changes in the commodity's price, but also help guard against fluctuations in the underlying currency, primarily the U.S. Dollar.

Example:
> Our investor plans on making a USD 10 million copper purchase, but needs to have the metal on hand in six months' time only. Since the deal will be executed six months down the road and our investor anticipates prices to rise, he will buy a long copper future. At the same time, he expects the U.S. Dollar to appreciate markedly against the Euro; he is eager to protect himself against such appreciation. He will sell Euro/dollar futures of matching value against the commercial transaction envisaged. If the expected development on the foreign currency exchanges materializes, our investor will be protected against a depreciating Euro by virtue of his foreign currency future. At the same time, the long copper future pro-

tects him against a higher price of copper. Both components afford him a predictable measure of protection and assurance looking forward.

Obviously, seeking blanket protection to the very last dollar would not be wise. Protection against potential loss must be kept within sensible limits. Of course, the basic premise should be to stay in conformity with market conditions or else the whole business of seeking protection would be futile.

13.3 What strategies are common in currency futures trading?

13.3.1 Hedging strategies

An investor plans to hedge against depreciation of his home currency. So he will sell a future of his currency against a foreign currency, and will realize a profit when the anticipated depreciation occurs.

Example:

> Our investor expects to be in receipt of USD 10 million three months from now. Since the U.S. Dollar is his home currency, he wishes to protect himself against a depreciating Euro and, to this end, sells Euro futures. This transaction is equivalent to a sale of the Euro and simultaneous purchase of the U.S. Dollar, enabling the investor to balance out any given difference.

Hedging strategies with currency futures are mostly employed by investors protecting large commercial transactions, enabling them to achieve predictability in their plans and calculations.

Betting on foreign currency is a different matter entirely. In this instance the bet is based solely on one currency's change relative to another's. Deals of the sort are done independent of commercial transactions for no other purpose than generating profits.

Example:

> Our investor anticipates the Euro to depreciate relative to the dollar, prompting him to sell Euro futures. By doing so, he synthetically acquires dollars. With the decline in the Euro and corresponding rise in the dollar, the investor stands to profit; in the opposite case he will suffer a loss.

The example illustrates how potential losses from a spot transaction (bond portfolio) can be compensated by taking protective action as described.

13.3.2 Strategies for speculation

This strategy involves the betting on a change in price of two currencies relative to each other, preferably through an exchange-traded FX future. If an investor anticipates higher prices he will buy a future, and he will sell a future if he anticipates a decline in the currency. The FX future is the instrument of choice for currency speculation because of its speedy and cost-effective characteristics that allows for it to be executed.

Example:
> Our investor expects the U.S. Dollar to appreciate against the Euro and takes a short 1position in Euro futures (analogous to a purchase of USD futures). His judgment is confirmed when the Euro begins to appreciate against the U.S. Dollar, assuring him of a profit. However if the Euro were to appreciate against the dollar, he would suffer a loss. In any case, the investor will participate in price movements on a 1:1 basis, as the future contract is a Delta–1 instrument.

Summary:
In order to ensure the effective management of a portfolio together with current futures positions, it is vital to stay on top of things, adhering to clear-cut strategies. This holds true in particular for commodity futures, foreign currency futures, the hedging of commercial transactions, and deals of a speculative nature. When hedging a commercial transaction, it is recommended to do so with regard to both, the commodity and the underlying currency.

14 Over the counter derivatives

This chapter deals with the following questions:
1. What is a swap?
2. What are Swaptions and IRGs?
3. What are exotic options?
4. What is a forward?

14.1 Non-exchange-traded derivatives

In this chapter we will take a look at derivatives not traded on the exchange.

These are contracts negotiated individually between the parties concerned, and therefore not standardized (individual bilateral financial agreements). As explained in the previous chapters, only standardized derivatives can easily be transferred to other parties via the exchange. The contracts to be discussed are used for (medium to long-term) speculation or to hedge an underlying trade, and we usually see professional/institutional investors carrying these non-exchange-traded derivatives in their portfolios. In the following sections we will describe a few examples.

14.2 What is a swap?

From a purely formal standpoint, a swap is a bilateral financial agreement about a payment stream between two parties. Or rather, an exchange ("swap") of payment streams is agreed, along with the nominal value and contractual terms.

Since only payment streams are exchanged, an important issue is the creditworthiness of the contractual parties, for it constitutes an integral part of the risk.

We distinguish between four different kinds of swaps:
- Interest (rate) swap
- Currency swap
- Stock index swap
- Commodity swap

Party 1   Party 2
e.g., bank   *Payment stream*   e.g., client

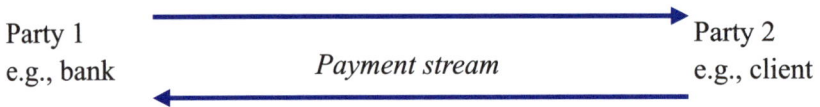

Figure 14.1: Swap

14.2.1 Interest rate swaps

The parties to an interest rate swap agree on swapping payment streams based on a fictitious par value; for instance, variable interest rates can be swapped against fixed interest rates. We speak of a payor swap if the client pays the fixed interest rate and of a payee swap if the client receives the fixed rate; while a basis swap involves an exchange of two variable interest rates. In terms of the volume traded (around € 50 trillion) the swaps market is larger than the bond market. This order of magnitude further emphasizes the importance of these instruments to hedgers and speculators.

Table 14-1: Designation of interest rate swaps

Interest rate side	Designation
Fixed interest rate	Payor swap
Variable interest rate	Receiver swap

Put in simple terms, one could say that an interest swap is somewhat comparable to exchanging a fixed-interest-rate bond against a variable-interest-rate bond (floater). In the case of a swap, however, netting is based on interest streams rather than nominal values. Upon conclusion of the deal the swap has a value of zero, as otherwise one party would have to compensate the other. The payor assumes that interest rates will either rise faster or fall slower than expected by the market, and pays the fixed interest rate out of this conviction. If his expectations come true he will realize a profit – if they don't, he will take a loss and the receiver as his counterparty will make a profit.

Thus we can see that market savvy is indispensable if you want to make money with swaps.

The following conditions must be agreed upon before taking a swap position:
• Term
• Beginning of term

- Par value
- Payor and payee of fixed interest
- Swap rate
- Reference interest rate
- Payment intervals
- Interest rate usance

14.2.2 Currency swap

This is an exchange of two different currencies. The swap can refer to the currency difference or the nominal value.

14.2.3 Stock index swap

Here, the exchange is based on the performance of two indices.

14.2.4 Commodity swap

In a commodity swap, payment streams are exchanged based on the development of commodity values.
Irrespective of the type of swap, there are the following variants:
- Fixed / fixed
- Fixed / variable
- Variable / variable

Example of a swap:

Example of a swap with a credit as underlying business

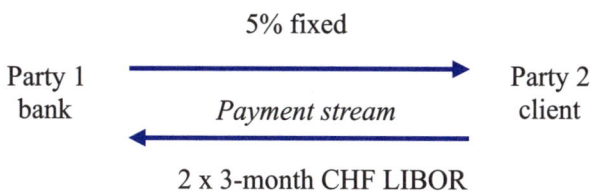

5% fixed

Party 1
bank

Party 2
client

Payment stream

2 x 3-month CHF LIBOR

Figure 14.2: Example of a swap

Example of a swap with a credit as underlying business

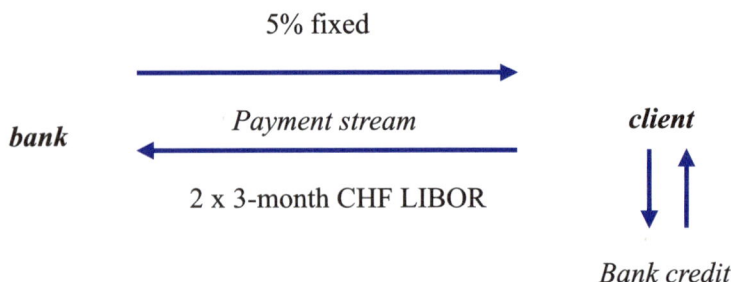

Figure 14.3: Example of a swap with a credit as underlying factor

A swap is based on an underlying trade. Accordingly, its purpose is to hedge an-other payment stream such as a credit liability. The swap enables the client to keep interest rates constant, by transferring his interest rate risk to another party.

In the aforementioned example, the client exchanges the fixed interest rate risk against a variable risk in the form of the 3-month CHF Libor. He generates a profit if the fixed interest rate is higher than the variable rate he has to pay or a loss if it is lower. Thus, the investor bets on the variable interest rate not to rise, and not to reach the 5 percent interest rate limit. He can use this position, for instance, to set up credit hedging positions (interest certainty) tied to the underly-ing trade (credit agreement).

14.2.5 Swap trading

Open, tradable swaps enable parties that have taken on a risk (such as banks) to pass on that risk to other parties. If a client wishes to execute a swap (counter-trade) he must raise the market price, as swaps are always valued based on the present situation.

In theory, and in a perfect market, a receiver swap always has the same value as a fixed-rate bond, minus the value of the floater. In other words, the swap ex-presses the difference between the discounted value of the fixed interest rate and the discounted value of the variable interest rate at the time $t = 0$. The value of the payer swap equals the negative value of the receiver swap.

14.2.6 Variable interest rates

The variable interest rates implied by swaps are based on the EURIBOR (Euro Interbank Offered Rate) and Libor (London Interbank Offered Rate) reference interest rates. The parties can agree on different terms of payment: In practice, it is often agreed that payments are due on a semiannual or quarterly basis, rather than only once a year.

14.2.7 When and how to apply swaps

Traditional swaps are tied to the underlying trades, and used to hedge these or speculate on a higher profit margin.
The most common motives are these:
• Locking in interest rates
• Credit management
• Modifications in the balance sheet
• Hedging against currency and interest rate risks
• Differential trades
• Exploring financing sources
• Taking advantage of global currency and interest rate constellations
• Locking in profits
• Taking advantage of supplier credits without facing any currency risk
• Diversification in bonds portfolios and hedging against exchange rate fluctuations

This shows that building a swap and transacting it successfully requires an excellent feeling for the market.

14.3 What are Swaptions and IRGs?

14.3.1 Swaptions

A Swaptions is an option on a swap. By paying a premium the buyer acquires the right but not the obligation to enter into a predefined swap trade with the seller, the terms of which have been agreed when closing the deal.

The following is specified:
- Maturity of option and term of swap
- Currency
- Strike price
- Par value
- Payer and receiver
- Interest rate usance
- Payment intervals
- Settlement mode

As we can see, investors can use an option to secure a swap to fall back on at a later date. This type of transaction is useful if a certain underlying trade is imminent and the investor fears that the terms of that trade will change to his disadvantage. The holder of the long position is then prepared to pay a premium to the short investor. Should he choose not to exercise the option he will suffer a loss equivalent to the premium paid (cf. exchange-traded options). The writer receives the premium and takes on the obligations of the counter-party to the swap.

14.3.2 IRGs

Another interesting product is the interest-rate guarantee (IRG). This is an option on a forward rate agreement (non-standardized interest-rate future) which gives the buyer (long) the right to buy or sell at a predefined interest rate. IRGs are always transacted European-style, which means that they cannot be exercised until the end of their maturity.

14.4 What are exotic options?

Exotic options are not traded on the exchange (as conditional derivatives) but represent bilateral financial agreements. They are negotiated individually between the contracting parties, and therefore not standardized. They offer the parties the possibility to include additional contractual terms. Contrary to traditional options where the payment pattern mainly depends on the underlying price, payment schemes for exotic options can differ greatly and, among other things, include several strike prices (so-called **rainbow options**).

Just like traditional options, exotic options include a call (right to buy) and a put (right to sell) position. As OTC options they are not traded on the derivatives exchange but agreed individually between bank trading departments and/or contracting parties.

Exotic options are particularly important for issuers of securitized derivatives as they are used to engineer and build structured products for retail investors. Consequently, a growing market for securitized derivatives enables the market for exotic derivatives to continue growing as well. Due to their construction, issuers can offer very specific risk-return profiles with lower hedging costs and higher participation rates (for the structured product). In most cases, structured products are engineered by combining a derivative product (or a constructed derivative contract) with a zero bond, or based on the derivative product only. Zero bonds are predominantly used for guaranty products.

14.4.1 What sorts of exotic options are there?

As previously mentioned, exotic options are options which are designed individually by adding or removing individual components (rights). Most of these options are exclusively traded by professional investors. In the following sections we will outline a few examples.

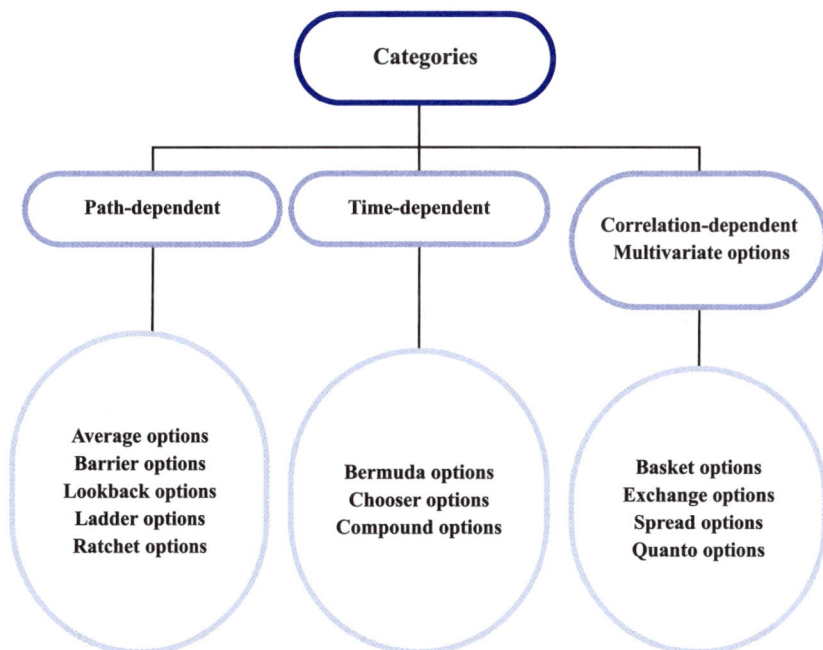

Figure 14.4: Overview of exotic options

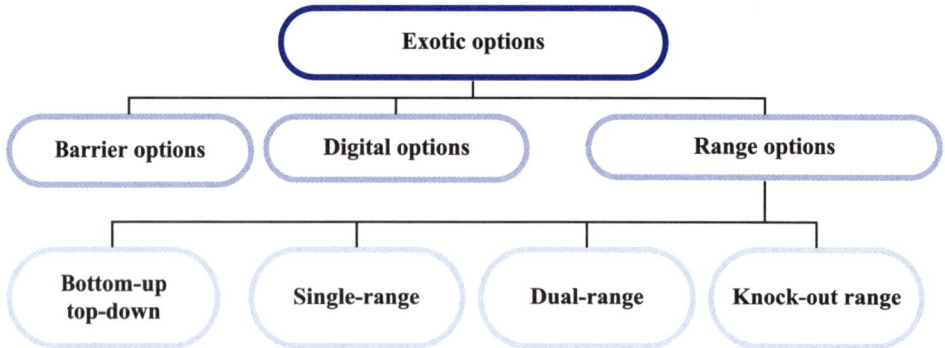

Figure 14.5: Types of exotic options

Among other things, we distinguish between **barrier options, digital options,** and **range options**.

We distinguish between path-dependent, time-dependent, and correlation-dependent or multivariate options, and between one-time payment and payment under a specific scheme. One example for that are **leveraged options** which render several times their intrinsic value upon repayment, and an exponential value upon expiration.

Barrier options

Barrier options are options that are activated or expire once the underlying reaches, exceeds, or falls below a defined barrier price. As these barriers can be above (up) or below (down) the current underlying price, there are eight possible forms of barrier options. They can all be issued as either European-type or American-type options.

Table 14-1: Knock-in / knock-out options

Event	Knock-in (option is activated)	Knock-out (option expires)
Underlying up	Up-and-in call/put	Up-and-out call/put
Underlying down	Down-and-in call/put	Down-and-out call/put

The intrinsic value of a barrier option is equal to that of a standard option, provided that the option is still in existence or has been activated. On principle, knock-out and knock-in options are lower-priced than standard options and therefore offer a higher profit potential. These options have emerged because there has been a strong demand for low-cost hedging. Another advantage of barrier options is the possibility to include a money-back element. Also, the barrier can be defined dynamically (→ dynamic barrier option), for instance, by setting the knock-out or knock-in level at € 100 for the first and € 110 for the second year. If the knock-out level is additionally linked to a certain period in time we speak of "Parisian options". A possible variant could be, for instance, that the underlying price must remain below the knock-out level for four weeks straight. Products of this type can be considered the epitome of exotic options.

Knock-out barrier: If the barrier is hit in the course of the option's maturity the option immediately expires worthless.

Knock-in barrier: After payment of the premium the option is not active yet. Rather, it is activated once the barrier is hit (during the option maturity), and will then be treated like any other standard option.

Reverse knock option We speak of reverse-knock options if any movement in the underlying will increase the probability of the barrier being hit, and the option increasing in value. With these options the barrier will always be in the money.

Advantages of barrier options: The premium to be paid is much lower than for standard options. At the same time, the product permits accurate hedging and precisely matching the expected market situation.

Disadvantages of barrier options: Investors need an alternative plan for the event that the option is knocked out and never knocked back in. Thus, it is necessary to keep monitoring the option.

Digital options
Digital options (sometimes also referred to as binary options) involve payment of a predefined amount if the price of the underlying exceeds or drops below the agreed strike price. Again, these options are available as both, the European or the American type.

They are called "digital" because they are exercised in the digital system – i.e., either 0 or 1. Usually this type of options is combined with other types and then generates a specific payment pattern.

One-touch and **double-touch** as well as **no-touch** and **double-no-touch** options are normally held until expiration and paid back on the delivery date.

Instant-one-touch- and **instant-double-touch** options involve immediate repayment in case the strike price is reached.

With **European-style digital calls** and **puts**, the trigger is only relevant on the expiration date.

Range options
The price of range options depends on how one or several underlying assets move within predefined limits.

The following possibilities exist:
- Bottom up/top down
- Singe range
- Dual range
- Knock-out range

Bermuda options
The Bermuda option is an option with several exercise points. If it is not exercised at one point, the right to exercise shifts to the next predefined date. A Bermuda option entails some kind of double right, as the remaining exercise points do not expire until the option is exercised.

Chooser options
The holder of chooser options can choose on a predefined date whether his option is a call or put option. The price of a chooser option rises as volatility increases, whereas the actual price level of the underlying is of minor concern. Thus, chooser options are an excellent instrument to set up volatility strategies. **Investors take advantage of the increase in volatility, without being too dependent of the price of the underlying asset.**

Chooser options are usually more expensive than comparable call or put options, but they are still less expensive than a combination trade such as a straddle would be. The earlier the investor makes his decision, the lower the price he will pay for a chooser option.

Asian options
Asian options are particularly exotic options. Throughout the option's maturity the buyer is paid a mean value of the underlying asset. We distinguish between arithmetical and geometrical Asian options. As implied in their names, different methods are used to determine the mean value.

Basics
In this chapter, we have provided a short overview of the most common exotic options. As they are not traded at Eurex or other derivative exchanges, we will end this overview here.

14.5 What is a forward?

A forward is an individual, unconditional derivative instrument similar to a future. It is "only" similar not equal because it cannot be traded on the exchange. The details of the contract are defined and agreed upon at the parties' discretion. Transactions of this kind are customarily done by banks and their clients, usually for the purpose of hedging an underlying trade. Contrary to a future (which is exchange-tradable), a forward entails a counterparty risk. Investors should keep this in mind, in particular when the two parties involved have very different backgrounds (such as a small or medium-size firm and a major bank). The risk involved cannot be transferred to a secondary market. Nevertheless there is a possibility to expand the transaction by a hedging trade which, however, must be viewed as an additional transaction (involving new risks and tying up yet more capital).

Summary:
Non-exchange-traded derivatives are bilateral financial agreements mainly used to hedge an underlying trade.
A swap is an exchange of payment streams, based on the fact that the two contracting parties have very different views of the market.
A Swaptions is an option on a swap, which the investor can exercise if things turn out to his advantage. The exercise of the option triggers the swap.
Exotic options are traded OTC, and are mainly used by issuers for the purpose of engineering structured products for the retail market. An important element of these options is the inclusion of additional rights, or the non-existence of "old" rights.
Forwards are bilateral, binding financial agreements which, due to their individual nature, are not traded on the exchange.
Derivative transactions of this kind are only set up and carried out by professional investors.

15 Credit derivatives

This chapter deals with the following questions:
1. What are the basics of credit derivatives?
2. What is a credit?
3. What kinds of credit derivatives are there?
4. What are the iTraxx® Futures at Eurex?
5. What are securitized credit derivatives?

15.1 What are the basics of credit derivatives?

Compared to the previously described derivatives, credit derivatives are relatively new in the market. Their purpose is to transfer credit risks from one party to another; the party assuming the risk is paid a premium. This allows for financial intermediaries to have the possibility to dispose of credit default risk (credits and loans) completely or in part. In addition, investors can use credit derivatives to hedge against a price collapse in corporate bonds, as would occur if the debtor defaults or its credit rating deteriorates.

15.2 What is a credit?

Let us begin by defining the term "credit derivative". The word credit has its origin from the Latin "credo" (belief) and "creditum" (something entrusted to someone). Thus, a creditor is someone acting upon his conviction that the liquid funds lent to the debtor will eventually return. There is a trust-based relationship between the two which is expressed by lending out assets. As not every debtor has sufficient creditworthiness for a creditor to entrust him with his money, the creditor attempts to protect against a credit default (failure to pay interest, lateness or default of repayment). Credit derivatives were developed specifically to cover that need. They are used as hedging instruments and help the creditor to protect from potential credit defaults associated with his credit portfolio.

15.3 What types of credit derivatives exist?

15.3.1 Traditional credit derivatives

Traditional credit derivatives are bilateral agreements between a buyer and a seller of protection. The seller gives the buyer protection from the credit risk, the buyer transfers the associated risk to the protection seller. The premiums to be paid are calculated based on the rating and possible external credit default risks, and are immediately due.

The premiums for credit derivatives which are based on ratings are usually expressed as spreads. The international market for these derivatives is very homogeneous, as pricing is based on the credit risk rather than interest rate levels and ratings are handled the same way everywhere. This homogeneity facilitates a comparison of credit risks on an international level, which further contributes to an active market. As a result of the possibility to transfer risk the market has been expanding, and in many ways has been developing into an efficient and consistent market.

The important point is to correctly specify the credit default or "credit event", as it is commonly referred to. Both parties must be able to clearly define this event and ascertain its occurrence, and both must understand how it was caused. When a credit event is triggered the payment stream from the protection seller to the protection buyer is interrupted (payment from the protection; the payment is on ice), and payments will not be effected until there is no doubt that a credit event has occurred and this credit event has been documented.

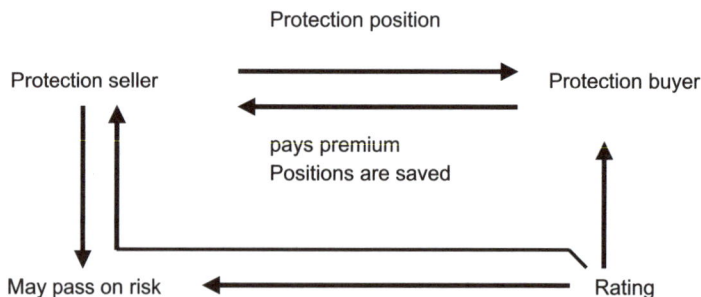

Figure 15.1: Credit derivative

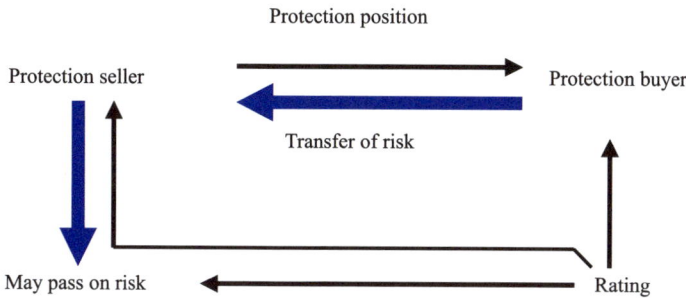

Figure 15.2: Credit derivative for a credit event (payment)

A credit event can be either of the following:
- Default or failure to pay
- Deterioration of creditworthiness
- Price drop of underlying product
- Restructuring of liabilities

Further points to be clarified include the precise nature of the debt and its nominal value.

15.3.2 Modern credit derivatives

Credit derivatives used to be tradable only as credit default swaps (CDS). As of 2007, they can be traded directly at Eurex.

In some ways, a CDS (the most widely traded derivative product) is similar to a put option. When the credit event occurs the option is activated and the credit risk sold. The term swap originated from the constellation in which a corporate bond would be exchanged ("swapped") against a government bond. Contrary to a swap of the classical type, however, in this case the exchange is only affected when a credit event occurs. Settlement can be made by physical delivery or in cash; the premium is due when the CDS contract is signed. Today CDS are no longer only offered by banks. In past years, hedge funds have begun to aggressively advance into this field.

CDS premiums depend on the reference credit position and its credit rating. A higher probability of default equates to a higher premium paid. For some years there have been standardized contract details for CDS, ensuring fast and smooth contract execution. In 1999, the International Swap and Derivatives Association (ISDA), which is headquartered in New York, issued comprehensive trading recommendations as well as the so-called ISDA Master Agreement, a standardized contract permitting both parties to ensure a fair solution.

A CDS must meet the following basic requirements:
- Reference entity
- Credit event protected (insolvency, rescheduling, etc.)
- Based on what assets can the credit event be ascertained?
- Effective date
- Term
- Nominal value
- Premium amount (usually given in basis points of nominal value)
- Type of payment due from protection seller upon credit event occurrence
- Physical delivery or cash settlement

15.4 What are the iTraxx® Futures at Eurex?

Since March 2007, Eurex has been offering investors the possibility to trade in credit futures on the three iTraxx Europe® indices, which are based on a forward contract. The credit indices are standardized and determined based on the cash equivalent of a portfolio of reference debtors. The index will rise when the market is bullish, and fall when it is bearish. Premiums are calculated based on the index; contracts have a nominal value of € 100,000 and must be settled in cash. The last trading day for these products is the fifth exchange trading day prior to the 20th calendar day of the contract month. As trading on the Eurex®-system is flexible and fast, contracts can be effectively processed at any time. While iTraxx® Futures are particularly interesting for investors wishing to speculate on the changes in the derivatives market, risk-averse investors will also find them useful in structuring their positions.

15.5 What are securitized credit derivatives?

Instruments securitizing credit risk are referred to as "Credit-Linked Notes" (CLN). They are a combination of a debenture bond and a default put. While CLN are issued like securities and also sold to retail clients, it is important to note that usually several debtors are pooled in one certificate. Investors (protection sellers) should be aware that repayment of the CLN is uncertain in case of a credit event: Depending on the specifics of the securitization, repayment may incomplete or defaulted entirely. Due to the higher risk, interest payments on the CLN are higher than for traditional debentures. Moreover, the issuer-related risk must not be underestimated. As debentures, CLN are also subject to the rating of the issuer. Potential risks could result from the issuer's possible insolvency.

An alternative is provided by Collateralized Debt Obligations (CDO), which are securities issued by a financial institution which has the respective bonds in its portfolio. In case of synthetic CDOs, the portfolio will contain credit derivatives (such as CDS) instead of bonds.

This short overview demonstrates that credit derivatives are generally used to transfer risk; this is what they originated from. Today, the credit risk market is very large and multifaceted. Credit derivatives are traded by professional investors, usually firms, while private investors mostly focus on CLNs. In any case it is important to ensure that a private investor is aware of the risks of such trades, and has the necessary liquidity to afford them. In a worst-case scenario – if a credit event occurs – the investor will suffer a total loss.

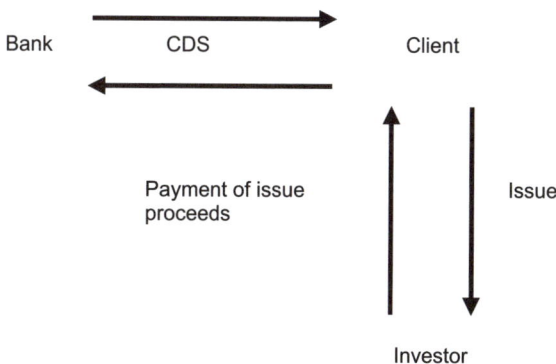

Figure 15.3: Credit-linked note

Summary:
Credit derivatives are instruments used to professionally cover credit default risks or risks resulting from a debtor's decreasing creditworthiness. Credit derivatives can be either bilateral contracts or Eurex-tradable futures. The background is always a possible decrease in a debtor's creditworthiness, resulting in a risk position which a protection seller will cover on behalf of a protection buyer in exchange for a premium. In case of default (credit event), the protection seller is assigned the protection buyer's risk position and the protection buyer has disposed of that risk.

16 Structuring complex portfolios with derivatives

This chapter deals with the following questions:
1. What are the basics and extensions of position management?
2. Was do the terms averaging and pyramiding mean?
3. What is a roll-over?
4. How is a portfolio set up?
5. What do we mean by trading presence?
6. What is risk controlling?

16.1 What are the basics of position management and what are possible expansion strategies?

Investors should always set up plans with clear targets, taking action only after such plans have been well thought out. Impulsive decisions and hurried moves should be avoided as they usually result in losses.

Before entering into a contract, every investor should consider the following questions:
- Does this trade really make sense?
- What is the risk/reward ratio?
- How much money am I going to put into this investment right now?
- How much money will I put into it later?
- How long do I want to hold this investment, and what additional risk am I prepared to take on?
- When will I close this position in case of profit?
- When will I close it out in case of losses?

Next, the investor should draw up a concept for speculation covering the answers to these questions. As a general rule, it is advisable to invest no more than 20 to 30 percent of one's liquid assets in speculative deals. Additional margins (required as collateral) should not exceed 30 to 50 percent of the actual investment sum, as this order of magnitude should be sufficient to cover potential losses. Further, the concept should be fairly detailed as it must help guide investors through their first commitments. Investors who have traded in derivatives for some time can probably do without a written concept since their broad experience will enable them to decide and respond appropriately.

Investors who are new in the field, however, should begin by drawing up and pursuing their strategy on paper. It is important to do this in writing and to be very honest with yourself, recording successes and failures alike. Even though fictitious, losses made on paper can teach you a lot. In this context we also want to emphasize that

- strategies must be tested out in different market situations
- entry and exit signals must be realistic and easy to recognize
- basic rules of statistics must be observed at all times.

If you lie to yourself on these points you will regret it in real-life trading.

You should not venture into real investments until gathering experience in a fictitious manner. Now you can handle emerging problems far more easily as you have already "lived" such situations on paper. However, don't fool yourself into thinking that you won't need to make any new decisions: Even the best concept for speculation and the best preparation cannot provide 100-percent protection from hectic and emotional decisions. The first rule, therefore, is: Keep calm and make your decisions based on facts.

16.2 What is averaging and pyramiding?

Another point to think through before starting is how to set up your derivatives positions. There are two basic approaches:

We speak of **averaging** if an investor keeps building the same number of contracts on one existing position. If this strategy succeeds it can be a good source of income. If it fails, however, you will exponentially increase your risk with each new position. We would therefore discourage you from taking this approach. It should be applied exclusively by experienced derivatives specialists and only after careful consideration.

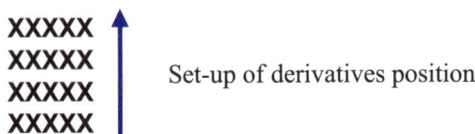

XXXXX
XXXXX   Set-up of derivatives position
XXXXX
XXXXX

Figure 16.1: Schematic depiction of averaging approach

The second approach is called **pyramiding:** Both existing and new (small) positions are based on top of each other so as to form a pyramid. This set-up is to be recommended as it represents a risk-weighted strategy in the classical sense.

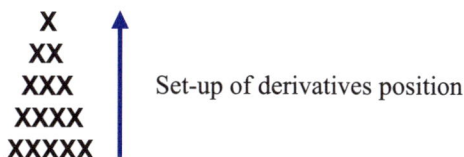

```
  X      ↑
 XX      │
XXX      │   Set-up of derivatives position
XXXX     │
XXXXX    │
```

Figure 16.2: Schematic depiction of pyramiding approach

However make sure to set up the pyramid correctly (see graph). If numerous positions are based on few facts you will again exponentially increase your risk and achieve the opposite of the desired effect. The Egyptian Pyramids were not built to stand on their tips either.

16.2.1 What can be possible purposes of expanding one's exposure?

Two basic courses of action are envisioned: Increasing one's profits or managing opposite positions.

Profit expansion

The investment is performing as expected and generating attractive profits. The investor decides to expand the position and to enter into additional contracts. In doing so he should not forget, however, that along with the higher profit potential each contract also increases the risk of losses.

In this case, the investor expands his position not because the market has developed adversely but because his strategy succeeds and he sees a chance to increase his gains. This also enables him to buffer his risk with the profits already made. Nevertheless, we would advise caution since in a worst-case scenario the investor's risk increases along with the number of trades he is committed to.

Position management in the face of adverse developments

The investment is not performing as expected. The investor "averages down" by adding more positions, thus increasing his loss potential but also the chance that the position will end up in the profit zone. It is therefore important to carefully assess whether this expansion is really worthwhile before going ahead with it. Averaging-down strategies of this kind should be a last resort only, as it is rarely advisable to expand the risk inherent in an original position. In most cases, the real problem is that the investor's initial expectations have not come true, and as there is no guarantee that this will happen after increasing exposure, it is often better to completely close the position instead. If an investor, based on his analysis, still decides to expand his position he should proceed with much caution.

At this point, let us remind you that every investor should think about potential expansion of a trade at the very start, i.e., when he opens a new position. He should define entry and exit points in terms of both time and monetary criteria.

Example of an expansion situation:

> An investor has taken a position in long future contracts. Unfortunately the underlying instrument has developed contrary to expectations and our investor is suffering losses. Nevertheless he wishes to maintain the position since, based on both fundamentals and chart indicators, he is convinced that the underlying instrument will appreciate. He decides to expand the position and cheapen his initial investment.

This is what he needs to keep in mind:
- There is some risk that he is misinterpreting the market situation.
- In setting up new positions, he exponentially increases his risk of losses.
- The investment volume at risk in the expanded position is higher than what he initially wanted to put at stake.
- Often, a position's first loss is the lowest.

By rebuilding the same position an investor can, at best, cheapen his initial investment price; at worst he will multiply his losses.

We therefore strongly contend that such strategies should only be pursued by very liquid investors.

Example of how to proceed about expanding a position:

> The investor holds 5 long index future contracts in his portfolio. He decides to extend his position by pyramiding, and buys another 3 contracts. If the expected market move sets in he will profit from 8 contracts. If his market expectation fails he will suffer a loss that will be exponentially higher than it would have been with his original 5-contracts position.

XXX

XXXXX

Figure 16.3: Schematic depiction of the exemplary expansion strategy (pyramiding)

If the index performs according to expectations the investor can set up more contracts. Contrary to the previous example, however, he will build them up in parallel with the market, thus profiting from the upward market trend. With 3 new contracts he can build upon his existing 5 which are already yielding profits. The risk of losses from his original position will be reduced by the profit already realized. Only after this profit has been consumed will the investor have the same risk profile as in our first example.

As these examples show, setting up positions with **the market is by far preferable.** Derivatives positions set up against the market can easily result in enormous losses.

16.3 What is a roll-over?

With a roll-over, an investor extends his position beyond the expiration date by closing out the original position and opening a new one. His motives can be either of these:
• Loss in the original position (due to failed market expectations)
• Preventing a premature assignment
• Good performance of the position
Let us have a closer look at each of them.

16.3.1 Roll-over due to adverse market trends

An investor has sold calls on the X-index (short call) at a strike price of 5,000 points, and received a premium of 50 points. One day before maturity the index reaches 5,100 points, whereas our investor had assumed it to remain below 5,050 points (premium + strike). Still, he believes the index to be overvalued. He therefore closes out the initial position (by buying it back) and once again sells calls on the X-index, this time at 5,100 points, for which he receives an additional premium. If this premium covers the premium he has paid for the repurchase we speak of a premium-neutral roll-over. If, however, the investor thinks that the index will appreciate even more he can "roll over" to a higher strike price (e.g., 5,300 points). In all probability this will not be a premium-neutral roll-over; rather, the investor is likely to either face additional expenses or else increase the number of contracts. The consequence is a risk increase, since our investor has expanded his original position beyond the level originally intended.

Buying to close 5 call contracts
Selling to open 10 call contracts
= Risk increase by 100 percent

This is the most common type of roll-over. As it results from a market expectation not fulfilled, we could also speak of a "forced roll-over". In practice however, such roll-overs can often pave the way back into the profit zone.

Before each roll-over, an analysis of the present and expected market situation is absolutely necessary. Only if both are conclusive should the roll-over be carried through. If the investor no longer counts on his initial market expectation to materialize, he will be better advised to close out and set up a new position.

16.3.2 Preventing premature assignment

An investor in short positions wishing to prevent premature assignment can roll over these positions to a later maturity date. Although they will gain time premium this way, it will rarely be his prime motive; rather, the roll-over is likely to help him avert premature assignment, as options with long remaining maturity – due to the time premium component – involve a lower risk of being assigned prematurely.

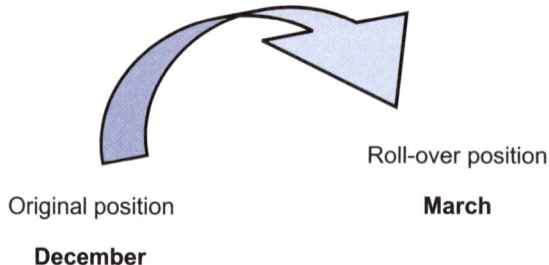

Roll-over position

March

Original position

December

Figure 16.4: Using a roll-over to prevent a premature assignment

16.3.3 Extending high-performing investments

An investor has taken the long position in a futures contact which is not performing in his favor. On the last trading day he sells that future and buys the one farther out. This way he profits from his existing strategy and maintains his position.

Long future – sale for the purpose of closing out
Long future – purchase for the purpose of opening

As we can see, a roll-over is used to extend the investor's position in derivatives. If this also involves an increase in quantity, the investor should consider the higher risk involved. On principle, however, derivatives investments can be extended indefinitely. Prerequisites are the existence of counterparties, liquidity of the investor, and a sensible strategy. In the case of futures, another factor to be considered is the cost of carry.

To sum up: Investors accumulating risk without seeing a chance of positive completion of the transaction act foolishly. Instead, we urgently recommend thinking about the fulfillment of a contract before entering into it. Should an investment fail to render the expected profit, the position should either be closed out and another one opened, or the investment strategy should be revisited. We strongly discourage investors from taking additional positions (possibly even before another investment) in hopes of achieving premium neutrality. An original position in the X share should not be transformed into new positions into the X and Y shares as well as the Z index, if you would not have made those investments in the absence of problems. In order to avoid the losses resulting from such risk expansion, you always need an emergency exit strategy which you should think about before even entering into the contract.

16.3.4 Cross roll-over

If an investor holds a call option on the X share which does not perform as expected, he can buy back that contract and open another position. Even if this cross roll-over is not a roll-over in the classical sense, as the underlying is substituted, it can be advisable for some investments.

Short call on X share → closing
Short call on Y share → opening

The investor backs up the closing of the original position in X by opening a position in Y, by which he gets rid of the original, poorly performing investment. Although there are two different underlying instruments involved, they are used for cross-financing.

16.4 How are positions set up?

Inexperienced (private) investors should begin by focusing on covered and long derivatives positions (except for futures) as those carry the smallest risk. The best way to get started is to acquire options on portfolios, i.e. write covered calls. This way, the new investor can develop a feeling for the market and its complexity. Covered call writing is useful to increase one's returns through the premiums received, and can be treated as a limited sale order – depending on how aggressively the strike prices are set.

Long positions can be an attractive alternative to classic, speculative short positions: At maximum, the investor can lose the sum invested, and there is no risk of having to post additional margin. Holding these positions also helps develop a feeling for the market, as well as for the structure and pricing of options. In short, they are quite suitable for investors taking their first steps in the derivatives market.

Other instruments on the derivatives market should be traded by savvy investors only. Note that portfolios consisting of options and futures usually generate more stable returns than those comprised of securities and options. Futures instruments enable investors to set up and structure their strategies more clearly and profitably, as they are better suited for taking advantage of rapid market changes than options are. At the same time, option-futures combinations enable investors to bring their money-losing positions back into the profit zone, or at least compensate the losses.

Example:

> An investor holds short calls on the X index which are deep in the money. Contrary to expectations, the index continues to rise. While the investor could choose between various roll-over strategies, another possibility is to expand the position by adding a futures-based strategy. To do this he buys X futures based on his call options. If the index continues to go up these futures will offset the losses incurred by the call positions. If the index falls they will incur losses while the calls will generate a profit. In pursuing strategies of this kind it is important to maintain scrutiny of one's positions and trade them precisely at the two break-even points.

16.4.1 Combinations

Combinations such as the counter-financing of derivatives trades should only be carried out by experienced investors. The same is true for derivatives positions combined with commodity and currency futures. It is also important to make sure that liquidity requirements can be met.

Trades in derivatives can be transacted in any exchange phase, provided they are carried out correctly. Sometimes it is necessary to close out a position in order to prevent additional risks and potentially higher losses, in line with the old saying that **"the first loss is often the smallest"**. Another important aspect is to keep monitoring external performance drivers such as volatility.

But the key to any derivatives trade is liquidity. It is important to always maintain sufficient liquidity to be able to keep positions open even if the market moves the other way. The greatest problem to happen to an investor is the inability to provide the collateral required: In that case he faces the threat of forced liquidation, following a margin call. His positions will be closed out and he will no longer be able to make money with them. Since investors are obliged to respond to a margin call it is extremely important they carry no more positions in their portfolio than they are able to cover. The same is true for technical know-how: Once you have lost track of developments you are headed for rough waters. The risk of losses then multiplies as you are powerless to stem the tide. Therefore, make sure to only keep as many positions open as you can survey and manage. As an investor you need to be able to analyze and assess the underlying instrument, and take appropriate and timely action!

For extreme situations you should always have emergency plans at hand, such as, for instance, selling 50 index-based futures if the stock market crashes. This way you are prepared for potential emergencies, which is particularly important when you hold large portfolios of spot market instruments. If prices change rapidly, due to extreme market developments, the only way to hedge a spot market portfolio rapidly and efficiently is with futures contracts. We would like to reiterate that you should always decide beforehand what exactly you will do in such a situation, so that on the actual date all you have to do is make the necessary adjustments. This ensures that you won't lose valuable time.

Also, it is important to ensure technical feasibility of your plans early on. Only if the necessary processes are immediately at hand in extreme situations will you be able to respond promptly with well-targeted counter-moves. Specifically, it is indispensable to have the necessary contact data for the respective trading departments at your fingertips. This is particularly important for large private investors which do not operate their own trading platforms.

We recommend putting down your emergency plan on paper, using a simple algorithm which you should absolutely stick to in case of emergency. This algorithm should include recommended action, volumes, contacts, contact data, and a recommendation for the event of intraday reversal (i.e., a complete reversal of prices within one day, e.g. from negative to positive).

16.4.2 Setting up a portfolio

On principle, a portfolio should be designed to support diversification. Also, it is important to consider which of the current market trends it should cover. Next, the securities portfolio can be expanded to include derivatives positions; for instance, by writing calls on stock positions you are no longer convinced of, or for which you expect a sideways market. Additional purchases can be realized via aggressive short put strategies. Hedging strategies with short futures or long puts on existing portfolios should be considered whenever a downturn is expected.

These examples may suffice to show that derivatives positions are useful to complement spot positions by ensuring stability and generating additional profits. Investors using derivatives to actively structure their portfolios are better able to fine-tune their spot trading: By means of the derivatives transactions they actively increase or decrease their commitments in the spot market, and explore opportunities to generate additional income and buffer potential risks. This way portfolios become more easily planned – due to the better predictability of expected effects – and more stable. The investor passes on part of his decisions to other parties (in the case of short trades). Only when he gets actively involved (close-out) does he take an ultimate decision. In all other cases, the decision originally made when taking the position will continue to be valid.

The following is an example of derivatives structures used to expand an assumed securities portfolio:

Table 16-1: Example portfolio and expansion through derivatives

Existing portfolio (excerpt)				Expansion
Underlying product	Portfolio:	Buying price	Current price	Derivative instrument
X-share	10,000	34.50	39.00	Short call strike 41
Y-share	15,000	43.10	41.90	Short put strike 41
M-share	7,000	89.45	91.23	Short call strike 92
Index certificate on L- index	15,000	54.40	67.10	Index future as additional component

The investor expands his strategies by adding covered calls, thus receiving premium payments and pursuing a yield strategy. The short puts are intended for expanding his portfolio in Y shares. With this strategy the investor lowers his initial price and continues to view his investment positively. The index certificate is extended to futures based on the same index. This way the investor creates an equally weighted opportunity-risk profile, but at the same time he is able to trade his portfolio while retaining the certificate as his long-term investment.

This simple example illustrates how derivatives positions can be used to expand and better control an existing portfolio. It also shows that combinations of securitized and other derivatives can offer substantial advantages. In practice we find such constructs fairly often. For instance, calls are written on discount and bonus certificates, or liquidity is increased by writing short options and investing the premiums in futures or securitized products.

By combining different opportunity-risk profiles, new investment opportunities can be explored. The same is true for combinations of commodity and currency futures.

In pursuing these strategies it is important to keep one thing in mind that combinations can only be successful as long as you maintain a good overview. Therefore, should you ever reach a point where you find your positions difficult to understand, close them out! Otherwise you may face enormous losses as you will not able to adequately respond to changes in the market.

16.5 What is trading presence?

At this point, allow us a few words on the subject of trading presence. Investors not continuously present at the exchange will often find it difficult to actively manage their position books. 100 percent trading presence is therefore strongly recommended. In all other cases, investors should mainly trade in covered options and focus on conservative strategies.

Another noteworthy point is that investors should familiarize themselves with the exchange at which they are trading. They should be familiar with its regulations and understand them well. There is no point in trading at an exotic derivatives exchange when you do not know the rules, contract specifications, and other drivers – this will involve additional risk which you cannot measure, and often not cover. By contrast, at one of the major American exchanges or at Eurex you will be able to get hold of the necessary information fast and reliably. Rules against trading violations ("mistrade") protect trading participants and, together with the supervisory bodies, ensure safe and orderly trading processes.

16.6 What is risk controlling?

Banks and brokers have "central staff functions" to control the risks associated with derivatives positions. Nevertheless, it is every investor's duty to keep an eye on his own risk. In particular it is important to closely monitor the size of the position book, which often happens to grow out of control – in particular with roll-over positions. This should be avoided at all cost, as otherwise deliberate and strategy-conform control is no longer possible. In other words, take care not to let a 10-contract position turn into a roll-over position of 100 contracts.

Investors should always be aware of the size of the underlying assets – only then will they be able to develop a feeling for the market and its size. Also, we strongly recommend working with trading limits (which are usually given by the brokers). Only if you set yourself a limit will you keep control of your risks. The same is true for providing security in the form of margins.

Finally, allow as a word on unpredictable market developments as may occur at any given time. While we do not suggest waiting for such developments to happen, investors should always have enough viable strategies at hand to counter such developments and avert forced liquidation, in particular as even critical market situations can be taken advantage of with speculative strategies.

Summary:
Strategies aimed at expanding investment positions always involve additional risk. Therefore, it is necessary to carefully think them through beforehand.
The term "averaging" refers to an approach where you set up the same number of contracts once again, whereas "pyramiding" means that you set them up in the form of a pyramid. Expansions are pursued either when investments are highly profitable, or as a last resort for loss-bringing positions. Often these strategies are pursued in combination with a roll-over, which is an extension of the position beyond its original maturity date.

17 Margining

This chapter deals with the following questions:
1. What is margining?
2. How is margin coverage ensured for options and futures?
3. What is risk-based margining?
4. How can margins be posted?
5. What are related clearing activities?
6. What is a margin call, and what are its consequences?

17.1 What is margining?

A margin is the collateral that the holder of a derivatives position has to deposit. Its purpose is to guarantee that the transaction will be fulfilled and the open position can be closed out. On principle, a margin is due for all exchange-traded derivative transactions. The only exception is long options, as their buyers acquire rights but no obligations. For all open positions, margins must be posted for the following exchange trading day. Under difficult conditions it is also possible that an additional margin is required within the same trading day, a process which is referred to as margin call.

Banks and brokers post margins in securities or cash (in different currencies, such as €, CHF, USD, CGP) and then freeze the corresponding amounts in securities or cash, broken down by customers, in the respective customer accounts. As a general rule, customers provide to their brokers and banks between 1.2 times and double the amount required by the exchange. This "artificial" increase is a further protective measure, both vis-à-vis the customer (by restricting his room to maneuver) and for the bank/broker itself.

Now what is the margin composed of? Principally, there are different margining systems such as risk-based margining, SPAN, TIMS, and others. In the following we will focus on risk-based margining as applied by Eurex.

Before our analysis, we would like to include a brief explanatory note. All transactions at Eurex exchanges are processed by Eurex Clearing AG. It guarantees business partners and clearing participants the execution of their transactions, and is in charge of calculating the respective margins.

17.2 What is risk-based margining?

For investors there is a clear advantage in only having to deposit an amount covering the risk associated with their position book, rather than the equivalent of the entire position. As combinations are taken account of, the risk is reduced and excess coverage is avoided. Products based on (nearly) identical underlying instruments are grouped in risk classes. For instance, all options on DAX® equities as well as ODAX and FDAX positions are comprised in the DAX® margin class. All risk classes are defined in analogy to this example. Possible margin credits and debits of the same class are offset against each other, a process which is referred to as cross-margining. It helps to keep liquidity high, as moving each position individually would incur a higher overall margin. If two or more margin classes with similar correlations are grouped together we speak of a margin group. Cross-margining is also carried out within such groups; for instance, the classes Euro-Bund Futures, Euro-Bobl Futures, and Euro-Schatz Futures are offset against each other.

Margins are determined daily for each trading member. They are also calculated intraday, taking account of current and imminent foreign exchange risks. If a trading member's account falls below the minimum maintenance margin, an intraday margin call is issued and he is asked to close the liquidity gap.

17.3 Why must a margin be posted and how is it calculated?

Margins are posted as a safeguard against the risk of accounts having to be closed out at their maximum level (worst-case scenario).

As a first step, all long and short positions on contracts with identical maturity dates are offset against each other ("netted"), resulting in a net long or short position. All net risk positions are consolidated and treated as one aggregated net risk position.

To determine the maximal close-out cost, past price trends for the contracts (or the underlying instrument) are used to assess possible further price developments. Volatility plays an essential role in this context. To calculate it correctly, Eurex Clearing AG takes into account all price fluctuations observed during the past 30 or 250 exchange trading days (i.e., the past month or year). Based on these fluctuations, margin parameters are determined expressing the maximum price deviation from one exchange trading day to the next. These parameters are adjusted as required.

Using these margin parameters, possible maximum and minimum prices for the individual underlying instruments and, on that basis, theoretical option premiums are determined. The volatility level used here is the implied volatility extracted from options' settlement prices.

17.4 What types of margins are common?

17.4.1 Premium margin

A premium margin must be posted for all options where the premium is due immediately. It must be backed by the writer with appropriate assets (eligible securities or cash). The premium margin covers the loss that would result if the writer bought back his positions on the same trading day.

There is no premium margin for options on futures. Here, the option premium is not due upon execution of the contract, but will be paid via the mark-to-market process.

Long positions do not require a premium margin either, as the buyer of the option's premium acquires a right but no obligation. Contrary to short positions, possible excess margins for long positions are taken into account when considering the overall balance of a position book.

17.4.2 Additional Margin

The purpose of the additional margin is to cover potential close-out costs as might accrue (in a worst-case scenario) before the next trading day.

Additional margins are required for all options and futures positions. In the case of futures positions, the additional margin is also referred to as initial margin (only outside Eurex). Upon completion of the derivatives contract, a certain amount is posted to cover the worst-case scenario for that position.

17.4.3 Variation margin

The variation margin is the daily profit-and-loss settlement for futures or options on futures. For this purpose, the mark-to-market method mentioned above is applied: Daily profits and losses are debited or credited to clearing members' accounts by Eurex Clearing AG. So, contrary to other types of margins, the variation margin is not collateral (in securities or other assets) but an actual cash entry.

If an investor has purchased a futures contract at 100 points and that future hits 110 points the next days, the additional 10 points – converted into the respective currency – are credited to the investor's account. Likewise, the holder of a short futures position is debited.

All positions are reevaluated this way on a daily basis. On the last trading day, the difference between the previous day's levels and the final settlement price is determined for all open positions.

17.4.4 Futures-spread margin

If a position book contains several futures positions based on the same underlying, long and short positions can be offset against each other, provided they have the same maturity. This process is referred to as "netting".

If any long or short positions remain because their maturity dates do not coincide, they can also be offset against each other. These positions are called "non-compensable non-spreads". The implicit risk resulting from the imbalance is covered with the so-called futures spread margin.

17.5 Margins for options

17.5.1 Long positions

The financial risk of long positions is covered by the premium paid, since the buyer acquires a risk but not an obligation.

17.5.2 Short positions

We distinguish between covered and uncovered short positions.

A holder of **covered** short positions also holds the underlying assets in his portfolio. For instance, if he holds short call options on the X stock, he will also carry that stock in his portfolio (in a 1:1 ratio). This only works for options not based on futures and with physical settlement. Options with cash settlement are always uncovered.

Options on stocks, ETF, and indices

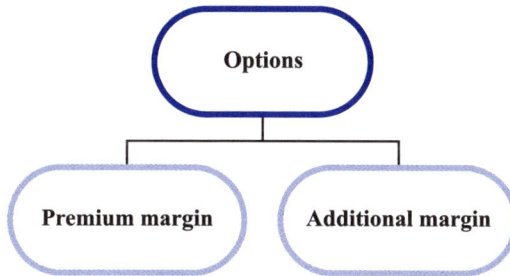

Futures

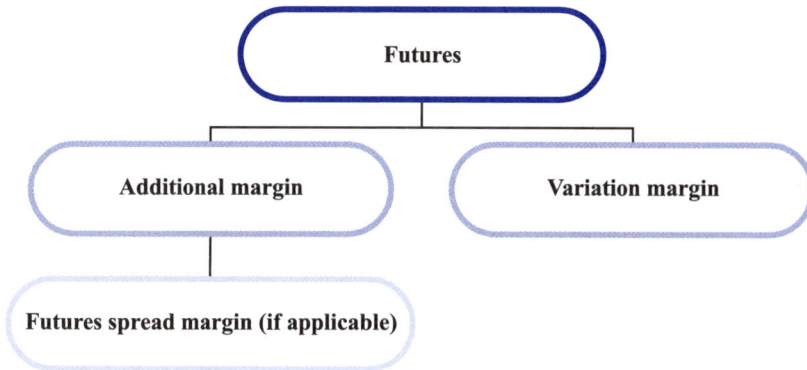

Options on futures

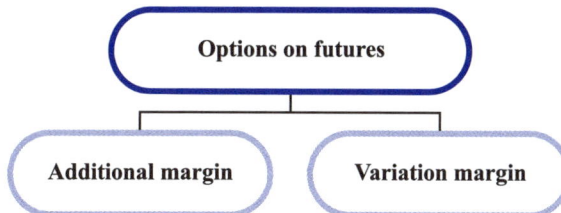

Figure 17.1: Overview of the different kinds of margins

If a long options investor exercises his position, a matching short position is randomly assigned. Delivery times depend on the contract and delivery mode.

For **uncovered** options, a margin will be required as described. The theoretical option premiums which are needed to calculate that margin are determined with different option pricing models (Black, Scholes and Cox, Ross & Rubinstein). As with options deeply out of the money, there is a risk of setting prices too low (since they can respond very strongly to abruptly increasing fluctuations in the underlying price) the so-called "short option adjustment" is applied, which may considerably increase the option premium originally calculated.

One element in this calculation is the out-of-the-money minimum set by the derivatives exchange:

> **Short option adjustment =**
> **Margin parameter x out-of-the-money minimum + daily settlement price**

17.5.3 Margin during delivery period

When an option is exercised, a further margin is due until delivery. Rather than to the option itself, this margin only refers to the underlying instrument to be delivered. The difference between its strike price and its closing price must be posted as premium margin. Market price fluctuations are taken account of by including the so-called additional margin.

17.6 Margins on futures

As explained before, profits and losses are offset on a daily basis through a cash entry, the so-called variation margin. This mechanism ensures that profits and losses cannot be accumulated.

In addition to this daily profit-and-loss settlement, however, additional collateral must be provided for the event that a possible close-out on the next trading day would incur losses. Contrary to the variation margin, which can be paid in cash only, this **additional margin** (frequently called **initial margin**) can be provided in the form of securities *or* cash (i.e., account balance). Its amount corresponds to what would be required to settle open contracts in a worst-case scenario.

- As a first step, all long and short positions with the same maturity dates are netted. If the result is a net long or short position, it is examined for possibilities to build spreads. For these, the so-called spread margin is applied (as explained above), which is lower than the additional margin for the remaining net positions. If neither netting nor spread-building is possible, only the additional margin is determined. In calculating the **spread margin** we distinguish between the spot-month spread margin and the back-month spread margin: The derivative contract with the nearest maturity date is referred to as "front contract", the respective month as "spot month". All other months are so-called "back months" and the corresponding contracts are referred to as "deferred contracts". Assuming that all contracts refer to the same month, spot margin is applied for the front contract – for a simple reason: As for the nearest option both revenues and volatility are highest, the risk involved increases with that option's duration. As a result, long and short positions may no longer correlate negatively, which means that the compensation might no longer be sufficient. Hence the margin increase, which becomes due at the start of the last trading month.
- If no spreads can be built, an **additional margin** is applied as outlined above, as the positions concerned carry the entire close-out risk until the following exchange trading day. At the time this book went to print the additional margin per contract for an FDAX® position was 550 FDAX® points (equivalent to $550 \times €\ 25 = €\ 13,750$).

17.7 Margining for futures-style options

As explained before, with traditional options the usual premium margin is applied. Not so for future-style options. In this case, premium payment is effected under the mark-to-market method (cf. section on variation margin). The additional margin, which covers possible close-out losses until the next exchange trading day, is calculated in analogy to traditional options.

Futures-style options are subject to futures-style premium posting: When they are exercised or expire, the partial premiums yet unpaid are offset, in addition to the daily profit-and-loss settlement. Thus, the option premium is only paid when the option is exercised or mature. The result is a liquidity advantage for the buyer: The debit or credit to his account is calculated based on the daily option prices. Since under this scheme the option writer forgoes the interest to be gained by reinvesting the option premiums, these options are traded at higher prices than traditional options. This approach ties up less capital. At Eurex, it is applied for options on futures (such as OGBL).

17.8 How are margins calculated for option positions?

If a position book contains several contracts on the same underlying instrument, the different risk levels can be balanced against one another using the cross margining method. Calculation of the margin is based on the assumed maximum price change for the underlying until the next exchange trading day (the so-called **margin parameter**), which is determined by using statistical findings on the volatility of the underlying product. By adding this parameter to the current price or subtracting it, respectively, the maximum or minimum market price for the underlying product can be determined and the extent of a possible upside or downside risk is revealed. At the end, all strike prices for a margin interval are determined.

17.8.1 Determining close-out costs

The more option combos are traded and appear in the position book, the greater the effect of cross-margining.

If several margin classes can be gathered in one margin group it is reevaluated based on equal or near-equal risks: First, for each margin class the upper and the lower half of the additional margin are determined. If the result is a negative value these margins are usually multiplied with the so-called "**offset percent**", which mostly equals zero – which means that they are deleted. Next, all additional margins for the upper half are added. The result is known as the "upside additional margin" of a margin group. The same procedure is followed for the lower half, resulting in the **downside additional margin** for the group. Both margins are compared against each other and the higher one is used as additional margin for that **margin group**.

17.9 Ensuring that the margin obligation is met

A margin can be deposited in cash or securities. While different currencies are admissible in principle, it is important to consider that the exchange risk can work to reduce the deposit. In addition, safety discounts can be applied to the securities deposited.

17.10 Settlement price

The settlement price is the last price of an exchange trading day. If no price has been established for a product, series, or contract, Eurex Clearing AG will determine a settlement price. Settlement prices on the last trading day are referred to as final settlement prices or exchange delivery settlement prices (EDSP).

17.11 The margin call from an investor's point of view

In this section we will outline by example the possible causes and sequence of a margin call from an investor's point of view. If an investor can no longer meet his obligations (i.e., provide collateral) his bank or broker will issue a margin call in writing. In the letter he will be asked to increase his amount of security in line with requirements, and be notified that otherwise forced liquidation of these positions will be inevitable. Should the investor still fail to meet margin requirements the positions in question will be liquidated once the grace period agreed upon expires. In practice it rarely happens that investors cannot or do not want to respond to a margin call. In order to avoid this whole process, banks and brokers have therefore established safety systems requiring an early response from investors. In the course of these procedures they will try to jointly find a solution with the investors concerned. If as a result the margin call can be avoided there will be no further action in this regard; only if investors still fail to meet their obligations will the formal margin call be issued. In the event of a forced liquidation, the bank or broker will close as many positions as necessary to meet overall margin requirements.

17.12 Forced liquidation from a bank's or broker's vantage point

If the worst case happens and forced liquidation becomes necessary it must be precisely documented. Business with the respective customers should be ended, if possible: As there is a considerable risk that the situation will repeat itself, the bank or broker should meet its duty of due diligence and discourage the customer from investing in derivatives any more. It is further important to ensure that only so many positions will be closed out as are required to cover margin requirements. Also, the close-out should stretch across the entire position book – that is, it should affect several small positions rather than one large position. Otherwise it might happen that the investor could realize a profit in the position that was closed out while suffering losses in the positions still open, a situation that would hardly be justifiable. If at all possible, liquidation specifics should be agreed upon with the investor. Should he be unwilling to cooperate, forced liquidation will be initiated and the investor should be informed in a timely manner about the consequences and the decisions taken. It is indispensable that the investor receive this information so he can respond promptly.

Summary:

A margin is an amount required to cover the margin requirements of the derivatives exchange. It is posted either in cash or in securities eligible as collateral for borrowings from Deutsche Bundesbank. The purpose of calculating margins is to exclude or cover all close-out risks until the following exchange trading day. Futures positions are evaluated every day after market close, and profits and losses are netted. The resulting margin, which is called variation margin, is compensated in cash. The respective entry is carried out every trading day after settlement prices have been calculated.

Appendix

A.1 Questions and answers

This chapter contains examination questions covering the foregoing subject matter; enabling teachers and trainers to ascertain whether students have reached their learning targets. All questions and answers refer to the topics covered in the previous chapters.

A.1.1 Questions

Question #1
Please comment on the statement that "derivatives are an invention of our time" and that "derivatives trading has existed since the 1980s".

Question #2
Please analyze the term "derivative" with regards to its origin, and explain how it is defined today in the context of financial markets.

Question #3
What are the two basic intentions behind investmenting in derivatives?

Question #4
"Interest rates and dividends affect derivatives pricing both directly and indirectly." Is this statement correct? Explain why.

Question #5
Is it correct to say that the interest structure curve is used predominantly in the United States and the yield curve mainly in Europe? Explain by comparing the application of the two models.

Question #6
What do we call the difference in interest rates at the long- and short-end?

Question #7
What is the difference between a future and a forward?

Question #8
What exactly is a future?

Question #9
Is it correct to say that an option includes a right of choice, which the seller is entitled to exercise?

Question #10
Please comment on the following statement that, "If an option is not exercised the buyer will get the option premium back on the last trading day".

Question #11
What components of option contracts are standardized?

Question #12
What market participants do we find at the derivatives exchange?

Question #13
Which one of the market participant holds one-sided, open positions?

Question #14
What were the Eurex predecessor organizations?

Question #15
Must a market maker must respond to every quote request; and why or why not?

Question #16
Please comment on the statement that, "There is no difference in clearing status".

Question #17
What are the two components included in the option premium?

Question #18
Can either of the components in Question 17 be negative?

Question #19
When is a call option In The Money (ITM)?

Question #20
Please comment on the statement that, "The price of an option increases exponentially in the course of its term".

Question #21
Please complete the following statement: Options with a short remaining lifetime…

Question #22
Please comment on the point that, "Premature exercise of an option is unfavorable, since the investor will lose the time premium".

Question #23
"Volatility indicates which way the price of a financial instrument is fluctuating." Is this statement correct; why?

Question #24
Please complete the following table. Might consider giving more instructions for *what* to fill in.

Parameter		Call option price	Put option price
Underlying product			
Volatility			
Remaining lifetime			
Market interest rate			
Dividend payout American-style European-style			

Question #25
Please complete the following statement:
For a long call and a short put, the Greek indicator rho is always...

Question #26
"The Black-Scholes model assumes a normal distribution for the change in value." Is this statement correct? Please explain why this a correct or incorrect observation.

Question #27
The Binominal Model distinguishes between recombinant and non-recombinant trees. Which of the two are used when assessing American-style options?

Question #28
Please name the four basic positions in options trading.

Question #29
What is the maximum profit a short options investor can achieve?

Question #30
Please complete the following table:

	Basic assumption	Deal specifics
Long put		
Short put		

Question #31
How do we calculate the hedge ratio of a delta hedge?

Question #32
What is a Short Straddle?

Question #33
Please comment on the statement that, "Investors holding a credit bear-spread assume a strongly bullish market".

Question #34
What do we mean when we speak of "ultra-short speculation"?

Question #35
Evaluate the position that, "In futures trading, an open trade is closed out by means of an offsetting trade".

Question #36
What types of delivery are possible in futures trading? Give an example for each.

Question #37
An investor in a long Euro Bund Future® assumes...

Question #38
How is the price of a Future calculated?

Question #39
Can one state that, "A futures price can have a positive or negative basis".

Question #40
What is an intra-contract spread?

Question #41
Explain the concept of cash-and-carry arbitrage?

Question #42
Please complete the table below:

An Option on a Future is settled as follows:

Option contract	Future
Long call	
Short call	
Long put	
Short put	

Question #43
Synthetic forms of derivatives result from combinations derivative instruments.
Please complete the table below:

Synthetic form of...	Combination of...		
	Call option	Put option	Future
Long call			
Short call			
Long put			
Short put			

Synthetic form of...	Combination of...		
	Call option	Put option	Future
Long future			
Short future			

Question #44
What is a deport?

Question #45
What is balanced out by the swap rate?

Question #46
Compare the concepts of Contango and Backwardation by examining the conditions in which both exist?

Question #47
At Eurex, can an expiration date be prior to the 15th of an expiration month?

Question #48
What is pyramiding?

Question #49
What is a roll-over, and when is this typically observed?

Question #50
What is margin, and what purpose does it serve?

Question #51
What is a margin call, and when does it occur?

Question #52
What is covered by additional margin, and under what circumstances is it necessitated?

Question #53
"Long options investors do not have to deposit margin." Is this statement correct?

Question #54
By whom are credit derivatives mostly traded?

Question #55
What is a swap?

Question #56
An investor intends to expand his positions by an equal number of new positions. What do you advise him to do?

Question #57
One of your investors is facing a margin call the following day. What do you do?

Question #58
Evaluate the position that, "A portfolio consisting of options and futures is more stable than one comprising options only".

Question #59
Does an options investor receive dividends for the underlying security?

Question #60
What is variation margin?

Question #61
Under what price of the underlying asset would maximum profit of a bear spread be experienced on the day of expiration?

Question #62
The forward rate of the Euro to the US Dollar entails a deport (I think this means for discount…). What does this mean?

Question #63
For a pair of currencies we find identical interest rates. What is the effect on the swap rate?

Question #64
Please complete the following statement: The seller of a future is obliged to…

Question #65
An investor wishes to hedge his DAX® depot. What are possible courses of action?

Question #66
What expiration dates do we find in Index Futures Trading at the Eurex?

Question #67
What is basis convergence, and when does it occur?

Question #68
What components are covered by the margin to be paid to the clearing house for opening and holding a derivatives position?

Question #69
What is an exchange minimum margin, and for which options is it calculated?

Question #70
What is CCW? What affect might taking this position have on an investor's portfolio?

A.1.2 Answers

The following are the answers to the questions posted before. We have tried to keep them precise yet succinct.

Answer to question #1
This statement is not entirely correct. While liquid trading in financial derivatives only began in the 1980s, the first forms of derivative trades were conducted as early as two thousand years before Christ. Derivative trades also existed under the Roman Empire. They originated from commodity futures contracts.

Answer to question #2
The term derivative originates from the Latin "derivare"; so a derivative is something "derived" from something else. With regard to our subject matter this means that in a derivatives transaction the object traded is a product "derived" from an underlying asset, and not the underlying itself.

The derivative transaction is linked to the underlying asset, for instance, in terms of pricing.

Answer to question #3
An investor in derivatives may either wish to safeguard an existing or future investment – in that case he is a hedger. Or he may wish to place his bets on an assumed market move, which would make him a speculator.

Answer to question #4
Yes, this assumption is correct. Dividends and interest rates affect the price of a derivative both directly and indirectly.

Answer to question #5
No, this statement is not correct. In the U.S. it is customary to specify yields (returns) while European traders apply interest rates.

Answer to question #6
This difference is referred to as term spread.

Answer to question #7
A forward is a non-standardized future. Elements of the contract are bilaterally agreed upon. Due to their individual nature, forwards are not traded on the exchange.

Answer to question #8
A future is an unconditional derivative contract, and thus binding for both parties. The buyer of a future expects the underlying asset to appreciate; the seller assumes a price drop. The future contract must be fulfilled upon term end. Only an offsetting trade can release a contracting party from its obligations.

Answer to question #9
No, this statement is not entirely correct. While an option does entail a right of choice, contrary to the future, this right resides on the buyer's and not the seller's side.

Answer to question #10
This statement is not correct. An option not exercised expires on its last trading day. The seller retains the option premium. He has thus achieved an absolute gain.

Answer to question #11
The components of options contracts that are standardized are the underlying asset, quantity, quality, strike price, lifetime, trading time, and trading place.

Answer to question #12
Typical market participants found at the derivatives exchange are speculators, arbitrageurs, spreaders, and hedgers.

Answer to question #13
A speculator holds one-sided, open positions. He commits to investments for one single purpose, which is to achieve a maximal gain. In exchange for that he deliberately takes on the risk involved.

Answer to question #14
The Eurex originated from a merger of DTB (Deutsche Terminbörse – German Derivatives Exchange) and SOFFEX (Swiss derivatives exchange).

Answer to question #15
No, the Market Maker only has to meet the obligations actually taken on. As a general rule, the Market Maker answers 50 to 85 percent of all quote requests. If their number exceeds 150 per day the Market Maker may refuse accepting any more.

Answer to question #16
This is wrong. There are three levels: general clearing license, direct clearing license, and non-clearing membership. The individual trading members' status depends on their guarantee capital.

Answer to question #17
An option premium comprises the option's time value and its intrinsic value.

Answer to question #18
No, they cannot. The intrinsic value can equal zero but it can never be negative.

Answer to question #19
An option is In The Money if it has an intrinsic value; which means that the price of the underlying asset must be higher than the option's strike price.

Answer to question #20
This statement is not correct. The price of an option *de*creases exponentially in the course of its term. On its last trading day, the option only is reduced to its intrinsic value. If the intrinsic value equals zero the option expires worthless.

Answer to question #21
… should be sold.

Answer to question #22
This statement is correct, because…

Answer to question #23
No, volatility expresses the intensity of price fluctuation but not its direction. Volatility is the statistical measure for the fluctuation in the underlying price around its mean value within a defined period of time.

Answer to question #24

Parameter		Option price Call	Option price Put
Underlying product	increases	increases	decreases
	decreases	decreases	increases
Volatility	increases	increases	increases
	decreases	decreases	decreases
Remaining lifetime	decreases	decreases	decreases
Market interest rate	increases	increases	decreases
	decreases	decreases	increases
Dividend payout American-style European-style		decreases remains unchanged	increases remains unchanged

Answer to question #25
… positive.

Answer to question #26
No, the change in value is distributed exponentially and interdependent (as Benoît Mandelbrot managed to prove).

Answer to question #27
Non-recombinant trees are used with path-independent options.

Answer to question #28
Long call
Short call
Long put
Short put

Answer to question #29
His maximum profit is the premium received when entering into the contract.

Answer to question #30

	Basic assumption	Deal specifics
Long put	Price of underlying asset will go down	Must pay premium, can possibly sell underlying
Short put	Price of underlying asset will remain constant or go up slightly	Receives premium (in his function as writer) and may have to accept underlying asset

Answer to question #31

$$\# \ of \ contracts = \frac{Number \ of \ shares}{Contract \ size} \times \frac{1}{delta \ of \ option}$$

Answer to question #32
A Short Straddle is a combination of options in which the calls and puts sold have the same strike price and maturity date. The investor assumes moderate price fluctuations for the underlying asset.

Answer to question #33
This statement is not correct. The investor assumes the market to slightly grow sideways.

Answer to question #34
These are very short, often even intra-day, trades. The investor expects a certain movement in the underlying asset.

Answer to question #35
This statement is correct. Possible elaboration sentence might be helpful – or source to discussion in book.

Answer to question #36
1. Physical delivery
   Example: bond future
2. Cash settlement
   Example: index future

Answer to question #37
… falling interest rates, because…

Answer to question #38
Spot price + cost of carry = futures price

Cost of carry = net financing cost (financing cost – lost profits)

$$Future\ Price = C_t + \left(C_t \times r_c \times \left(\frac{T-t}{360} \right) - d_{t,T} \right)$$

C_t = Underlying (e.g., index level)
r_c = Money market interest rate (percent, current/360)
t = Valuta of cash market positions
T = Fulfillment day of a future
$T{-}t$ = Remaining lifetime of a future
$d_{t,T}$ = Dividend payment expected for the period t to T

Answer to question #39
Yes, a futures price can have a negative or positive basis.

Answer to question #40
An intra-contract spread is a spread operation in identical futures with different expiration dates.

Answer to question #41
Cash-and-carry arbitrage is used to offset market imbalances: The investor sells the future (as it is overpriced) and buy the spot instrument (as it appears too low-priced in relation to the future). His profit is the difference between the two.

Answer to question #42

Option contract	Future
Long call	Long future
Short call	Short future
Long put	Short future
Short put	Long future

Answer to question #43

Synthetic form of a ...	Combination of...		
	Call option	Put option	Future
Long call		Long	Long
Short call		Short	Short
Long put	Long		Short
Short put	Short		Long

Synthetic form of a ...	Combination of...		
	Call option	Put option	Future
Long future	Long	Short	
Short future	Short	Long	

Answer to question #44
A deport is a discount used in foreign exchange trading. Its opposite is a report (rate increase).

Answer to question #45
The difference between two currencies is balanced out.

Answer to question #46
These terms refer to commodity futures: A future that is more expensive than the spot instrument is traded "with contango"; if its price is lower it is traded "with backwardation".

Answer to question #47
No, expiration dates are always on the 3rd Friday of the expiration month, which means they can be on the 15th of that month at the earliest.

Answer to question #48
Pyramiding means that in the context of an expansion strategy derivative contracts are set up in the form of a pyramid A smaller number of contracts is based on a larger number.

XXX
XXXX
XXXXX

Answer to question #49
A roll-over is an extension of the derivative instrument beyond its original expiration date. The "old" position is closed out and a new position is opened. If this is achieved at no additional expense we speak of a premium-neutral roll-over.

Answer to question #50
A margin is the collateral posted for derivative trades. It must be deposited in cash or as securities (with a safety discount). If an investor is no longer capable of raising the margin required he faces a margin call by the bank or broker.

Answer to question #51
A margin call is a formal request to increase the collateral deposited. If an investor does not properly respond to a margin call he may face forced liquidation of his positions.

Answer to question #52
Additional margin is used to cover the potential close-out costs which, in a worst-case scenario, may accrue before the following trading day.

Answer to question #53
Yes, this statement is correct. After the premium has been paid there is no further risk to be covered for the worst case.

Answer to question #54
Credit derivatives are mainly traded by large and institutional investors. They are used to cover credit default risks.

Answer to question #55
A swap is an off-market derivative contract under which two payment streams are exchanged. Swaps usually refer to an underlying trade.

Answer to question #56
The investor should clearly be discouraged from pursuing this course of action. By doubling his positions he would exponentially increase his risk. As a possible last resort he might consider expanding his position by pyramiding.

Answer to question #57
Above all, the investor must be notified immediately and informed about the risks involved. Should he be able to increase the margin he will be able to keep his existing positions open; however, the pros and cons of this approach should be weighed carefully. If the margin cannot be increased the investor should be discouraged from maintaining active positions. Should he be unwilling to take that advice it is imperative that the whole process be documented in detail.

Answer to question #58
This statement is correct. As futures count among the delta 1 instruments, the portfolio will be more stable this way (provided that a consistent strategy is pursued).

Answer to question #59
No, an options investor does not receive dividends.

Answer to question #60
The variation margin is the daily profit and loss settlement for futures positions. It is deposited in cash. The respective entry is made in the customer's account every evening after market close.

Answer to question #61
The underlying price must be listed close to the strike of the put option sold.

Answer to question #62
It means that it will be cheaper to buy a forward of the currency (Euro) than to buy it in the cash market.

Answer to question #63
The swap rate will be zero since there is no interest rate difference to balance.

Answer to question #64
... deliver to the futures buyer, on the specified delivery date, the underlying asset in the quantity and quality specified.

Answer to question #65

He can set up strategies based on either long puts or short futures. Another alternative is to sell his positions; although this is less advisable. While in this way he will dispose of the risk he will also forgo all profit chances,and have to pay transaction costs.

Answer to question #66

Regular expiration dates are the following three quarter-end months.

Answer to question #67

Basis convergence occurs on the last trading day for futures. At this time there is no more cost of carry; and the futures price thus equals the spot price.

Answer to question #68

This margin ensures the trading participants' capability and willingness to meet their obligations (and therefore covers the fulfillment risk). It is calculated assuming a worst-case scenario.

Answer to question #69

The exchange minimum margin is the minimal margin requested by the derivatives exchange itself, without any surcharges. Among others, it is calculated for options deeply out of the money. As a general rule (according to Eurex Risk Based Margining) it is a fourth of the margin parameters plus the value (settlement price) of the option.

Answer to question #70

CCW stands for covered call writing – referring to a short call covered by an existing securities portfolio. This strategy is also referred to as "return-increasing strategy". What matters to the investor is the premium he receives. If he has to deliver the securities he can do so out of his own portfolio.

A.2 Glossary

Additional Margin Additional margin is designed to cover the additional potential close-out costs of an open position. Such potential losses would arise if the least favorable expected price Developments were to materialize within the next exchange trading day (a worst-case loss), starting from the current price for futures contracts held within the respective account. It is used for short options and non-spread (outright) futures positions.

American-style option An option that can be exercised on any exchange trading day before expiration.

At-the-money An option whose exercise price corresponds approximately to the current price of the underlying.

Ask The price at which one can sell an option – or other financial instrument.

Arbitrage When one takes advantage of price differences between two, relative, financial instruments on the same trading day (e.g., during the same trading hours) by simultaneously buying and selling the opposite positions; which creates a theoretically risk-free profit.

Arbitrageur The investor who partakes in arbitrage activities.

Backwardation Formally, it is the situation where, and the amount by which, the price of a commodity for future delivery is *lower* than the spot price; or a distant future delivery price lower than a nearer future delivery.

Basis	The difference between the price of the underlying instrument and the futures price.
Basis convergent	The condition when future and spot prices are equal.
Beta	The beta factor reflects the sensitivity of a single share, or portfolio, relative to the overall market movement.
Bid	The price at which one can sell an option – or other financial instrument.
Binomial Model	In finance, the **binomial options pricing model** (BOPM) provides a generalized numerical method for the valuation of options. The binomial model was first proposed by Cox, Ross and Rubinstein, and also carries the namesake Cox-Ross-Rubinstein Model.
Black-Scholes Model	An option-pricing model developed by Fischer Black, Myron Scholes, and Robert Merton for assessing the price of European options on stocks. The result is obtained by applying the Black-Scholes PDE to European put and call options (as it cannot be used in American style options). There are extensions of the model for dividend-paying stocks.
Call	An option contract that gives the buyer the right to buy a fixed number of units of the underlying instrument at a set price on, or up to, a set date (i.e., physical delivery). The right to physical delivery can be replaced by cash settlement (e.g., for equity index derivatives).

Cash Settlement	Settling a contract whereby a cash sum is paid or received instead of physically delivering the underlying instrument. In the case of an option contract, the cash settlement is determined by the difference between the option exercise price and the final settlement price of the underlying instrument. In the case of a financial futures contract, the cash settlement is calculated as the difference between the final settlement price and the daily settlement price of the contract on the previous exchange trading day.
CCW	Covered Call Writing, is a short position whereby the underlying has been deposited as a security for the transaction.
CTD	"Cheapest to deliver".
Closing	Closing or close out an open options or futures position with a counter transaction is referred to as closing out (closing transaction).
Contract size	Minimum size, in the units underlying, for a derivatives transaction.
Contango	A term used in the futures market to describe an *upward* sloping forward curve.
Convenience Yield	An adjustment to the cost of carry in the non-arbitrage pricing formula for forward prices in markets with trading constraints.
Cost of Carry (CoC)	The cost of "carrying" or holding a position.
Credit Derivatives	A financial instrument or derivative whose price and value derives from the creditworthiness of the obligations of a third party, which is isolated and traded.
European-style option	An option which cannot be exercised until its last trading day.

Exotic derivatives	**Exotic derivatives** refers to a specific type of financial asset, which is not standardized compared to traditional options.
Expiration Date	The date on which an option right can no longer be exercised. On the Eurex, this is the 3rd Friday of every month.
Future	A standardized contract comprising the delivery or receipt of a specific amount of a financial instrument at a set price on a certain date in the future.
Future Style Options	A margin collecting activity on options on futures, whereby variation and additional margin are collected/paid out daily.
Future-Spread-Margin	This margin must be pledged to cover the maximum anticipated loss that could be incurred on a futures spread position within the next exchange trading day.
Hedging	Using a strategy to protect a portfolio, or planned investments, against unfavorable price changes. **Hedging** is a strategy designed to minimize exposure to an unwanted business risk, while still allowing the business to profit from an investment activity.
Hedger	An investor that engages in hedging activities; thus one who is risk averse and attempting to minimize risks by taking positions that mitigate their effects.
In the money	An option is ITM when either, in a call option, the price of the underlying instrument is higher than the exercise price, or, a put option, the price of the underlying instrument is lower than the exercise price.
Initial Margin	Margin required for holding a futures position.

Intrinsic value

The intrinsic value of an option corresponds to the difference between the current market price and the option's exercise price, insofar as this represents an advantage for the buyer. The intrinsic value is always greater than, or equal to, zero.

Margin

The provision of collateral, which must be pledged to guarantee the fulfillment of contracts.

Margin Call

When the margin posted in the margin account is below the **minimum margin requirement**, the broker or exchange issues a **margin call**. The investor now either has to increase the margin that he has deposited, or he can close out his position. He can do this by selling the securities, options, or futures if he is long; and by buying them back if he is short.

Mark to Market

Daily re-evaluation of positions in financial futures or options on futures after the close of trading, to calculate the daily profit or loss.

Option

The right to buy (call option) or to sell (put option) a specific number of units of a specific underlying instrument at a fixed price on, or up to, a specified date.

Options price

The price paid for the option-right (also referred to as "premium").

Out-of-the-money

An option is OTM either on a *call option* when the price of the underlying instrument is lower than the exercise price, or a *put option* when the price of the underlying instrument is higher than the exercise price.

OTC

"Over the counter", options where the prices are not fixed by the exchange, but is agreed to by the parties entering into the deal.

Premium Margin	The Premium Margin must be pledged by the holder of a short options position, and must be maintained until exercise or expiration. It covers the seller's close-out costs, as measured by the settlement price. Premium Margin is continuously adjusted. Option buyers do not have to pledge any margin. By paying the option premium they have acquired a right, but have not undertaken any obligations. Their maximum risk is that the contract can expire worthless. Hence the risk is limited to the option premium.
Put	An option contract that gives the holder the right to sell a fixed number of units of the underlying instrument at a set price on or up to a set date (e.g., with physical delivery). The right to physical delivery can be replaced by cash settlement (i.e., for equity index derivatives).
Risk Based Margining	Risk Based Margining means the Eurex Margin System.
Roll-Over	The prolongation of a derivatives position by "rolling over" the investment to another period, and with another expiration date.
Settlement	The process of exchanging the consideration for financial instruments once a transaction has been executed.
Short Position	The open seller's position in a forward contract.
Spread-Position	In the case of an option transaction, the simultaneous purchase and sale of option contracts with different exercise prices and/or different expiration dates. In the case of financial futures, the simultaneous purchase and sale of futures contracts with different maturity dates or underlying instruments.

Strike Price	The price (also, exercise price) agreed to by parties in an option contract that underlying assets will be delivered on upon the time when the option is exercised.
Straddle	Long or short position with an equal number of calls and puts on the same underlying instrument, each with the same exercise price and expiration date.
Strangle	Long or short position with an equal number of calls and puts on the same underlying instrument, with the same expiration date, but with different exercise prices.
SWAP	An agreement to exchange one set of cash flows for another.
Synthetic position	Using other derivatives to reproduce an option or futures contract.
Theta	Is the influence of time on the value of the option price.
Time value	Time value comprises that part of an option's price that reflects the option's remaining lifetime. The longer the remaining lifetime, the higher the option price. This is due to the amount of time which still remains; during which the price of the underlying instrument can rise or fall (the rule stated here may not apply to certain deep-in-the-money puts).
Underlying	A stock, index, or other financial instrument on which an options or futures contract is based.
Variation Margin	The profit or loss arising from the daily revaluation of futures contracts (mark-to-market). Variation Margin is settled daily – in cash.

Volatility   The extent of the actual or anticipated fluctuations
                                in the returns of a financial instrument. The volatil-
                                ity of a financial instrument can vary, depending on
                                the period of time over which it is measured. Either
                                the historical or implied volatility can be calculated.

A.3 Single stock futures

Futures on	Product-ID	Country Code	Contract Seize	Minimum Price Change
ABB	ABBF	CH	100	0.01
Abertis Infraestructuras	ABEF	ES	100	0.01
ABN Amro Holding	AARF	NL	100	0.01
Acciona	ANAF	ES	10	0.01
Accor	ACRF	FR	100	0.01
Acerinox	ACEF	ES	100	0.01
ACS Actividades de Construcción y Servicios	OCIF	ES	50	0.01
Actelion	ATLF	CH	10	0.01
Adecco	ADEF	CH	100	0.01
Adidas	ADSG	DE	100	0.01
AEGON	AENF	NL	100	0.01
AEM	EAMF	IT	1,000	0.0005
AGF	AGEF	FR	100	0.01
Agfa-Gevaert	AGFF	BE	100	0.01
Ahold	AHOF	NL	100	0.01
Air France-KLM	AFRF	FR	100	0.01
Air Liquide	AIRG	FR	100	0.01
Akzo Nobel	AKUF	NL	100	0.01
Alcatel-Lucent	CGEF	FR	100	0.01
Alleanza Assicurazioni	AZAF	IT	500	0.0005
Allianz SE	ALVF	DE	10	0.01
Allied Irish Banks	ALBF	IE	100	0.01
Alpha Bank	ACBF	GR	100	0.01
ALSTOM RGPT	AOMF	FR	50	0.01
Altadis	TABF	ES	100	0.01
Altana	ALTF	DE	100	0.01
Anglo Irish Bank Corporation	CKLF	IE	100	0.01
Antena 3 de Televisión	YT2F	ES	100	0.01
Arkema	V1SF	FR	100	0.01
ASML Holding	ASMF	NL	100	0.01
Assicurazioni Generali	ASGF	IT	100	0.0005
Atos Origin	AXIF	FR	100	0.01
Autogrill	AULF	IT	500	0.0005
Autostrade	AOPF	IT	500	0.0005
AXA	AXAF	FR	100	0.01

Futures on	Product-ID	Country Code	Contract Seize	Minimum Price Change
Bâloise Holding	BALF	CH	100	0.01
BAM Groep	BGPF	NL	100	0.01
Banca Carige	BCAF	IT	500	0.0005
Banca Intesa	IESF	IT	1,000	0.0005
Banca Italease	B4IF	IT	100	0.0005
Banca Lombarda e Piemontese	BLFF	IT	100	0.0005
Banca Monte dei Paschi di Siena	MPIF	IT	1,000	0.0005
Banca Popolare di Milano	BPMF	IT	100	0.0005
Banca Popolare di Verona	BPVF	IT	500	0.0005
Banca Popolare Italiana	BPRF	IT	500	0.0005
Banche Popolari Unite	BPDF	IT	500	0.0005
Banco Bilbao Vizcaya Argentaria	BBVF	ES	100	0.01
Banco BPI	BPIF	PT	500	0.01
Banco Comercial Português	BCPF	PT	500	0.01
Banco de Valencia	BDVF	ES	50	0.01
Banco Espirito Santo	BATF	PT	100	0.01
Banco Pastor	BPQF	ES	50	0.01
Banco Popular Español	POPF	ES	100	0.01
Banco Sabadell	BDSF	ES	50	0.01
Banco Santander Central Hispano	SANF	ES	100	0.01
Bank of Greece	BGCF	GR	10	0.01
Bank of Ireland	BIRF	IE	100	0.01
Bank of Piraeus	BKPF	GR	100	0.01
Bankinter	BAKF	ES	100	0.01
BASF	BASF	DE	100	0.01
Bayer	BAYF	DE	100	0.01
BB Biotech	BIOF	CH	50	0.01
Beiersdorf	BEIF	DE	50	0.01
Belgacom	BX7F	BE	100	0.01
Bilfinger Berger	GBFF	DE	50	0.01
BMW	BMWF	DE	100	0.01
BNP Paribas	BNPF	FR	100	0.01
Böhler-Uddeholm	UDHF	AT	10	0.01
Bourbon	GBBF	FR	50	0.01
Bouygues	BYGF	FR	100	001
BRISA Auto-Estradas de Portugal	BRQF	PT	100	0.01
Buhrmann	BUHF	NL	100	0.01
Bulgari	BUIF	IT	1,000	0.0005
Business Objects	BUVF	FR	100	0.01
bwin Interactive Entertainment	BW9F	AT	50	0.01
C&C Group	GCCF	IE	500	0.01

Futures on	Product-ID	Country Code	Contract Seize	Minimum Price Change
Capgemini	CGMF	FR	100	0.01
Capitalia	BCRF	IT	1,000	0.0005
Cargotec	C1CF	FI	50	0.01
Carrefour	CARF	FR	100	0.01
Casino Guichard	CAJF	FR	100	0.01
Cattolica di Assicurazioni	CASF	IT	50	0.0005
Celesio	CLSF	DE	100	0.01
CEPSA Compañia Española de Petroleos	CPSF	ES	50	0.01
CGG Compagnie Générale de Géophysique	GDGF	FR	10	0.01
Christian Dior	CDIF	FR	100	0.01
Ciba Spezialitätenchemie Holding	CIBF	CH	10	0.01
Cie Financière Richemont	CFRG	CH	100	0.01
CIMPOR Cimentos de France	CPVF	PT	500	0.01
Cintra	UFGF	ES	100	0.01
Clariant	CLNF	CH	100	0.01
CNP Assurances	XNPF	FR	100	0.01
Coca-Cola Hellenic Bottling	HCBF	GR	100	0.01
Colruyt	EFCF	BE	50	0.01
Commerzbank	CBKF	DE	100	0.01
Continental	CONG	DE	100	0.01
Converium Holding	CHRF	CH	100	0.01
Corio	CL6F	NL	50	0.01
Corporación Financiera Alba	CSVF	ES	50	0.01
Corporación MAPFRE	CMAG	ES	500	0.01
COSMOTE Mobile Telecommunications	CRMF	GR	100	0.01
Crédit Agricole	XCAG	FR	100	0.01
Credit Suisse Group	CSGF	CH	100	0.01
CRH	CRGF	IE	50	0.01
CSM	CSMF	NL	50	0.01
DaimlerChrysler	DCXF	DE	100	0.01
Dassault Systèmes	DSYF	FR	100	0.01
DCC	DCCF	IE	100	0.01
Delhaize Group	DHZF	BE	100	0.01
DEPFA Bank	DEPF	DE	100	0.01
Deutsche Bank	DBKF	DE	100	0.01
Deutsche Börse	DB1F	DE	100	0.01
Deutsche Post	DPWF	DE	100	0.01
Deutsche Postbank	DPBF	DE	100	0.01
Deutsche Telekom	DTEF	DE	100	0.01
Dexia	DXBF	FR	100	0.01
E.ON	EOAG	DE	100	0.01

Futures on	Product-ID	Country Code	Contract Seize	Minimum Price Change
EADS	EADF	FR	100	0.01
Ebro Puleva	AZUF	ES	100	0.01
EFG Eurobank Ergasias	EFGF	GR	50	0.01
Eiffage	EF3F	FR	10	0.01
Elan Corporation	DRXF	IE	100	0.01
Electricité de France	E2FF	FR	100	0.01
Elisa Communications	EIAF	FI	100	0.01
Enagás	EG4F	ES	100	0.01
Endesa	ELEG	ES	100	0.01
Enel	ENLF	IT	500	0.0005
Energias de France	EDPF	PT	100	0.01
Eni	ENTF	IT	500	0.0005
Ericsson	ERCF	SE	500	0.01
Erste Bank	EBOF	AT	100	0.01
Essilor International	EFXF	FR	100	0.01
Eurazeo	RFXF	FR	50	0.01
Euronext	ENXF	NL	100	0.01
Eutelsat	E3BF	FR	100	0.01
Fastweb	EB7F	IT	100	0.0005
FCC Fomento de Con-strucciones y Contratas	FCCF	ES	50	0.01
Fiat	FIAF	IT	500	0.0005
Finmeccanica	FMNF	IT	100	0.0005
Fondiaria-Sai	SOAF	IT	50	0.0005
Fortis	FO4F	NL	100	0.01
Fortum	FOTF	FI	100	0.01
France Télécom	FTEF	FR	100	0.01
Fraport	FRAF	DE	50	0.01
Fresenius pref.	FREG	DE	100	0.01
Fresenius Medical Care	FMEG	DE	100	0.01
Fugro	FUGF	NL	100	0.01
Gamesa	GTQF	ES	100	0.01
Gas Natural SDG	GANF	ES	100	0.01
Gaz de France	GZFF	FR	100	0.01
GEA Group	G1AF	DE	100	0.01
Geberit	GBRF	CH	10	0.01
Gecina	GFCF	FR	50	0.01
Gestevisión-Telecinco	RWWF	ES	100	0.01
Getronics	GTOG	NL	100	0.01
Givaudan	GIVF	CH	10	0.01
Grafton Group	GN5F	IE	100	0.01
Groupe Bruxelles Lambert	EAIF	BE	100	0.01
Groupe Danone	BSNF	FR	100	0.01
Grupo Ferrovial	FERF	ES	100	0.01
Hagemeyer	HMYF	NL	100	0.01
Hannover Rück	HNRF	DE	100	0.01

Futures on	Product-ID	Country Code	Contract Seize	Minimum Price Change
Havas	HAVF	FR	100	0.01
HeidelbergCement	HEFF	DE	50	0.01
Heidelberger Druckmaschinen	HDDF	DE	50	0.01
Heineken	HNKF	NL	100	0.01
Heineken Holding	HEHF	NL	100	0.01
Hellenic Telecommunic ADS	OTEF	GR	100	0.01
Henkel	HENF	DE	100	0.01
Hermes International	HMIF	FR	10	0.01
Hochtief	HOTF	DE	100	0.01
Holcim	HOLG	CH	100	0.01
Huhtamaki	HUKF	FI	100	0.01
Hypo Real Estate Holding	HRXF	DE	100	0.01
HypoVereinsbank	HVMF	DE	100	0.01
IAWS Group	IW4F	IE	100	0.01
Iberdrola	IBEF	ES	100	0.01
Iberia Lineas Aereas de España	IBLF	ES	500	0.01
IFIL Investments	IILF	IT	500	0.0005
Imerys	NKFF	FR	50	0.01
IMMOEAST	I4MF	AT	100	0.01
IMMOFINANZ Immobilien Anlagen	IMOF	AT	500	0.01
InBev	ITKF	BE	100	0.01
Independent News & Media	IPDF	IE	500	0.01
Inditex	IXDG	ES	100	0.01
Indra Sistemas	IDAF	ES	100	0.01
Infineon	IFXF	DE	100	0.01
ING	INNF	NL	100	0.01
Inmobiliaria Colonial	COFF	ES	50	0.01
Irish Life & Permanent	ILBF	IE	50	0.01
Italcementi	ITAF	IT	50	0.0005
IVG Immobilien	IVGF	DE	50	0.01
JCDecaux	DCSF	FR	50	0.01
Julius Bär	BAEF	CH	10	0.01
K+S	SDXF	DE	50	0.01
KBC Groep	KDBF	BE	50	0.01
Kerry Group	KYGF	IE	50	0.01
Kesko	KEKF	FI	50	0.01
Kingspan Group	KRXF	IE	100	0.01
Klépierre	LIFF	FR	10	0.01
KONE	KC4F	FI	50	0.01
Koninklijke DSM	DSMF	NL	100	0.01
Kudelski	KUDF	CH	100	0.01
Kühne + Nagel	KNIF	CH	50	0.01

Futures on	Product-ID	Country Code	Contract Seize	Minimum Price Change
Lafarge	CILF	FR	100	0.01
Lagardère	LAGF	FR	100	0.01
LANXESS	LXSF	DE	100	0.01
Legrand	LRCF	FR	100	0.01
Linde	LING	DE	100	0.01
Lindt & Sprüngli	LISF	CH	1	0.01
Logitech	LOGF	CH	100	0.01
Lonza Group	LONF	CH	100	0.01
L'Oréal	LORF	FR	100	0.01
Lottomatica	N4GF	IT	100	0.0005
Lufthansa	LHAF	DE	100	0.01
Luxottica Group	LUXF	IT	100	0.0005
LVMH	MOHF	FR	100	0.01
M6 Metropole Television	MMTF	FR	50	0.01
MAN	MANF	DE	100	0.01
Maurel & Prom	ETXF	FR	100	0.01
Mediaset	MDSF	IT	1,000	0.0005
Mediobanca	ME9F	IT	500	0.0005
Mediolanum	MUNF	IT	500	0.0005
Meinl European Land	ODDF	AT	100	0.01
Merck	MRKF	DE	100	0.01
Metro	MEOF	DE	100	0.01
Metrovacesa	MVCF	ES	50	0.01
Metso	VLMF	FI	50	0.01
Michelin	MLXF	FR	100	0.01
Mittal Steel	ISPF	FR	100	0.01
Mobistar	MOSF	BE	50	0.01
MTU Aero Engines Holding	MTXF	DE	100	0.01
Münchener Rück	MU2F	DE	10	0.01
Natexis Banques Populaires	KNFG	FR	100	0.01
National Bank of Greece	NAGF	GR	100	0.01
Neopost	NP6F	FR	50	0.01
Neste Oil	NEFF	FI	100	0.01
Nestlé	NESF	CH	10	0.01
Nobel Biocare	NOBF	CH	10	0.01
Nokia	NO3F	FI	100	0.01
Nordea Bank	NDBF	SE	100	0.01
Novartis	NOVF	CH	100	0.01
Océ	OCEF	NL	100	0.01
OKO Bank	OKBF	FI	100	0.01
OMV	OMVF	AT	100	0.01
OPAP	GF8F	GR	100	0.01
Outokumpu	OUTF	FI	100	0.01
Pargesa Holding	PARF	CH	10	0.01
Parmalat	P4IF	IT	500	0.0005
Pernot-Ricard	PERF	FR	100	0.01

Futures on	Product-ID	Country Code	Contract Seize	Minimum Price Change
Peugeot	PEUF	FR	100	0.01
Philips	PH1F	NL	100	0.01
Phonak	PHBF	CH	50	0.01
Pirelli & C	PILF	IT	1,000	0.0005
Porsche	PORG	DE	10	0.01
Portugal Telecom SGPS	PTCF	PT	100	0.01
PPR	PPXF	FR	100	0.01
PSP Swiss Property	PSPF	CH	50	0.01
Public Power	PU8F	GR	100	0.01
Publicis Groupe	PU4F	FR	100	0.01
Puma	PUMF	DE	10	0.01
Q-Cells	QCEF	DE	100	0.01
Qiagen	QIAF	DE	100	0.01
Raiffeisen International	RAWF	AT	50	0.01
Randstad Holding	RSHF	NL	50	0.01
Rautaruukki	RKKF	FI	50	0.01
Red Eléctrica de España	RE2F	ES	50	0.01
Reed Elsevier	ELVF	NL	100	0.01
Renault	RNLF	FR	100	0.01
Repsol YPF	REPF	ES	100	0.01
Rheinmetall	RHMF	DE	50	0.01
Rhodia	RHDF	FR	500	0.01
Roche Holding	ROGF	CH	100	0.01
Rodamco Europe	RCEF	NL	100	0.01
Royal Dutch Shell	R6CF	NL	100	0.01
Royal KPN	KPNF	NL	100	0.01
Royal Numico	NUTF	NL	100	0.01
RWE	RWEF	DE	100	0.01
Ryanair	RY4F	IE	500	0.01
Sacyr Vallehermoso	VHMF	ES	50	0.01
Safran	SEJF	FR	100	0.01
Saint-Gobain	GOBF	FR	100	0.01
Saipem	SPEF	IT	50	0.0005
Salzgitter	SZGF	DE	100	0.01
Sampo	SMPF	FI	100	0.01
Sanofi-Aventis	SNWF	FR	100	0.01
SanomaWSOY	SWSF	FI	100	0.01
Sanpaolo IMI	PA5F	IT	500	0.0005
SAP	SAPG	DE	50	0.01
SBM Offshore	IHCG	NL	100	0.01
Schindler Holding	SINF	CH	50	0.01
Schneider Electric	SNDF	FR	100	0.01
SCOR	SCOH	FR	50	0.01
Seat Pagine Gialle	SP7F	IT	1,000	0.0005
Serono	SEOF	CH	10	0.01
SES Global	SESF	LU	100	0.01

Futures on	Product-ID	Country Code	Contract Seize	Minimum Price Change
SGS Surveillance Holding	SGSF	CH	10	0.01
Siemens	SIEF	DE	100	0.01
Sika	SIKF	CH	10	0.01
Snam Rete Gas	SNFF	IT	1,000	0.0005
Société BIC	BIFF	FR	50	0.01
Société Des Autoroutes Paris-Rhin-Rhône	RK9F	FR	50	0.01
Société Générale	SGEG	FR	100	0.01
Sodexho Alliance	SJ7F	FR	100	0.01
Sogecable	XSOF	ES	50	0.01
Solarworld	SWVG	DE	50	0.01
Solvay	SOLF	BE	100	0.01
Stada Arzneimittel	SAZF	DE	50	0.01
STMicroelectronics	SGMF	FR	100	0.01
Stora Enso	ENUF	FI	100	0.01
Stork	VMSF	NL	50	0.01
Straumann Holding	STMF	CH	10	0.01
Südzucker	SZUF	DE	50	0.01
Suez	LYOF	FR	100	0.01
Sulzer	SUNF	CH	10	0.01
Swatch B	UHFF	CH	10	0.01
Swatch Group	UHRF	CH	100	0.01
Swiss Life Holding	SLHF	CH	10	0.01
Swiss Re	RUKF	CH	10	0.01
Swisscom	SCMG	CH	10	0.01
Syngenta	SYNG	CH	10	0.01
Synthes	SYSF	CH	10	0.01
Technip	THPF	FR	50	0.01
Telecom Italia	TQIF	IT	1,000	0.0005
Telefónica	TEFF	ES	100	0.01
Telekom Austria	TA1F	AT	100	0.01
TeliaSonera	TLSF	FI	500	0.01
Tenaris	TENF	LU	100	0.01
Terna	UEIF	IT	1,000	0.0005
TF1	FSEF	FR	100	0.01
Thalès	CSFF	FR	100	0.01
Thomson	TNMF	FR	100	0.01
ThyssenKrupp	TKAG	DE	100	0.01
TietoEnator	TTEF	FI	100	0.01
Titan Cement	TICF	GR	50	0.01
TNT	TNTF	NL	100	0.01
TOTAL	TOTG	FR	100	0.01
TUI	TUIF	DE	100	0.01
UBS	UBSG	CH	100	0.01
UCB	UNCF	BE	100	0.01
Umicore	NVJF	BE	50	0.01

Futures on	Product-ID	Country Code	Contract Seize	Minimum Price Change
Unibail	UBLF	FR	100	0.01
UniCredito Italiano	CR5F	IT	1,000	0.0005
Unilever	UNIH	NL	100	0.01
Union Fenosa	UEFF	ES	100	0.01
Unipol	UNFF	IT	500	0.0005
UPM-Kymmene	RPLF	FI	100	0.01
Valeo	VSAF	FR	100	0.01
Valiant Holding	VATF	CH	10	0.01
Vallourec	VACF	FR	10	0.01
Vedior	VEDF	NL	100	0.01
Veolia Environnement	VVDF	FR	100	0.01
Verbund – Österreichische Elektrizitätswirtschaft	OEWF	AT	10	0.01
Vinci	SQUF	FR	100	0.01
Vivendi Universal	VVUF	FR	100	0.01
Voestalpine	VASF	AT	50	0.01
VW	VOWF	DE	100	0.01
Wärtsilä	MTAF	FI	100	0.01
WENDEL Investissement	MFXF	FR	50	0.01
Wereldhave	WERF	NL	50	0.01
Wienerberger	WIBF	AT	50	0.01
Wincor Nixdorf	WING	DE	50	0.01
Wolters Kluwer	WOSF	NL	100	0.01
YIT	YITF	FI	100	0.01
Zardoya-Otis	ZDOF	ES	50	0.01
Zodiac	ZDCF	FR	50	0.01
Zurich Financial Services	ZURF	CH	10	0.01

Contract standards
Equities of leading European and national indexes such as the Dow Jones EURO STOXX 50® Index, Dow Jones STOXX® 600 Index, DAX®, and SMI®.

Contract sizes
1, 10, 50, 100, 500 or 1'000 equities.

Settlement
Cash settlement, payable on the first exchange day following the Last Trading Day.

Minimum price change
EUR 0.0005, EUR 0.01 or CHF 0.01.

Contract months

Up to 36 months: The twelve nearest successive calendar months as well as the two following annual months of the December cycle thereafter.

Last trading day

The third Friday, for futures on Italian equities the day before the third Friday of each maturity month, if this is an exchange day; otherwise the exchange day immediately preceding that day. Close of trading in the maturing futures on the Last Trading Day is at 17:45 CET.

Daily settlement price

Established by Eurex. The Daily Settlement Prices for Single Stock Futures are derived from the closing price of the underlying determined during the closing auction plus the respective cost of carry.

Further details are available in the clearing conditions on **www.eurexchange. com.**

Final settlement price

Established by Eurex; based on the closing price determined within the electronic trading system of the domestic cash market for the respective underlying on the Last Trading Day.

Trading hours

09:00–17:45 CET.

A.4 Equity options

Contract	Settlement Day
Standard	$t+3$
German equity options	$t+2$
Finnish equity options	$t+4$

Contract standards
Equities of leading European and national indexes such as the Dow Jones EURO STOXX 50® Index, Dow Jones STOXX® 600 Index, DAX® and SMI® as well as other international equities.

Contract sizes
10, 50, 100, 500 or 1,000 equities.

Settlement
Physical delivery of 10, 50, 100, 500 or 1,000 equities of the underlying two, three or four exchange days after exercise:

Minimum price change
EUR 0.0005, EUR 0.01 or CHF 0.01.

Contract months
Up to 12 months: The three nearest successive calendar months and the three following quarterly months of the March, June, September and December cycle thereafter.

Up to 24 months: The three nearest successive calendar months, the three following quarterly months of the March, June, September and December cycle thereafter, and the two following semi-annual months of the June and December cycle thereafter.

Up to 60 months: The three nearest successive calendar months, the three (for Spanish equity options nine) following quarterly months of the March, June, September and December cycle thereafter, and the four (for Spanish equity options the nearest) following semi-annual months of the June and December cycle thereafter, and the two following annual months of the December cycle thereafter.

Exercise Prices (Standard)	Remaining Lifetime		
Exercise Price in EUR or CHF	< 3 months	4 – 12 months	> 12 months
up to 2	0.05	0.10	0.20
2 – 4	0.10	0.20	0.40
4 – 8	0.20	0.40	0.80
8 – 20	0.50	1.00	2.00
20 – 52	1.00	2.00	4.00
52 – 100	2.00	4.00	8.00
100 – 200	5.00	10.00	20.00
200 – 400	10.00	20.00	40.00
> 400	20.00	40.00	80.00

Last trading day
Last Trading Day is the third Friday, for Italian equity options the day before the third Friday, of each expiration month, if this is an exchange day; otherwise, the exchange day immediately preceding that day.

Close of trading in the expiring option series on the Last Trading Day is at 17:30 CET, for Swiss equity options at 17:20 CET and for Spanish equity options 17:35 CET.

If for German equity options a dividend resolution is passed on the Last Trading Day, the exchange day preceding that day is deemed as the Last Trading Day.

Daily settlement price
Established by Eurex. The Daily Settlement Prices for equity options are determined through the binomial model according to Cox/Ross/Rubinstein. If necessary, dividend expectations, current interest rates or other payments are taken into consideration.

Further details are available in the clearing conditions on **www.eurexchange. com.**

Exercise
American-style; an option can be exercised up to the beginning of the Post-Trading Restricted Period (20:00 CET) on any exchange day during the lifetime of the option.

German equity options cannot be exercised on a day on which a dividend resolution is passed.

Exercise Prices (Spanish Equity Options)	
Exercise Price in EUR	**Exercise Price Intervalsin EUR**
Up to 1	0.05
1–5	0.10
5–10	0.25
10–20	0.50
20–50	1.00
50–100	2.00
100–200	5.00
200–400	10.00
>400	20.00

Number of exercise prices

Upon the admission of the options, at least seven exercise prices shall be made available for each due date with a term of up to 24 months for each call and put, such that three exercise prices are in-the-money, one is at-the-money and three are out-of-the-money.

Upon the admission of the options, at least five exercise prices shall be made available for each due date with a term of more than 24 months for each call and put, such that two exercise prices are in-the-money, one is at-the-money and two are out-of-the-money.

Option premium

The EUR or CHF equivalent is payable in full, on the first exchange day following the trade date.

Trading Hours	
Contract	**Trading Hours**
Standard	09:00–17:30 CET
Swiss equity options	09:00–17:20 CET
Spanish equity options	09:00–17:35 CET

Options on	Product-ID	Country code	Contract seize	Minimum Price Change	Contract Month
ABB	ABBN	CH	100	0.01	60
ABN Amro Holding	AAR	NL	100	0.01	60
Accor	ACR	FR	100	0.01	60
Actelion	ATLN	CH	10	0.01	24
Adecco	ADEN	CH	100	0.01	24
Adidas	ADS	DE	100	0.01	24
AEGON	AEN	NL	100	0.01	60
AGF	AGF	FR	100	0.01	60
Ahold	AHO	NL	100	0.01	60
Air Liquide	AIR	FR	100	0.01	60
Aixtron	AIX	DE	100	0.01	24
Akzo Nobel	AKU	NL	100	0.01	60
Alcatel-Lucent	CGE	FR	100	0.01	60
Allianz SE	ALV	DE	10	0.01	60
Altana	ALT	DE	100	0.01	24
ASML Holding	ASM	NL	100	0.01	60
Assicurazioni Generali	ASG5	IT	100	0.0005	60
Autostrade	AOP5	IT	500	0.0005	24
AXA	AXA	FR	100	0.01	60
Bâloise Holding	BALN	CH	100	0.01	24
Banca Intesa	IES5	IT	1,000	0.0005	24
Banco Bilbao Vizcaya Argentaria	BBVD	ES	100	0.01	60
ABB	ABBN	CH	100	0.01	60
ABN Amro Holding	AAR	NL	100	0.01	60
Accor	ACR	FR	100	0.01	60
Actelion	ATLN	CH	10	0.01	24
Adecco	ADEN	CH	100	0.01	24
Adidas	ADS	DE	100	0.01	24
AEGON	AEN	NL	100	0.01	60
AGF	AGF	FR	100	0.01	60
Ahold	AHO	NL	100	0.01	60
Air Liquide	AIR	FR	100	0.01	60
Aixtron	AIX	DE	100	0.01	24
Akzo Nobel	AKU	NL	100	0.01	60
Alcatel-Lucent	CGE	FR	100	0.01	60
Allianz SE	ALV	DE	10	0.01	60
Altana	ALT	DE	100	0.01	24
ASML Holding	ASM	NL	100	0.01	60
Assicurazioni Generali	ASG5	IT	100	0.0005	60
Autostrade	AOP5	IT	500	0.0005	24
AXA	AXA	FR	100	0.01	60
Bâloise Holding	BALN	CH	100	0.01	24
Banca Intesa	IES5	IT	1,000	0.0005	24
Banco Bilbao Vizcaya Argentaria	BBVD	ES	100	0.01	60

Options on	Product-ID	Country code	Contract seize	Minimum Price Change	Contract Month
Banco Santander Central Hispano	BSD2	ES	100	0.01	60
BASF	BAS	DE	100	0.01	60
Bayer	BAY	DE	100	0.01	60
Bayer Basket	BAYE	DE	100	0.01	30
Beiersdorf	BEI	DE	50	0.01	24
BMW	BMW	DE	100	0.01	24
BNP Paribas	BNP	FR	100	0.01	60
Bouygues	BYG	FR	100	0.01	60
Buhrmann	KNP	NL	100	0.01	60
Capgemini	CGM	FR	100	0.01	60
Carrefour	CAR	FR	100	0.01	60
Casino Guichard	CAJ	FR	100	0.01	60
Celesio	CLS	DE	100	0.01	24
Ciba Spezialitäten-chemie Holding	CIBN	CH	10	0.01	24
Cie Financière Richemont	CFR	CH	100	0.01	24
Cisco Systems	CIS	US	100	0.01	12
Citigroup	TRV	US	100	0.01	12
Clariant	CLN	CH	100	0.01	24
Commerzbank	CBK	DE	100	0.01	24
Continental	CON	DE	100	0.01	24
Converium Holding	CHRN	CH	100	0.01	24
Crédit Agricole	XCA	FR	100	0.01	60
Credit Suisse Group	CSGN	CH	100	0.01	60
DaimlerChrysler	DCX	DE	100	0.01	60
DEPFA Bank	DEP	DE	100	0.01	24
Deutsche Bank	DBK	DE	100	0.01	60
Deutsche Börse	DB1	DE	100	0.01	24
Deutsche Post	DPW	DE	100	0.01	24
Deutsche Postbank	DPB	DE	100	0.01	24
Deutsche Telekom	DTE	DE	100	0.01	60
Dexia	DXB	FR	100	0.01	60
E.ON	EOA	DE	100	0.01	60
EADS	EAD	FR	100	0.01	60
Electricité de France	E2F	FR	100	0.01	60
Elisa Communications	EIA	FI	100	0.01	12
EMC	EMP	US	100	0.01	12
Endesa	ENA	ES	100	0.01	60
Enel	ENL5	IT	500	0.0005	60
Eni	ENT5	IT	500	0.0005	60
Epcos	EPC	DE	100	0.01	24
Ericsson	ERCB	SE	500	0.01	60
Fiat	FIA5	IT	500	0.0005	24
Fortis	FO4	NL	100	0.01	60

Options on	Product-ID	Country code	Contract seize	Minimum Price Change	Contract Month
Fortum	FOT	FI	100	0.01	12
France Télécom	FTE	FR	100	0.01	60
Fresenius Medical Care	FME	DE	100	0.01	24
Fresenius pref.	FRE3	DE	100	0.01	24
Gaz de France	GZF	FR	100	0.01	60
Geberit	GEBN	CH	10	0.01	24
General Electric	GEC	US	100	0.01	12
Getronics	GTO	NL	100	0.01	60
Givaudan	GIVN	CH	10	0.01	24
Groupe Danone	BSN	FR	100	0.01	60
Hagemeyer	HMY	NL	100	0.01	60
Hannover Rück	HNR1	DE	100	0.01	24
Heineken	HNK	NL	100	0.01	60
Henkel	HEN3	DE	100	0.01	24
Hochtief	HOT	DE	100	0.01	24
Holcim	HOLN	CH	100	0.01	24
Hypo Real Estate Holding	HRX	DE	100	0.01	24
HypoVereinsbank	HVM	DE	100	0.01	24
Iberdrola	IBE	ES	100	0.01	60
IBM	IBM	US	100	0.01	12
Infineon	IFX	DE	100	0.01	60
ING	INN	NL	100	0.01	60
Intel	INL	US	100	0.01	12
Julius Bär	BAER	CH	10	0.01	24
KarstadtQuelle	KAR	DE	100	0.01	24
Koninklijke DSM	DSM	NL	100	0.01	60
Kudelski	KUD	CH	100	0.01	24
Kühne+Nagel	KNIN	CH	50	0.01	24
Lafarge	CIL	FR	100	0.01	60
LANXESS	LXS	DE	100	0.01	24
Linde	LIN	DE	100	0.01	24
Logitech	LOGN	CH	100	0.01	24
Lonza Group	LONN	CH	100	0.01	24
L'Oréal	LOR	FR	100	0.01	60
Lufthansa	LHA	DE	100	0.01	24
LVMH	MOH	FR	100	0.01	60
MAN	MAN	DE	100	0.01	24
Mediaset	MDS5	IT	1,000	0.0005	24
Merck	MRK	DE	100	0.01	24
Metro	MEO	DE	100	0.01	24
Microsoft	MSF	US	100	0.01	12
Mittal Steel	ISPA	FR	100	0.01	60
MLP	MLP	DE	100	0.01	24
Mobilcom	MOB	DE	100	0.01	24
Münchener Rück	MUV2	DE	10	0.01	60

Options on	Product-ID	Country code	Contract seize	Minimum Price Change	Contract Month
Neste Oil	NEF	FI	100	0.01	12
Nestlé	NESN	CH	10	0.01	60
Nobel Biocare	NOBE	CH	10	0.01	24
Nokia	NOA3	FI	100	0.01	60
Nordea Bank	NDB	SE	100	0.01	24
Novartis	NOVN	CH	100	0.01	60
Numico	NUT	NL	100	0.01	60
OC Oerlikon Corporation	UNAX	CH	10	0.01	24
Oracle	ORC	US	100	0.01	12
Pernot-Ricard	PER	FR	100	0.01	60
Petroplus Holdings AG	PPHN	CH	100	0.01	24
Peugeot	PEU	FR	100	0.01	60
Philips	PHI1	NL	100	0.01	60
Phonak	PHBN	CH	50	0.01	24
Porsche	POR3	DE	10	0.01	24
PPR	PPX	FR	100	0.01	60
Publicis Groupe	PU4	FR	100	0.01	60
Puma	PUM	DE	10	0.01	24
Qiagen	QIA	DE	100	0.01	24
Reed Elsevier	ELV	NL	100	0.01	60
Renault	RNL	FR	100	0.01	60
Repsol YPF	REP	ES	100	0.01	60
Roche Holding	ROG	CH	100	0.01	60
Rodamco Europe	RCE	NL	100	0.01	60
Royal Dutch Shell	ROY	NL	100	0.01	60
Royal KPN	KPN	NL	100	0.01	60
RWE	RWE	DE	100	0.01	60
Saint-Gobain	GOB	FR	100	0.01	60
Salzgitter	SZG	DE	100	0.01	24
Sampo	SMPA	FI	100	0.01	12
Sanofi-Aventis	SNW	FR	100	0.01	60
Sanpaolo Imi	PAO5	IT	500	0.0005	60
SAP	SAP	DE	50	0.01	60
SBM Offshore	SBMO	NL	100	0.01	60
Schering	SCH	DE	100	0.01	24
Schneider Electric	SND	FR	100	0.01	60
Serono	SEO	CH	10	0.01	24
SGS Surveillance Holding	SGSN	CH	10	0.01	24
Siemens	SIE	DE	100	0.01	60
Société Générale	SGE	FR	100	0.01	60
Sodexho Alliance	SJ7	FR	100	0.01	60
Solarworld	SWV	DE	50	0.01	24
STMicroelectronics	SGM	FR	100	0.01	60
Stora Enso	ENUR	FI	100	0.01	12

Options on	Product-ID	Country code	Contract seize	Minimum Price Change	Contract Month
Suez	LYO	FR	100	0.01	60
Sulzer	SUN	CH	10	0.01	24
Sun Microsystems	SSY	US	100	0.01	12
Swatch Group	UHRN	CH	100	0.01	24
Swiss Life Holding	SLHN	CH	10	0.01	24
Swiss Re	RUKN	CH	10	0.01	60
Swisscom	SCMN	CH	10	0.01	24
Syngenta	SYNN	CH	10	0.01	24
Synthes	SYST	CH	10	0.01	24
Telecom Italia	TQI5	IT	1,000	0.0005	60
Telecom Italia RNC	TQIR	IT	1,000	0.0005	24
Telefónica	TNE5	ES	100	0.01	60
TeliaSonera	TLSN	FI	500	0.01	12
TF1	FSE	FR	100	0.01	60
Thalès	CSF	FR	100	0.01	60
Thomson	TNM	FR	100	0.01	60
ThyssenKrupp	TKA	DE	100	0.01	24
TietoEnator	TTEB	FI	100	0.01	12
Time Warner	AOL	US	100	0.01	12
TNT	TNT	NL	100	0.01	60
TomTom	OEM	NL	100	0.01	60
TOTAL	TOTB	FR	100	0.01	60
TUI	TUI	DE	100	0.01	24
UBS	UBSN	CH	100	0.01	60
UniCredito Italiano	CRI5	IT	1,000	0.0005	60
Unilever	UNI	NL	100	0.01	60
UPM-Kymmene	RPL	FI	100	0.01	12
Van der Moolen	VMH	NL	100	0.01	60
Vedior	VED	NL	100	0.01	60
Veolia Environnement	VVD	FR	100	0.01	60
Vinci	SQU	FR	100	0.01	60
Vivendi Universal	VVU	FR	100	0.01	60
VW	VOW	DE	100	0.01	24
Wolters Kluwer	WOS	NL	100	0.01	60
Zurich Financial Services	ZURN	CH	10	0.01	60

Low exercise price options (LEPOS)

This section only lists the differences with respect to the regular contract specifications for equity options, whereas for every equity option a Low Exercise Price Option (LEPO) is available.

Contract months
Up to 6 months: The nearest calendar month and the two following quarterly months of the March, June, September and December cycle thereafter.

Daily settlement price
Established by Eurex. The Daily Settlement Prices for Low Exercise Price Options are determined through the binomial model according to Cox/Ross/Rubinstein. If necessary, dividend expectations, current interest rates or other payments are taken into consideration.

Further details are available in the clearing conditions on **www.eurexchange. com.**

Exercise prices
Exercise price of a LEPO is the smallest exercise price of an option available in the Eurex® system.

For example, for securities with exercise prices with two decimal places, LEPOs with an exercise price of EUR 0.01 or CHF 0.01, respectively, will be set up. Options with an exercise price with one decimal place have an exercise price of EUR 0.1 or CHF 0.1, respectively.

A.5 Equity index derivatives

Equity index futures

Contract Standards		
Contract	**Product-ID**	**Underlying**
DJ EURO STOXX 50® Index Futures	FESX	DJ EURO STOXX 50® Index
DJ STOXX 50® Index Futures	FSTX	DJ STOXX 50® Index
DJ STOXX® 600 Index Futures	F600	DJ STOXX® 600 Index
DJ STOXX® Mid 200 Index Futures	F2MI	DJ STOXX® Mid 200 Index
DJ Global Titans 50ˢᴹ Index Futures	FGTI	DJ Global Titans 50ˢᴹ Index
DJ Italy Titans 30ˢᴹ Index Futures	F1TA	DJ Italy Titans 30ˢᴹ Index
DAX® Futures	FDAX®	DAX®, the blue chip index of Deutsche Börse AG
MDAX® Futures	F2MX	MDAX®, the international mid cap index of Deutsche Börse AG
TecDAX® Futures	FTDX	TecDAX®, the international technology index of Deutsche Börse AG
SMI® Futures	FSMI	SMI®, the blue chip index of SWX Swiss Exchange
SMIM® Futures	FSMM	SMI® Mid, the mid cap index of SWX Swiss Exchange
OMXH25 Futures	FFOX	OMXH25, Finnish equity index
DJ EURO STOXX® **Sector Index Futures**	**Produkt ID**	**DJ EURO STOXX®** **Sector Underlying**
Automobiles & Parts Futures	FESA	Automobiles & Parts Index
Banks Futures	FESB	Banks Index
Basic Resources Futures	FESS	Basic Resources Index
Chemicals Futures	FESC	Chemicals Index
Construction & Materials Futures	FESN	Construction & Materials Index
Financial Services Futures	FESF	Financial Services Index
Food & Beverage Futures	FESO	Food & Beverage Index
Health Care Futures	FESH	Health Care Index
Industrial Goods & Services Futures	FESG	Industrial Goods & Services Index
Insurance Futures	FESI	Insurance Index
Media Futures	FSTV	Media Index
Oil & Gas Futures	FSTU	Oil & Gas Index

Contract Standards		
Contract	**Product-ID**	**Underlying**
Personal & Household Goods Futures	FESZ	Personal & Household Goods Index
Retail Futures	FESR	Retail Index
Technology Futures	FESY	Technology Index
Telecommunications Futures	FEST	Telecommunications Index
Travel & Leisure Futures	FESV	Travel & Leisure Index
Utilities Futures	FESU	Utilities Index
DJ STOXX® 600 **Sector Index Futures**	**Product ID**	**DJ STOXX® 600** **Sector Underlying**
Automobiles & Parts Futures	FSTA	Automobiles & Parts Index
Banks Futures	FSTB	Banks Index
Basic Resources Futures	FSTS	Basic Resources Index
Chemicals Futures	FSTC	Chemicals Index
Construction & Materials Futures	FSTN	Construction & Materials Index
Financial Services Futures	FSTF	Financial Services Index
Food & Beverage Futures	FSTO	Food & Beverage Index
Health Care Futures	FSTH	Health Care Index
Industrial Goods & Services Futures	FSTG	Industrial Goods & Services Index
Insurance Futures	FSTI	Insurance Index
Media Futures	FSTM	Media Index
Oil & Gas Futures	FSTE	Oil & Gas Index
Personal & Household Goods Futures	FSTZ	Personal & Household Goods Index
Retail Futures	FSTR	Retail Index
Technology Futures	FSTY	Technology Index
Telecommunications Futures	FSTT	Telecommunications Index
Travel & Leisure Futures	FSTV	Travel & Leisure Index
Utilities Futures	FSTU	Utilities Index

Contract values
EUR 5, EUR 10, EUR 25, EUR 50, EUR 100, EUR 200 or CHF 10 per index point of the underlying.

Settlement
Cash settlement, payable on the first exchange day following the Final Settlement Day.

Price quotation and minimum price change
The Price Quotation is in points with one decimal place. The Minimum Price Change is 0.1 points, 0.5 points or 1 point.

Contract	Contract Value	Minimum Price Change	
		Points	Value
DJ EURO STOXX 50® Index Futures	EUR 10	1	EUR 10
DJ STOXX 50® Index Futures	EUR 10	1	EUR 10
DJ STOXX® 600 Index Futures	EUR 200	0.1	EUR 20
DJ STOXX® Mid 200 Index Futures	EUR 200	0.1	EUR 20
DJ EURO STOXX® Sector Index Futures	EUR 50	0.1	EUR 5
DJ STOXX® 600 Sector Index Futures	EUR 50	0.1	EUR 5
DJ Global Titans 50ˢᴹ Index Futures	EUR 100	0.1	EUR 10
DJ Italy Titans 30ˢᴹ Index Futures	EUR 10	1	EUR 10
DAX® Futures	EUR 25	0.5	EUR 12.50
MDAX® Futures	EUR 5	1	EUR 5
TecDAX® Futures	EUR 10	1	EUR 10
SMI® Futures	CHF 10	1	CHF 10
SMIM® Futures	CHF 10	1	CHF 10
OMXH25 Futures	EUR 10	0.1	EUR 1

Contract months

Up to 9 months: The three nearest quarterly months of the March, June, September and December cycle.

Last trading day and final settlement day

Last Trading Day is the Final Settlement Day. Last Trading Day for SMI® and SMIM® Futures is the exchange day preceding the Final Settlement Day. Final Settlement Day is the third Friday of each maturity month if this is an exchange day; otherwise the exchange day immediately preceding that day. Close of trading in the maturing futures on the Last Trading Day is at:

Contract	Close of Trading
DJ EURO STOXX 50® Index Futures	12:00 CET
DJ STOXX 50® Index Futures	
DJ STOXX® 600 Index Futures	
DJ STOXX® Mid 200 Index Futures	
DJ EURO STOXX® Sector Index Futures	
DJ STOXX® 600 Sector Index Futures	
DJ Global Titans 50ˢᴹ Index Futures	17:00 CET
DJ Italy Titans 30ˢᴹ Index Futures	09:05 CET
DAX® Futures	Beginning of the Xetra® intraday auction starting
MDAX® Futures	at 13:00 CET (for MDAX® Futures at 13:05 CET).
TecDAX® Futures	
SMI® Futures	17:27 CET
SMIM® Futures	17:20 CET
OMXH25 Futures	17:30 CET

Daily settlement price

The Daily Settlement Prices for the current maturity month of SMI® and SMIM® Futures are determined during the closing auction of the respective futures contract.

For all other equity index futures, the Daily Settlement Price for the current maturity month is derived from the volume-weighted average of the prices of all transactions during the minute before 17:30 CET (reference point), provided that more than five trades transacted within this period.

For the remaining maturity months, the Daily Settlement Price for a contract is determined based on the average bid/ask spread of the combination order book.

Further details are available in the clearing conditions on **www.eurexchange. com.**

Final settlement price

Established by Eurex on the Final Settlement Day according to the following rules:

Contract	Final Settlement Price
DJ EURO STOXX 50® Index Futures DJ STOXX 50® Index Futures DJ STOXX® 600 Index Futures DJ STOXX® Mid 200 Index Futures DJ EURO STOXX® Sector Index Futures DJ STOXX® 600 Sector Index Futures	Average of the respective DJ STOXX® Index values calculated between 11:50 and 12:00 CET.
DJ Global Titans 50ˢᴹIndex Futures	Average of the DJ Global Titans 50ˢᴹ Index values calculated between 16:50 and 17:00 CET.
DJ Italy Titans 30ˢᴹ Index Futures	Value of the index, based on Borsa Italiana opening prices of the DJ Italy Titans 30ˢᴹ Index component shares.
DAX® Futures MDAX® Futures TecDAX® Futures	Value of the index, based on Xetra® auction prices of the respective index component shares. The intraday auction starts at 13:00 CET (for MDAX® Futures at 13:05 CET).
SMI® Futures SMIM® Futures	Value of the SMI® respectively SMIM®, based on virt-x respectively SWX Swiss Exchange opening prices of the respective index component shares.
OMXH25 Futures	Value of the index, based on Helsinki Stock Exchange volumeweighted average prices of the OMXH25 component shares from 08:40 until 17:30 CET.

Trading Hours	
Contract	**Trading Hours**
Standard	08:00–22:00 CET
SMI® Futures	09:00–17:27 CET
SMIM® Futures	09:00–17:20 CET

Admission for trading in the U.S.
Dow Jones EURO STOXX 50® Index Futures
Dow Jones STOXX 50® Index Futures
Dow Jones EURO STOXX® Banks Index Futures
Dow Jones STOXX® 600 Banks Index Futures
Dow Jones Global Titans 50℠ Index Futures
Dow Jones Italy Titans 30℠ Index Futures
DAX® Futures

A.6 Equity index options

Contract Standards		
Contract	**Product ID**	**Underlying**
DJ EURO STOXX 50® Index Options	OESX	DJ EURO STOXX 50® Index
DJ STOXX 50® Index Options	OSTX	DJ STOXX 50® Index
DJ STOXX® 600 Index Options	O600	DJ STOXX® 600 Index
DJ STOXX® Mid 200 Index Options	O2MI	DJ STOXX® Mid 200 Index
DJ Global Titans 50ᔢᴹ Index Options	OGTI	DJ Global Titans 50ˢᴹ Index
DJ Italy Titans 30ˢᴹ Index Options	OESX	DJ Italy Titans 30ˢᴹ Index
DAX® Options	ODAX®	DAX®, the blue chip index of Deutsche Börse AG
MDAX® Options	O2MX	MDAX®, the international mid cap index of Deutsche Börse AG
TecDAX® Options	OTDX	TecDAX®, the international technology index of Deutsche Börse AG
SMI® Options	OSMI	SMI®, the blue chip index of SWX Swiss Exchange
SMIM® Options	OSMM	SMIM®, the mid cap index of SWX Swiss Exchange
OMXH25 Options	OFOX	OMXH25, Finnish equity Index
DJ EURO STOXX® **Sector Index Options**	**Product ID**	**DJ EURO STOXX®** **Sector Underlying**
Automobiles & Parts Options	OESA	Automobiles & Parts Index
Banks Options	OESB	Banks Index
Basic Resources Options	OESS	Basic Resources Index
Chemicals Options	OESC	Chemicals Index
Construction & Materials Options	OESN	Construction & Materials Index
Financial Services Options	OESF	Financial Services Index
Food & Beverage Options	OESO	Food & Beverage Index
Health Care Options	OESH	Health Care Index
Industrial Goods & Services Options	OESG	Industrial Goods & Services Index
Insurance Options	OESI	Insurance Index
Media Options	OESM	Media Index
Oil & Gas Options	OESE	Oil & Gas Index
Personal & Household Goods Options	OESZ	Personal & Household Goods Index
Retail Options	OESR	Retail Index
Technology Options	OESY	Technology Index
Telecommunications Options	OEST	Telecommunications Index
Travel & Leisure Options	OESV	Travel & Leisure Index
Utilities Options	OESU	Utilities Index

Contract Standards		
Contract	**Product ID**	**Underlying**
DJ STOXX® 600	**Product ID**	**DJ STOXX® 600**
Sector Index Options		**Sector-Basiswert**
Automobiles & Parts Index	OSTA	Automobiles & Parts Index
Banks Index	OSTB	Banks Index
Basic Resources Index	OSTS	Basic Resources Index
Chemicals Index	OSTC	Chemicals Index
Construction & Materials Index	OSTN	Construction & Materials Index
Financial Services Index	OSTF	Financial Services Index
Food & Beverage Index	OSTO	Food & Beverage Index
Health Care Index	OSTH	Health Care Index
Industrial Goods & Services Index	OSTG	Industrial Goods & Services Index
Insurance Index	OSTI	Insurance Index
Media Index	OSTM	Media Index
Oil & Gas Index	OSTE	Oil & Gas Index
Personal & Household Goods Index	OSTZ	Personal & Household Goods Index
Retail Index	OSTR	Retail Index
Technology Index	OSTY	Technology Index
Telecommunications Index	OSTT	Telecommunications Index
Travel & Leisure Index	OSTV	Travel & Leisure Index
Utilities Index	OSTU	Utilities Index

Contract values
EUR 5, EUR 10, EUR 50, EUR 100, EUR 200 or CHF 10 per index point of
the underlying.

Settlement
Cash settlement, payable on the first exchange day following the Final Settlement
Day.

Price quotation and minimum price change
The Price Quotation is in points with one decimal place. The Minimum Price
Change is 0.1 points.

Contract months
Up to 12 months: The three nearest successive calendar months, the three following quarterly months of the March, June, September and December cycle
thereafter.

Up to 24 months: The three nearest successive calendar months, the three following quarterly months of the March, June, September and December cycle thereafter, and the two following semi-annual months of the June and December cycle thereafter.

Up to 60 months: The three nearest successive calendar months, the three following quarterly months of the March, June, September and December cycle thereafter, the four following semi-annual months of the June and December cycle thereafter and the two following annual months of the December cycle thereafter.

Up to 119 months: The three nearest successive calendar months, the three following quarterly months of the March, June, September and December cycle thereafter, the four following semi-annual months of the June and December cycle thereafter and the seven following annual months of the December cycle thereafter.

Contract	Contract Value	Minimum Price Change	Minimum Price Change	Contract
		Points	Value	Months
DJ EURO STOXX 50® Index Options	EUR 10	0.1	EUR 1	119
DJ STOXX 50® Index Options	EUR 10	0.1	EUR 1	24
DJ STOXX®600 Index Options	EUR 200	0.1	EUR 20	24
DJ STOXX® Mid 200 Index Options	EUR 200	0.1	EUR 20	24
DJ EURO STOXX® Sector Index Options	EUR 50	0.1	EUR 5	24
DJ STOXX® 600 Sector Index Options	EUR 50	0.1	EUR 5	24
DJ Global Titans 50ˢᴹ Index Options	EUR 100	0.1	EUR 10	24
DJ Italy Titans 30ˢᴹ Index Options	EUR 10	0.1	EUR 1	24
DAX® Options	EUR 5	0.1	EUR 0.50	60
MDAX® Options	EUR 5	0.1	EUR 0.50	24
TecDAX® Options	EUR 10	0.1	EUR 1	24
SMI® Options	CHF 10	0.1	CHF 1	60
SMIM® Options	CHF 10	0.1	CHF 1	24
OMXH25 Options	EUR 10	0.1	EUR 1	12

Last trading day and final settlement day

Last Trading Day is the Final Settlement Day. Last Trading Day of SMI® and SMIM® Options is the exchange day preceding the Final Settlement Day.

Final Settlement Day is the third Friday of each expiration month if this is an exchange day; otherwise the exchange day immediately preceding that day. Close of trading in the expiring option series on the Last Trading Day is at:

Contract	Close of Trading
DJ EURO STOXX 50® Index Options DJ STOXX 50® Index Options DJ STOXX® 600 Index Options DJ STOXX® Mid 200 Index Options DJ EURO STOXX® Sector Index Options DJ STOXX® 600 Sector Index Options	12:00 CET
DJ Global Titans 50℠Index Options	17:00 CET
DJ Italy Titans 30℠ Index Options	09:05 CET
DAX® Options MDAX® Options TecDAX® Options	Beginning of the Xetra® intraday auction starting at 13:00 CET (for MDAX® Options at 13:05 CET)
SMI® Options SMIM®-Options	17:20 CET
OMXH25 Options	17:30 CET

Daily settlement price
Established by Eurex. The Daily Settlement Prices for equity index options are determined through the Black/ Scholes 76 model. If necessary, dividend expectations, current interest rates or other payments are taken into consideration.
Further details are available in the clearing conditions on **www.eurexchange.com**.

Final settlement price
Established by Eurex on the Final Settlement Day according to the following rules:

Contract	Final Settlement Price
DJ EURO STOXX 50® Index Options DJ STOXX 50® Index Options DJ STOXX® 600 Index Options DJ STOXX® Mid 200 Index Options DJ EURO STOXX® Sector Index Options DJ STOXX® 600 Sector Index Options	Average of the respective DJ STOXX® Index values calculated between 11:50 and 12:00 CET.

Contract	Final Settlement Price
DJ Global Titans 50^{SM} Index Options	Average of the DJ Global Titans 50ˢᴹ Index values calculated between 16:50 and 17:00 CET.
DJ Italy Titans 30ˢᴹ Index Options	Value of the index, based on Borsa Italiana opening prices of the DJ Italy Titans 30ˢᴹ Index component shares.
DAX® Options MDAX® Options TecDAX® Options	Value of the index, based on Xetra® auction prices of the respective index component shares. The intraday auction starts at 13:00 CET (for MDAX® Options at 13:05 CET).
SMI® Options SMIM® Options	Value of the index, based on virt-x respectively SWX Swiss Exchange opening prices of the respective index component shares.
OMXH25 Options	Value of the index, based on Helsinki Stock Exchange volume-weighted average prices of the OMXH25 component shares from 08:40 until 17:30 CET.

Exercise

European-style; an option can only be exercised on the Final Settlement Day of the respective option series until the end of the Post-Trading Full Period (21:00 CET).

Exercise Prices	Exercise Price Intervals in Index Points for Contract Months with a Remaining Lifetime of				
Contract	< 3 months	4–12 months	13–24 months	25–36 months	> 36 months
DJ EURO STOXX® 50 Index Options	50	50	50	50	100
DJ STOXX 50® Index Options	50	50	100	–	–
DJ STOXX® 600 Index Options	5	5	10	–	–
DJ STOXX® Mid 200 Index Options	5	5	10	–	–
DJ EURO STOXX® Sector Index Options	5	10	20	–	–
DJ STOXX® 600 Sector Index Options	5	10	20	–	–
DJ Global Titans 50ˢᴹ Index Options	5	10	20	–	–
DJ Italy Titans 30ˢᴹ Index Options	50	50	100	–	–
DAX® Options	50	50	100	200	200
MDAX® Options	50	50	100	–	–
TecDAX® Options	5	10	20	–	–
SMI® Options	50	50	100	200	200
SMIM® Options	5	10	10	–	–
OMXH25 Options	25	25	–	–	–

Number of exercise prices

Upon the admission of the options, at least seven exercise prices shall be made available for each due date with a term of up to 24 months for each call and put, such that three exercise prices are in-the-money, one is at-the-money and three are out-of-the-money.

Upon the admission of the options, at least five exercise prices shall be made available for each due date with a term of more than 24 months for each call and put, such that two exercise prices are in-the-money, one is at-the-money and two are out-of-the-money.

Option premium

The EUR or CHF equivalent of the premium in points is payable in full, on the first exchange day following the trade date.

Trading Hours	
Contract	**Trading Hours**
Standard	09:00–17:30 CET
SMI® /SMIM® Options	09:00–17:20 CET

A.7 Weekly options

Contract Standards		
Contract	**Product ID**	**Underlying**
DJ EURO STOXX 50®, 1st Friday Weekly Options	OES1	DJ EURO STOXX 50® Index
DJ EURO STOXX 50®, 2nd Friday Weekly Options	OES2	
DJ EURO STOXX 50®, 4th Friday Weekly Options	OES4	
DJ EURO STOXX 50®, 5th Friday Weekly Options	OES5	
DAX®, 1st Friday Weekly Options	ODX1	DAX®, the blue chip index
DAX®, 2nd Friday Weekly Options	ODX2	of Deutsche Börse AG
DAX®, 4th Friday Weekly Options	ODX4	
DAX®, 5th Friday Weekly Options	ODX5	
SMI®, 1st Friday Weekly Options	OSM1	SMI®, the blue chip index
SMI®, 2nd Friday Weekly Options	OSM2	of SWX Swiss Exchange
SMI®, 4th Friday Weekly Options	OSM4	
SMI®, 5th Friday Weekly Options	OSM5	

Contract values
EUR 5, EUR 10 or CHF 10 per index point of the underlying.

Settlement
Cash settlement, payable on the first exchange day following the Last Trading Day.

Price quotation and minimum price change
The Price Quotation is in points, with one decimal place. The Minimum Price Change is 0.1 points.

Contract months
1st, 2nd and 4th Friday Weekly Options: One month for all contracts expiring on the 1st, 2nd and 4th Friday of a calendar month. At the start of trading on each Friday, the Weekly Options for the same week of the following month will be listed.

5th Friday Weekly Options: More than one month for contracts expiring on the 5th Friday of a calendar month. For months without a 5th Friday, the option expiration will fall on the next 5th Friday.

Contract	Contract Value	Minimum Price Change	
		Points	Value
DJ EURO STOXX 50®, 1st Friday Weekly Options DJ EURO STOXX 50®, 2nd Friday Weekly Options DJ EURO STOXX 50®, 4th Friday Weekly Options DJ EURO STOXX 50®, 5th Friday Weekly Options	EUR 10	0.1	EUR 1
DAX®, 1st Friday Weekly Options DAX®, 2nd Friday Weekly Options DAX®, 4th Friday Weekly Options DAX®, 5th Friday Weekly Options	EUR 5	0.1	EUR 0.50
SMI®, 1st Friday Weekly Options SMI®, 2nd Friday Weekly Options SMI®, 4th Friday Weekly Options SMI®, 5th Friday Weekly Options	CHF 10	0.1	CHF 1

Last trading day and final settlement day

Last Trading Day is the Final Settlement Day. Last Trading Day of SMI® Weekly Options is the exchange day preceding the Final Settlement Day. Final Settlement Day of the Weekly Options is the by the respective expiry determined Friday, if this is an exchange day; otherwise the exchange day immediately preceding that Friday. Close of trading in the expiring option series on the Last Trading Day is at:

Contract	Close of Trading
DJ EURO STOXX 50®, 1st Friday Weekly Options DJ EURO STOXX 50®, 2nd Friday Weekly Options DJ EURO STOXX 50®, 4th Friday Weekly Options DJ EURO STOXX 50®, 5th Friday Weekly Options	12:00 CET
DAX®, 1st Friday Weekly Options DAX®, 2nd Friday Weekly Options DAX®, 4th Friday Weekly Options DAX®, 5th Friday Weekly Options	Beginning of the Xetra® intraday auction starting at 13:00 CET.
SMI®, 1st Friday Weekly Options SMI®, 2nd Friday Weekly Options SMI®, 4th Friday Weekly Options SMI®, 5th Friday Weekly Options	17:20 CET

Daily settlement price

Established by Eurex. The Daily Settlement Prices for Weekly Options are determined through the Black/ Scholes 76 model. If necessary, dividend expectations, current interest rates or other payments are taken into consideration.

Further details are available in the clearing conditions on **www.eurexchange.com.**

Final settlement price

Established by Eurex on the Final Settlement Day according to the following rules:

Contract	Final Settlement Price
DJ EURO STOXX 50®, 1st Friday Weekly Options DJ EURO STOXX 50®, 2nd Friday Weekly Options DJ EURO STOXX 50®, 4th Friday Weekly Options DJ EURO STOXX 50®, 5th Friday Weekly Options	Average of the DJ EURO STOXX 50® Index values calculated between 11:50 and 12:00 CET.
DAX®, 1st Friday Weekly Options DAX®, 2nd Friday Weekly Options DAX®, 4th Friday Weekly Options DAX®, 5th Friday Weekly Options	Value of DAX , based on Xetra® auction prices of the index component shares. The intraday auction starts at 13:00 CET.
SMI®, 1st Friday Weekly Options SMI®, 2nd Friday Weekly Options SMI®, 4th Friday Weekly Options SMI®, 5th Friday Weekly Options	Value of SMI®, based on virt-x opening prices of the SMI® component shares

Exercise

European-style; an option can only be exercised on the Final Settlement Day of the respective option series until the end of the Post-Trading Full Period (21:00 CET).

Exercise prices

The exercise price intervals for Weekly Options are as follows:

Exercise Price Months with a Remaining Lifetime of	Intervalls in Minimum Number of Exercise Prices	Intervalls in Index Points
1–12	7	50

Option premium

The EUR or CHF equivalent of the premium in points is payable in full, on the first exchange day following the trade date.

Trading Hours	
Contract	**Trading Hours**
DJ EURO STOXX 50®, 1st Friday Weekly Options DJ EURO STOXX 50®, 2nd Friday Weekly Options DJ EURO STOXX 50®, 4th Friday Weekly Options DJ EURO STOXX 50®, 5th Friday Weekly Options	09:00–17:30 CET
DAX®, 1st Friday Weekly Options DAX®, 2nd Friday Weekly Options DAX®, 4th Friday Weekly Options DAX®, 5th Friday Weekly Options	09:00–17:30 CET
SMI®, 1st Friday Weekly Options SMI®, 2nd Friday Weekly Options SMI®, 4th Friday Weekly Options SMI®, 5th Friday Weekly Options	09:00–17:20 CET

A.8 Volatility index derivatives

Volatility index futures

Contract Standards			
Contract	**Product ID**	**Underlying**	**Currency**
VDAX-NEW® Futures	FVDX	VDAX-NEW®	EUR
VSMI® Futures	FVSM	VSMI®	CHF
VSTOXX® Futures	FVSX	VSTOXX®	EUR

Contract values
EUR 1,000 or CHF 1,000 per index point of the underlying.

Settlement
Cash settlement, payable on the first exchange day following the Final Settlement Day.

Price quotation and minimum price change
The Price Quotation is in points with two decimal places.
   The Minimum Price Change is 0.05 points, equivalent to a value of EUR 50 or CHF 50.

Contract months
Up to 5 months: The three nearest calendar months and the following quarterly months of the February, May, August and November cycle thereafter.

Last trading day and final settlement day
Last Trading Day is the Final Settlement Day. Final Settlement Day is 30 calendar days before the expiration day of the underlying options (i.e. 30 days before the third Friday of the expiration month of the underlying options, if this is an exchange day). This is usually the Wednesday before the second last Friday of the respective maturity month, if this is an exchange day; otherwise the exchange day

immediately preceding that day. Close of trading in the maturing futures on the Last Trading Day is at:

Contract	Close of Trading
VDAX-NEW® Futures	13:00 CET
VSMI® Futures	10:00 CET
VSTOXX® Futures	12:00 CET

Daily settlement price

The Daily Settlement Prices for the current maturity month of volatility index futures are determined during the closing auction of the respective futures contract.

For the remaining maturity months, the Daily Settlement Price for a contract is determined based on the average bid/ask spread of the combination order book.

Further details are available in the clearing conditions on **www.eurexchange. com.**

Final settlement price

Established by Eurex on the Final Settlement Day; based on the average of the index values of the respective underlying on the Last Trading Day between:

Contract	Time Frame
VDAX-NEW® Futures	12:30 and 13:00 CET
VSMI® Futures	09:00 and 10:00 CET
VSTOXX® Futures	11:30 and 12:00 CET

Trading Hours	
Contract	**Trading Hours**
Standard	09:00 – 17:30 CET
VSMI® Future	09:00 – 17:20 CET

A.9 Exchange traded funds® derivatives

EXTF futures

Contract Standards			
Contract	**Product ID**	**Underlying**	**Currency**
DAX® EX Futures	EXSF	DAX® EX	EUR
DJ EURO STOXX 50® EX Futures	EXWF	DJ EURO STOXX 50® EX	EUR
iShares DJ EURO STOXX 50® Futures	EUNF	iShares DJ EURO STOXX 50 ®	EUR
XMTCH on SMI® Futures	XMTF	XMTCH on SMI®	CHF

Contract size
100 index fund shares of the underlying.

Settlement
Physical delivery of 100 index fund shares two, for XMTCH on SMI® Futures three exchange days after the Last Trading Day.

Minimum price change
EUR 0.01 or CHF 0.01.

Contract months
Up to 9 months: The three nearest quarterly months of the March, June, September and December cycle.

Last trading day
The third Friday of each maturity month, if this is an exchange day; otherwise the exchange day immediately preceding that day. Close of trading in the maturing futures on the Last Trading Day is at 17:30 CET, for XMTCH on SMI® Futures at 17:20 CET.

Daily settlement price
The Daily Settlement Prices for EXTF futures are derived from the closing price of the underlying determined during the closing auction plus the respective cost of carry.

Further details are available in the clearing conditions on **www.eurexchange. com.**

Tender price
Established by Eurex; based on the closing price determined within the electronic trading system of the domestic cash market for the respective underlying on the Last Trading Day. If such a price cannot be determined, the volume-weighted average of the three last traded prices within the electronic trading system of the domestic cash market for the respective underlying will be consulted.

Trading Hours	
Contract	**Trading Hours**
Standard	09:00–22:00 CET
XMTCH on SMI® Futures	09:00–17:20 CET

EXTF options

Contract Standards			
Contract	**Product ID**	**Underlying**	**Currency**
DAX® EX Options	EXS1	DAX® EX	EUR
DJ EURO STOXX 50® EX Options	EXW1	DJ EURO STOXX 50® EX	EUR
iShares DJ EURO STOXX 50® Options	EUN2	iShares DJ EURO STOXX 50®	EUR
XMTCH on SMI® Options	XMT	XMTCH on SMI®	CHF

Contract size
100 index fund shares of the underlying.

Settlement
Physical delivery of 100 index fund shares two, for XMTCH on SMI® Options three exchange days after the Last Trading Day.

Minimum price change
EUR 0.01 or CHF 0.01.

Contract months
Up to 24 months: The three nearest successive calendar months, the three following quarterly months of the March, June, September and December cycle thereafter, and the two following semi-annual months of the June and December cycle thereafter.

Last trading day
The third Friday of each expiration month, if this is an exchange day; otherwise the exchange day immediately preceding that day. Close of trading in the expiring option series on the Last Trading Day is at 17:30 CET, for XMTCH on SMI® Options at 17:20 CET.

Daily settlement price
Established by Eurex. The Daily Settlement Prices for EXTFs options are determined through the binomial model according to Cox/Ross/Rubinstein. If necessary, dividend expectations, current interest rates or other payments are taken into consideration.

Further details are available in the clearing conditions on **www.eurexchange. com.**

Exercise
American-style; an option can be exercised up to the beginning of the Post-Trading Restricted Period (20:00 CET) on any exchange day during the lifetime of the option.

EUR-denominated EXTF options may be exercised on any exchange day with the exception of the day preceding the day of the dividend payout, respectively with the exception of the day preceding the day of the tax contribution.

Exercise Price	Exercise Price Intervals in EUR or CHF for Contract Months with a Remaining Lifetime of		
Exercise Prices in EUR or CHF	<3 months	4–12 months	>12 months
Up to 2	0.05	0.10	0.20
2–4	0.10	0.20	0.40
4–8	0.20	0.40	0.80
8–20	0.50	1.00	2.00
20–52	1.00	2.00	4.00
52–100	2.00	4.00	8.00
100–200	5.00	10.00	20.00
200–400	10.00	20.00	40.00
> 40	20.00	40.00	80.00

Number of exercise prices

Upon the admission of a contract, at least seven exercise prices shall be made available for each term for each call and put, such that three exercise prices are in-the-money, one is at-the-money and three are out-of-the-money.

Option premium

The EUR or CHF equivalent is payable in full on the first exchange day following the trade date.

Trading Hours	
Contract	**Trading Hours**
Standard	09:00 – 17:30 CET
XMTCH on SMI® Options	09:00 – 17:20 CET

A.10 Credit derivatives

Credit futures

Contract Standards			
Contract	**Product ID**	**Underlying**	**Currency**
iTraxx® Europe 5-year Index Futures	F5EO	The current iTraxx® Europe 5-year Index Series	EUR
iTraxx® Europe Hi Vol 5-year Index Futures	F5HO	The current iTraxx® Europe Hi Vol 5-year Index Series	EUR
iTraxx® Europe Crossover 5-year Index Futures	F5CO	The current iTraxx® Europe Crossover 5-year Index Series	EUR

Contract value
EUR 100,000

Settlement
Cash settlement, payable on the first exchange day following the Final Settlement Day.

Price quotation
In percentage, with three decimal places for the iTraxx® Europe 5-year Index Futures and with two decimal places for the iTraxx® Europe Hi Vol and iTraxx® Europe Crossover 5-year Index Futures as the sum of
- the basis, determined as the Σni, whereby ni represents the weight of the i'th reference entity in the underlying index series, which has not experienced an actual credit event (basis = 100, as long as no credit event has occured);
- the present value change calculated on the basis;
- the accrued premium since the effective date of the underlying index series based on the coupon fixed for the underlying index series;
- and, if applicable, the proportional recovery rate of the i'th reference entity in the underlying index series which experienced an actual credit event.

Minimum price change
iTraxx® Europe 5-year Index Futures
The Minimum Price Change is 0.005 percent, equivalent to a value of EUR 5.

iTraxx® Europe Hi Vol 5-year Index Futures and iTraxx® Europe Crossover 5-year Index Futures
The Minimum Price Change is 0.01 percent, equivalent to a value of EUR 10.

Contract months
The nearest semi-annual month of the March and September cycle will be available for trading.

Last trading day
The 5th exchange day following the 20th of the respective contract month.

Daily settlement price
The Daily Settlement Price for the current maturity month is determined during the closing auction of the respective futures contract.

For the remaining maturity month the Daily Settlement Price for a contract is determined based on the average bid/ask spread of the combination order book. Further details are available in the clearing conditions on **www.eurexchange.com.**

Final settlement price
The Final Settlement Price is established at 17:00 CET on the Last Trading Day in percent as the sum of
- the basis determined as the Σn_i, whereby n_i represents the weight of the i'th reference entity in the underlying index series, which has not experienced an actual credit event (basis = 100, as long as no credit event has occured);
- the present value change of the underlying index series resulting from the change of the credit spread in relation to the basis. The present value calculation on the final settlement day is based on the official iTraxx® Index levels as published by IIC at 17:00 CET and the deal spread (coupon) of the underlying index. The mid spread reflecting the mid point between the bid and ask spreads of the official iTraxx® Index levels are considered for the present value calculation.
- the accrued premium calculated from the effective date of the underlying index series based on the coupon fixed for the underlying index series;
- and, if applicable, the proportional recovery rate of the reference entity in the underlying index series, which experienced an actual credit event; The calculated Final Settlement Price will be determined with four decimal places and rounded to the next possible price interval (0.0005; 0.001 or a multiple thereof).

Trading hours
08:30–17:30 CET.

Occurrence of a credit event
Upon occurrence of a credit event, the credit futures contract will continue to trade in its original form including the reference entity subject to the credit event. In addition, Eurex will list a futures contract based on the new version of the underlying index (for example 124 reference entities).

For all details regarding the handling of a credit event as well as the determination of Final Settlement Prices, please refer to the full contract specifications published on **www.eurexchange.com.**

A.11 Interest rate derivatives

Fixed income futures

Contract standards
Notional short-, medium- or long-term debt instruments issued by the Federal Republic of Germany or the Swiss Confederation with remaining terms and a coupon of:

Contract	Product ID	Remaining Term	Coupon	Currency
		Years	Percent	
Euro-Schatz-Futures	FGBS	1.75 to 2.25	6	EUR
Euro-Bobl-Futures	FGBM	4.5 to 5.5	6	EUR
Euro-Bund-Futures	FGBL	8.5 to 10.5	6	EUR
Euro-Buxl® -Futures	FGBX	24.0 to 35.0	4	EUR
CONF-Futures	CONF	8.0 to 13.0	6	CHF

Contract values
EUR 100,000 or CHF 100,000.

Settlement
A delivery obligation arising out of a short position may only be fulfilled by the delivery of certain debt securities issued by the Federal Republic of Germany or the Swiss

Confederation with a remaining term on the Delivery Day within the remaining term of the underlying.

In the case of callable bonds issued by the Swiss Confederation, the first and last call dates must be between eight and 13 years.

Such debt securities must have a minimum issue amount of:

Contract	Minimum Issue Amount
Euro-Schatz-Futures	EUR 5 billion
Euro-Bobl-Futures	EUR 5 billion
Euro-Bund-Futures	EUR 5 billion
Euro-Buxl® -Futures	EUR 10 billion
CONF-Futures	CHF 500 million

Price quotation and minimum price change
The Price Quotation is in percent of the par value.

Contract	Minimum Price Change	
	Percent	Value
Euro-Schatz-Futures	0.005	EUR 5
Euro-Bobl-Futures	0.01	EUR 10
Êuro-Bund-Futures	0.01	EUR 10
Euro-Buxl®-Futures	0.02	EUR 20
CONF-Futures	0.01	CHF 10

Contract months
Up to 9 months: The three nearest quarterly months of the March, June, September and December cycle.

Delivery day
The tenth calendar day of the respective quarterly month, if this day is an exchange day; otherwise, the exchange day immediately succeeding that day.

Notification
Clearing members with open short positions must notify Eurex on the Last Trading Day of the maturing futures which debt instrument they will deliver. Such notification must be given by the end of the Post-Trading Full Period (20:00 CET).

Last trading day

Two exchange days prior to the Delivery Day of the relevant maturity month. Close of trading in the maturing futures on the Last Trading Day is at 12:30 CET.

Daily settlement price

The Daily Settlement Prices for the current maturity month of CONF Futures are determined during the closing auction of the respective futures contract.

For all other fixed income futures, the Daily Settlement Price for the current maturity month is derived from the volume-weighted average of the prices of all transactions during the minute before 17:15 CET (reference point), provided that more than five trades transacted within this period.

For the remaining maturity months the Daily Settlement Price for a contract is determined based on the average bid/ask spread of the combination order book.

Further details are available in the clearing conditions on **www.eurexchange. com.**

Final settlement price

Established by Eurex on the Last Trading Day at 12:30 CET; based on the volume-weighted average price of all trades during the final minute of trading provided that more than ten trades occurred during this minute; otherwise the volume-weighted average price of the last ten trades of the day, provided that these are not older than 30 minutes. If such a price cannot be determined, or does not reasonably reflect the prevailing market conditions, Eurex will establish the Final Settlement Price.

Trading Hours	
Contract	**Trading Hours**
Standard	08:00–22:00 CET
CONF Futures	08:30–17:00 CET

Fixed Income Futures have been admitted for trading in the U.S.

Options on fixed income futures

Contract standards
Futures on notional short-, medium- or long-term debt instruments issued by the Federal Republic of Germany with remaining terms and a coupon of:

Contract	Product ID	Basiswert	Remaining Term of the Underlying	Coupon
Options on			Years	Percent
Euro-Schatz-Futures	OGBS	Euro-Schatz Futures	1.75 to 2.25	6
Euro-Bobl-Futures	OGBM	Euro-Bobl Futures	4.5 to 5.5	6
Euro-Bund-Futures	OGBL	Euro-Bund Futures	8.5 to 10.5	6

Contract value
One fixed income futures contract.

Settlement
The exercise of an option on fixed income futures results in the creation of a corresponding position in the fixed income futures for the option buyer as well as the seller to whom the exercise is assigned. The position is established after the Post-Trading Full Period of the exercise day, and is based on the agreed exercise price.

Price quotation and minimum price change
The Price Quotation is in points.

Contract	Minimum Price Change	Minimum Price Change
Options on	Points	Value
Euro-Schatz-Futures	0.005	EUR 5
Euro-Bobl-Futures	0.01	EUR 10
Euro-Bund-Futures	0.01	EUR 10

Contract months
Up to 6 months: The three nearest successive calendar months, as well as the following quarterly month of the March, June, September and December cycle thereafter.

Calendar months: The maturity month of the underlying futures contract is the quarterly month following the expiration month of the option.

Quarterly months: The maturity month of the underlying futures contract and the expiration month of the option are identical.

Last trading day
Six exchange days prior to the first calendar day of the option expiration month. Close of trading in the expiring option series on the Last Trading Day is at 17:15 CET.

Daily settlement price
Established by Eurex. The Daily Settlement Prices for options on fixed income futures are determined through the binomial model according to Cox/Ross/Rubinstein.

Further details are available in the clearing conditions on **www.eurexchange. com.**

Exercise
American-style; an option can be exercised up to the beginning of the Post-Trading Restricted Period (20:00 CET) on any exchange day during the lifetime of the option, or until 18:00 CET on the Last Trading Day.

Exercise Prices	Exercise Intervals
Options on	**Points**
Euro-Schatz-Futures	0.1
Euro-Bobl-Futures	0.25
Euro-Bund-Futures	0.50

Number of exercise prices
Upon the admission of the options, at least nine exercise prices shall be made available for each term for each call and put, such that four exercise prices are in-the-money, one is at-the-money and four are out-of-the-money.

Option premium
The premium is settled using the futures-style method.

Trading hours
08:00 –19:00 CET.

One-Month EONIA futures (FEO1)

Contract standards
Average rate of the effective overnight reference rate for the euro (EONIA – Euro Over Night Index Average) – calculated by the European Central Bank (ECB) – for a period of one calendar month.

Contract value
EUR 3 million.

Settlement
Cash settlement, payable on the first exchange day following the Final Settlement Day.

Price quotation and minimum price change
The Price Quotation is in percent, with three decimal places, expressed as 100 minus the traded average effective EONIA rate of interest. The Minimum Price Change is 0.005 percent, equivalent to a value of EUR 12.50.

Contract months
Up to 12 months: The present calendar month and the eleven nearest calendar months.

Last trading day and final settlement day
Last Trading Day is the Final Settlement Day. Final Settlement Day is the last exchange day of the respective maturity month, provided that on that day the daily effective overnight reference rate for the euro (EONIA) is calculated by the European Central Bank; otherwise, the exchange day immediately preceding that day. Close of trading in the maturing futures on the Last Trading Day is at 19:00 CET.

Daily settlement price
The Daily Settlement Price for the current maturity month of One-Month EONIA Futures is derived from the volume-weighted average of the prices of all transactions during the minute before 17:15 CET (reference point), provided that more than five trades transacted within this period.

For the remaining maturity months, the Daily Settlement Price for a contract is determined based on the average bid/ask spread of the combination order book. Further details are available in the clearing conditions on **www.eurexchange.com.**

Final settlement price
Established by Eurex on the Final Settlement Day after 19:00 CET; based on the compounded average of the effective overnight reference rate for the euro (EONIA) as calculated by the European Central Bank on a daily basis for the period of the contract. To fix the Final Settlement Price the compounded EONIA average rate will be arithmetically rounded to the nearest price interval (0.005; 0.01 or a multiple thereof) and then subtracted from 100.

Trading hours
08:00–19:00 CET.

Matching of trades (pro rata matching)
Orders and quotes are matched according to the principle of pro rata matching, which is exclusively based on the principle of price priority.
 One-Month EONIA Futures have been admitted for trading in the U.S.

Three-Month EURIBOR futures (FEU3)

Contract standards
European Interbank Offered Rate (EURIBOR) for threemonth euro term deposits.

Contract value
EUR 1 million.

Settlement
Cash settlement, payable on the first exchange day following the Final Settlement Day.

Price quotation and minimum price change
The Price Quotation is in percent, with three decimal places, expressed as 100 minus the traded rate of interest. The Minimum Price Change is 0.005 percent, equivalent to a value of EUR 12.50.

Contract months
Up to 36 months: The twelve nearest quarterly months of the March, June, September and December cycle.

Last trading day and final settlement day

Last Trading Day is the Final Settlement Day. Final Settlement Day is two exchange days prior to the third Wednesday of the respective maturity month, provided that on that day FBE/ACI has determined the EURIBOR reference interest rate pertaining to three-month euro term deposits; otherwise, the exchange day immediately preceding that day. Close of trading in the maturing futures on the Last Trading Day is at 11:00 CET.

Daily settlement price

The Daily Settlement Price for the current maturity month of Three-Month EURIBOR Futures is derived from the volume-weighted average of the prices of all transactions during the minute before 17:15 CET (reference point), provided that more than five trades transacted within this period.

For the remaining maturity months, the Daily Settlement Price for a contract is determined based on the average bid/ask spread of the combination order book. Further details are available in the clearing conditions on **www.eurexchange.com.**

Final settlement price

Established by Eurex on the Final Settlement Day at 11:00 CET; based on the reference interest rate (EURIBOR) for three-month euro term deposits as determined by FBE/ACI. To fix the Final Settlement Price, the EURIBOR rate is rounded to the nearest price interval (0.005; 0.01 or a multiple thereof), and is then subtracted from 100.

Trading hours

08:00–19:00 CET.

Matching of trades (pro rata matching)

Orders and quotes are matched according to the principle of pro rata matching, which is exclusively based on the principle of price priority.

Three-Month EURIBOR Futures have been admitted for trading in the U.S.

Options on Three-Month EURIBOR Futures (OEU3)

Contract standards

Three-Month EURIBOR Futures.

Contract value

One Three-Month EURIBOR Futures contract.

Settlement
The exercise of an option on the Three-Month EURIBOR Futures contract results in the creation of a corresponding position in the Three-Month EURIBOR Futures for the option buyer as well as the seller to whom the exercise is assigned. The position is established after the Post-Trading Full Period of the exercise day, and is based on the agreed exercise price.

Price quotation and minimum price change
The Price Quotation is in points, with three decimal places. The Minimum Price Change is 0.005 points, equivalent to a value of EUR 12.50.

Contract months
Up to 12 months: The four nearest quarterly months of the March, June, September and December cycle.

The maturity month of the underlying futures contract and the expiration month of the option are identical.

Last trading day
Two exchange days prior to the third Wednesday of the respective expiration month, provided that on that day FBE/ACI has determined the EURIBOR reference interest rate pertaining to three-month euro term deposits; otherwise, the exchange day immediately preceding that day. Close of trading in the expiring option series on the Last Trading Day is at 11:00 CET.

Daily settlement price
Established by Eurex. The Daily Settlement Prices for options on Three-Month EURIBOR Futures are determined through the binomial model according to Cox/ Ross/Rubinstein.

Further details are available in the clearing conditions on **www.eurexchange. com.**

Exercise
American-style; an option can be exercised up to the beginning of the Post-Trading Restricted Period (20:00 CET) on any exchange day during the lifetime of the option.

Exercise prices
Option series have exercise prices with intervals of 0.1 points (for example, 95.4; 95.5; 95.6).

Number of exercise prices

Upon the admission of the options, at least 21 exercise prices shall be made available for each term for each call and put, such that ten exercise prices are in-the-money, one is at-the-money and ten are out-of-the-money.

Option premium

The premium is settled using the futures-style method.

Trading hours

08:00 – 19:00 CET.

Options on Three-Month EURIBOR Futures have been admitted for trading in the U.S.

A.12 Derivatives exchanges worldwide – An overview

Country	Exchanges	Time
America	American Stock Exchange	09:30–16:00 (ET)
	CBOE Futures Exchange (CFE)	09:30–16:15 (ET)
	Chicago Mercantile Exchange (Electronic-Globex)	SO 18:00–FR (17:00) (ET)
	Chicago Mercantile Exchange (Floor-Based)	08:20–15:00 (ET)
	Eurex US	MO 08:00 – FR 17:00 (ET)
	ISE Options Exchange	09:30–16:00 (ET)
	New York Mercantile Exchange (NYMEX)	00:20–16:15 (ET);
		16:45–21:15 (ET);
	OneChicago (One)	21:30–23:00 (ET)
	Pacific Exchange (PSE)	09:30–16:15 (ET)
	Philadelphia Stock Exchange (PHLX)	09:30–16:30 (ET)
		09:30–16:00 (ET)
Canada	Montreal Exchange	Options: 09:30–16:15 (ET);
		Futures: 06:00–16:15 (ET)
Belgium	Euronext Brussels (Belfox)	09:30–17:30 (CET)
	Euronext France (Monep/Matif)	08:00– 20:00 (CET)
Germany & Switzerland	EUREX	07:30–20:00 (CET)
Italy	Borsa Italiana (IDEM)	09:00–17:40 (CET)
NL	Euronext NL Derivatives (FTA)	09:30–17:30 (CET)
Spain	Spanish Futures & Options Exchange (MEFF)	09:00–17:35 (CET)
UK	LIFFE Commodities	08:00–17:30 (GMT)
	LIFFE Options & Futures	08:00–17:30 (GMT)
Australia	Sydney Futures Exchange (SNFE)	00:00–08:00;
		09:50–16:30;
		17:10–23:59 (Sydney)
Hong Kong	Hong Kong Futures Exchange (HKFE)	09:45–12:30;
		14:30–16:15 (HKT)

Country	Exchanges	Time
Japan	Osaka Securities Exchange (OSE.JPN)	09:00–11:00; 12:30–15:10 (Japan)
Singapore	Singapore Exchange (SGX)	07:45–19:05 (Singapur)
S. Korea	Korea Stock Exchange (KSE)	09:00–15:15 (S. Korea) Futures and Options

A.13 Eurex-Disclaimer

Eurex offers services directly to members of the Eurex exchanges. Those who desire to trade any products available on the Eurex market or who desire to offer and sell any such products to others, should consider legal and regulatory requirements of those jurisdictions relevant to them, as well as the risks associated with such products, before doing so.

Eurex derivatives (other than Dow Jones EURO STOXX 50® Index Futures contracts, Dow Jones STOXX 50® Index Futures contracts, Dow Jones STOXX® 600 Index Futures contracts, Dow Jones STOXX® Mid 200 Index Futures contracts, Dow Jones EURO STOXX® Banks Sector Futures contracts, Dow Jones STOXX® 600 Banks Sector Futures contracts, Dow Jones Global Titans 50℠ Index Futures contracts, DAX® Futures contracts, MDAX® Futures contracts, and Eurex interest rate derivatives) are currently not available for offer, sale or trading in the United States or by United States persons.

Trademarks and service marks

Buxl®, DAX®, Eurex®, Eurex Bonds®, Eurex Repo®, Euro GC Pooling®, Eurex Strategy Wizard℠, FDAX®, iNAV®, MDAX®, ODAX®, SDAX®, StatistiX®, TecDAX®, VDAX-NEW®, Xetra® and XTF Exchange Traded Funds® are registered trademarks of DBAG.

Xemac® is a registered trademark of Clearstream Banking AG. Vestima® is a registered trademark of Clearstream International S.A.

RDXxt® is a registered trademark of Wiener Börse AG (Vienna Stock Exchange).

iTraxx® is a registered trademark of International Index Company Limited (IIC) and has been licensed for the use by Eurex. IIC does not approve, endorse or recommend Eurex or iTraxx® Europe 5-year Index Futures, iTraxx® Europe HiVol 5-year Index Futures and iTraxx® Europe Crossover 5-year Index Futures.

Eurex is solely responsible for the creation of the Eurex iTraxx® Credit Futures contracts, their trading and market surveillance. ISDA® neither sponsors nor endorses the product's use. ISDA® is a registered trademark of the International Swaps and Derivatives Association, Inc.

SMI®, SMIM® and VSMI® are registered trademarks of SWX Swiss Exchange.

STOXX®, Dow Jones STOXX® 600 Index, Dow Jones STOXX® Large 200 Index, Dow Jones STOXX® Mid 200 Index, Dow Jones STOXX® Small 200 Index, Dow Jones STOXX® TMI Index, VSTOXX® Index, Dow Jones EURO STOXX® Select Dividend 30 Index, Dow Jones EURO STOXX®/STOXX® 600 Sector Indexes as well as the Dow Jones EURO STOXX 50® Index and Dow Jones STOXX 50® Index are service marks of STOXX Ltd. and/or Dow Jones & Company, Inc.

Dow Jones and Dow Jones Global Titans 50^{SM} Index are service marks of Dow Jones & Company, Inc. The derivatives based on these indexes are not sponsored, endorsed, sold or promoted by STOXX Ltd. or Dow Jones & Company, Inc., and neither party makes any representation regarding the advisability of trading or of investing in such products.

The names of other companies and third party products may be trademarks or service marks of their respective owners.

A.14 Eurex – one of the leading derivatives exchanges in the world

As a leading derivatives exchange, one of Eurex's key strengths is the open, low-cost electronic access to the global exchange network. We provide access to a broad range of global benchmark products, including the most liquid fixed income markets worldwide. Every day, participants in our global Eurex network trade more than seven million contracts, from around 700 different locations.

Alongside our fully-computerized trading platform, we also operate an automated and integrated clearing house. Acting as a central counterparty, Eurex Clearing AG guarantees the performance of all trades entered into at the Eurex exchanges. The same guarantee is extended to cover Eurex Bonds, Eurex Repo, and all cash securities listed at the Frankfurt Stock Exchange (Xetra® and floor) or at the Irish Stock Exchange (ISE).

This structure lets you benefit from a high-quality, cost-efficient value creation chain, covering trading, clearing, and settlement through a uniform systems platform.

Products

We offer an extensive product portfolio covering the most diverse of asset classes: In the **equity derivatives** sector, you have a choice of more than 400 futures contracts on all constituents of the Dow Jones (EURO) STOXX 50® and DAX® indexes, all Dow Jones STOXX® 600 constituents denominated in euro or Swiss francs, as well as on all component issues of the SMI® and RDXxt® indexes. In addition, more than 200 options on stocks from the major European industrial countries are traded.

Our **equity index derivatives** comprise futures and options on major global, pan-European and national blue-chip indexes, such as the Dow Jones EURO STOXX 50® Index, the DAX®, Deutsche Börse AG's benchmark index, the Swiss benchmark index SMI® as well as the RDXxt®, the Russian benchmark index. In addition, we offer numerous sector index derivatives based on the Dow Jones STOXX® 600 and Dow Jones EURO STOXX® indexes. The product range is completed by futures and options on pan-European and national large cap, mid cap and small cap indexes, on the Dow Jones STOXX® 600 Index and the Dow Jones EURO STOXX® Select Dividend 30 Index.

You can use **volatility index derivatives** to build pure volatility exposure, or to hedge the volatility risk of your equity positions. Our volatility futures are based on various volatility indexes covering the pan-European stock markets: the VSTOXX® (reflecting the volatility of the Dow Jones EURO STOXX 50® index) the VDAX-NEW® (based on the DAX®), and the VSMI® (based on the SMI®).

Launched in March 2007, Eurex **credit derivatives** allow you to hedge against credit events, such as corporate defaults or failure to pay. With this new and innovative derivatives category, we have added yet another asset class to provide you with new ways to manage your risks at lowest cost.

Our **interest rate derivatives** cover the entire German yield curve, from one day right to 35 years, as well as the Swiss yield curve between eight and 13 years. This segment comprises the Euro-Buxl®, Euro-Bund, Euro-Bobl and Euro-Schatz Futures, which rank amongst the most actively traded derivatives contracts worldwide. Our options on Euro-Bund, Euro-Bobl and Euro-Schatz Futures offer additional investment opportunities within our fixed income segment.

Wholesale trading functionality

Using the Wholesale Trading Functionality – which is integrated in the Eurex® system – you can enter over-thecounter (OTC) trades concluded outside the exchange. You can thus benefit from the flexibility of OTC trading, while at the same time still taking advantage of standardized clearing and settlement processes:

- Block Trades (OTC trades in futures and options)
- Vola Trades (delta hedges for options)
- Exchange for Physicals for Equity Index Futures Trades
- Exchange for Physicals for Fixed Income Futures Trades
- Exchange for Swap Trades (futures contracts as a hedge against cash market trades or interest rate swaps)
- Flexible Options and
- Flexible Futures

Moreover, you can use the Block Auction Functionality to anonymously request prices for large-sized orders.

Market-making

We support the provision of liquidity through the refund of transaction fees to each exchange participant fulfilling the requirements of our Market-Making schemes. Customers directly benefit from a large number of exchange participants having specialized – thanks to the incentives provided – in providing liquidity and enhancing transparency.

Price determination

Our market model is order-driven: Orders placed by market participants are executed with equal priority as quotes entered into the Eurex® system, applying the same rules. With the exception of money-market derivatives, orders are executed according to the principle of price/time priority. This means that orders are ranked according to their limit and the time of entry, with market orders always having the highest priority.Orders and quotes in money-market derivatives are matched on a pro rata basis. Under the pro rata matching algorithm, the entry time of an order has no impact on its execution priority: Incoming orders are executed in accordance with their relative size, compared to other orders in the book, which have the same limit.

Price information for all Eurex products is available on our website www. eurexchange.com. For information on market depth, please go to **Market Data > Delayed Quotes**.

Access

You can trade directly on Eurex, as an admitted exchange participant, or you can access the market as a customer of an admitted participant. Direct trading is possible as a General Clearing Member (GCM), a Direct Clearing Member (DCM), or a Non-Clearing Member (NCM). The difference between the three forms of membership is in their clearing status – the way in which they participate in the clearing process.

Around 400 Eurex participants worldwide enable their customers to trade indirectly – either through traditional order execution or via automated order routing. A list of admitted exchange participants, together with the brokerage services they offer, is available on **www.eurexchange.com**.

Training

Our Capital Markets Academy offers an extensive range of seminars and internationally recognized exams for traders, back office staff, security administrators, system administrators, as well as for institutional and private investors. Various courses of study compliment Deutsche Börse AG's training offer.

For more details, please contact us by e-mail (academy@eurexchange.com), or call the Capital Markets Academy on T +49-69-211-137 67. Our seminar program is also available online: **www.eurexchange.com > Education**.

Publications

A broad range of information on our products and services is available for download from our website, at **www.eurexchange.com > Documents > Publications**.

A.15 List of Literature

DeRosa, David F.: Options on Foreign Exchange, 2nd edition, New York, 2000

DeRosa, David: Currency Derivatives, New York 1998

Fabozzi, Frank J.: The Handbook of Financial Instruments, New Jersey 2002

Hicks, Alan: Managing Currency Risk Using Foreign Exchange Options, o.O. 2000

Hull, John C.: Fundamentals of Futures and Options Markets, 5th edition, New Jersey 2005

Hull, John C.: Options, Futures and Other Derivatives, 6th edition, New Jersey 2005

Jabbour, George; Budwick, Phillip: The Option Trader Handbook: Strategies and Trade Adjustments, New Jersey 2004

Kolb, Robert W.; Overdahl, James A.: Financial Derivatives, 3rd edition, New Jersey 2002

McCafferty Thomas A.: All About Options, 2nd edition, New York 1998

McInish, Thomas H.: Capital Markets, Oxford 2000

Uszczapowski, Igor: Optionen und Futures verstehen, DTV-Beck, München, 5. A. 2005

Rudolph, Bernd; Schäfer, Klaus: Derivative Finanzmarktinstrumente, Berlin 2005

Saliba, Anthony J.: The Options Workbook, 2nd edition, Chicago 2002

Sarno, Lucio; Taylor, Mark P.: The Economics of Exchange Rates, Cambridge 2002

Seethaler, Peter; Steitz, Markus: Praxishandbuch Treasury-Management, Wiesbaden 2007.

Sercu, Piet; Uppal, Raman: International Financial Markets and the firm, London 1995

Shamah, Shani: A Currency Options Primer, West Sussex 2004

Sherris, Michael: Money & Capital Markets: Pricing, Yields & Analysis, 2nd edition, Crows Nest 1996

Spremann, Klaus, Gantenbein, Pascal: Zinsen, Anleihen, Kredite, Oldenbourg, München, 4. A. 2007

Smithson, Charles W.: Managing Financial Risk: A Guide to Derivative Products, Financial Engineering, and Value Maximization, 3rd edition, New York, 1998

Walmsley, Julian: New Financial Instruments, 2nd edition, o.O., 1998

Williams, Michael; Hoffman, Amy: Fundamentals of Options Market, New York 2001

Subject Index